# Seven NoSQL Databases in a Week

Get up and running with the fundamentals and functionalities of seven of the most popular NoSQL databases

**Aaron Ploetz**
**Devram Kandhare**
**Sudarshan Kadambi**
**Xun (Brian) Wu**

**BIRMINGHAM - MUMBAI**

# Seven NoSQL Databases in a Week

Copyright © 2018 Packt Publishing

**Commissioning Editor:** Amey Varangaonkar
**Acquisition Editor:** Prachi Bisht
**Content Development Editor:** Eisha Dsouza
**Technical Editor:** Nirbhaya Shaji
**Copy Editors:** Laxmi Subramanian and Safis Editing
**Project Coordinator:** Kinjal Bari
**Proofreader:** Safis Editing
**Indexer:** Tejal Daruwale Soni
**Graphics:** Jisha Chirayil
**Production Coordinator:** Aparna Bhagat

First published: March 2018

Production reference: 1270318

Published by Packt Publishing Ltd.
Livery Place
35 Livery Street
Birmingham
B3 2PB, UK.

ISBN 978-1-78728-886-7

www.packtpub.com

*To my wife, Coriene, for all of her constant love and support. And to my parents, Brian and Mary Jo Ploetz and Christine and Rick Franda, for all the sacrifices they made to ensure that I always had access to a computer while growing up.*

*– Aaron Ploetz*

*To Goraksha Bharam for his sacrifices and support in my life. To my teachers, who introduced me to this beautiful world of knowledge. And to my grandmother.*

*– Devram Kandhare*

*I would like to thank my parents for providing me the foundation that make work like this possible. I would like to thank my sister, wife, and son for their support and encouragement and for the joy and happiness they bring to my life.*

*– Sudarshan Kadambi*

*I would like to thank my parents who always give me the inspiration, drive, and encouragement. I would also like to thank my wife and kids, Bridget and Charlotte, for their patience and support throughout this endeavor.*

*– Xun (Brian) Wu*

mapt.io

Mapt is an online digital library that gives you full access to over 5,000 books and videos, as well as industry leading tools to help you plan your personal development and advance your career. For more information, please visit our website.

# Why subscribe?

- Spend less time learning and more time coding with practical eBooks and Videos from over 4,000 industry professionals

- Improve your learning with Skill Plans built especially for you

- Get a free eBook or video every month

- Mapt is fully searchable

- Copy and paste, print, and bookmark content

# PacktPub.com

Did you know that Packt offers eBook versions of every book published, with PDF and ePub files available? You can upgrade to the eBook version at www.PacktPub.com and as a print book customer, you are entitled to a discount on the eBook copy. Get in touch with us at service@packtpub.com for more details.

At www.PacktPub.com, you can also read a collection of free technical articles, sign up for a range of free newsletters, and receive exclusive discounts and offers on Packt books and eBooks.

# Contributors

## About the authors

**Aaron Ploetz** is the NoSQL Engineering Lead for Target, where his DevOps team supports Cassandra, MongoDB, Redis, and Neo4j. He has been named a DataStax MVP for Apache Cassandra three times, and has presented at multiple events, including the DataStax Summit and Data Day Texas. He earned a BS in Management/Computer Systems from the University of Wisconsin-Whitewater, and a MS in Software Engineering from Regis University. He and his wife, Coriene, live with their three children in the Twin Cities area.

*I'd like to thank Dr. David Munro, who inspired me, Ron Bieber, who believed in me and introduced me to the world of distributed databases, and my lovely wife, Coriene, who provided constant support and encouragement during this endeavor. Seriously, without Coriene none of this would have been possible.*

**Devram Kandhare** has 4 years of experience of working with the SQL database—MySql and NoSql databases—MongoDB and DynamoDB. He has worked as database designer and developer. He has developed various projects using the Agile development model. He is experienced in building web-based applications and REST API.

*I'd like to thank my grandparents, Mamaji, Shriniwas Gadre, and Mudit Tyagi, for their love and guidance. Most importantly I want to thank my parents, my sister, Amruta, my loving and supportive wife, Ashvini, and my friend Prashant; without them none of this would have been possible.*

**Sudarshan Kadambi** has a background in distributed systems and database design. He has been a user and contributor to various NoSQL databases and is passionate about solving large-scale data management challenges.

*I would like to thank my parents for providing me the foundations that make work like this possible. I would like to thank my sister, wife, and son for their support and encouragement and for the joy and happiness they bring to my life.*

**Xun (Brian) Wu** has more than 15 years of experience in web/mobile development, big data analytics, cloud computing, blockchain, and IT architecture. He holds a master's degree in computer science from NJIT. He is always enthusiastic about exploring new ideas, technologies, and opportunities that arise. He has previously reviewed more than 40 books from Packt Publishing.

*I would like to thank my parents who always give me inspiration, drive and encouragement. I would also like to thank my wife and kids, Bridget and Charlotte, for their patience and support throughout this endeavor.*

# Packt is searching for authors like you

If you're interested in becoming an author for Packt, please visit `authors.packtpub.com` and apply today. We have worked with thousands of developers and tech professionals, just like you, to help them share their insight with the global tech community. You can make a general application, apply for a specific hot topic that we are recruiting an author for, or submit your own idea.

# Table of Contents

# Preface

The book will help you understand the fundamentals of each database, and understand how their functionalities differ, while still giving you a common result – a database solution with speed, high performance, and accuracy.

## Who this book is for

If you are a budding DBA or a developer who wants to get started with the fundamentals of NoSQL databases, this book is for you. Relational DBAs who want to get insights into the various offerings of the popular NoSQL databases will also find this book to be very useful.

## What this book covers

Chapter 1, *Introduction to NoSQL Databases*, introduces the topic of NoSQL and distributed databases. The design principles and trade-offs involved in NoSQL database design are described. These design principles provide context around why individual databases covered in the following chapters are designed in a particular way and what constraints they are trying to optimize for.

Chapter 2, *MongoDB*, covers installation and basic CRUD operations. High-level concepts such as indexing allow you to speed up database operations, sharding, and replication. Also, it covers data models, which help us with application database design.

Chapter 3, *Neo4j*, introduces the Neo4j graph database. It discusses Neo4j's architecture, use cases, administration, and application development.

Chapter 4, *Redis*, discusses the Redis data store. Redis' unique architecture and behavior will be discussed, as well as installation, application development, and server-side scripting with Lua.

Chapter 5, *Cassandra*, introduces the Cassandra database. Cassandra's highly-available, eventually consistent design will be discussed along with the appropriate use cases. Known anti-patterns will also be presented, as well as production-level configuration, administration, and application development.

Chapter 6, *HBase*, introduces HBase, that is, the Hadoop Database. Inspired by Google's Bigtable, HBase is a widely deployed key-value store today. This chapter covers HBase's architectural internals, data model, and API.

Chapter 7, *DynamoDB*, covers how to set up a local and AWS DynamoDB service and perform CRUD operations. It also covers how to deal with partition keys, sort keys, and secondary indexes. It covers various advantages and disadvantages of DynamoDB over other databases, which makes it easy for developers to choose a database for an application.

Chapter 8, *InfluxDB*, describes InfluxDB and its key concepts and terms. It also covers InfluxDB installation and configuration. It explores the query language and APIs. It helps you set up Telegraf and Kapacitor as an InfluxDB ecosystem's key components to collect and process data. At the end of the chapter, you will also find information about InfluxDB operations.

# To get the most out of this book

This book assumes that you have access to hardware on which you can install, configure, and code against a database instance. Having elevated admin or sudo privileges on the aforementioned machine will be essential to carrying out some of the tasks described.

Some of the NoSQL databases discussed will only run on a Linux-based operating system. Therefore, prior familiarity with Linux is recommended. As OS-specific system administration is not within the scope of this book, readers who are new to Linux may find value in seeking out a separate tutorial prior to attempting some of the examples.

The **Java Virtual Machine (JVM)**-based NoSQL databases will require a **Java Runtime Environment (JRE)** to be installed. Do note that some of them may require a specific version of the JRE to function properly. This will necessitate updating or installing a new JRE, depending on the database.

The Java coding examples will be easier to do from within an **Integrated Developer Envorinment (IDE)**, with Maven installed for dependency management. You may need to look up additional resources to ensure that these components are configured properly.

In Chapter 6, *HBase*, you can install the Hortonworks sandbox to get a small HBase cluster set up on your laptop. The sandbox can be installed for free from https://hortonworks. com/products/sandbox/.

In Chapter 8, *InfluxDB*, to run the examples you will need to install InfluxDB in a UNIX or Linux environment. In order to run different InfluxDB API client examples, you also need to install a programming language environment and related InfluxDB client packages:

1. Run the InfluxDB Java client: Install JDK and an editor (Eclipse or IntelliJ).
2. Run the InfluxDB Python client: Install Python.
3. Run the InfluxDB Go client: Install Go and the InfluxDB Go client; you can use JetBrains Goland to run the Go code.

# Download the example code files

You can download the example code files for this book from your account at www.packtpub.com. If you purchased this book elsewhere, you can visit www.packtpub.com/support and register to have the files emailed directly to you.

You can download the code files by following these steps:

1. Log in or register at www.packtpub.com.
2. Select the **SUPPORT** tab.
3. Click on **Code Downloads & Errata**.
4. Enter the name of the book in the **Search** box and follow the onscreen instructions.

Once the file is downloaded, please make sure that you unzip or extract the folder using the latest version of:

- WinRAR/7-Zip for Windows
- Zipeg/iZip/UnRarX for Mac
- 7-Zip/PeaZip for Linux

The code bundle for the book is also hosted on GitHub at https://github.com/PacktPublishing/Seven-NoSQL-Databases-in-a-Week. In case there's an update to the code, it will be updated on the existing GitHub repository.

We also have other code bundles from our rich catalog of books and videos available at https://github.com/PacktPublishing/. Check them out!

# Download the color images

We also provide a PDF file that has color images of the screenshots/diagrams used in this book. You can download it here: `http://www.packtpub.com/sites/default/files/downloads/SevenNoSQLDatabasesinaWeek_ColorImages.pdf`.

# Conventions used

There are a number of text conventions used throughout this book.

`CodeInText`: Indicates code words in text, database table names, folder names, filenames, file extensions, pathnames, dummy URLs, user input, and Twitter handles. Here is an example: "Now is also a good time to change the initial password. Neo4j installs with a single default admin username and password of `neo4j/neo4j`."

A block of code is set as follows:

```
# Paths of directories in the installation.
#dbms.directories.data=data
#dbms.directories.plugins=plugins
#dbms.directories.certificates=certificates
#dbms.directories.logs=logs
#dbms.directories.lib=lib
#dbms.directories.run=run
```

When we wish to draw your attention to a particular part of a code block, the relevant lines or items are set in bold:

```
# Paths of directories in the installation.
#dbms.directories.data=data
#dbms.directories.plugins=plugins
#dbms.directories.certificates=certificates
#dbms.directories.logs=logs
#dbms.directories.lib=lib
#dbms.directories.run=run
```

Any command-line input or output is written as follows:

```
sudo mkdir /local
sudo chown $USER:$USER /local
cd /local
mv ~/Downloads/neo4j-community-3.3.3-unix.tar.gz .
```

**Bold**: Indicates a new term, an important word, or words that you see onscreen. For example, words in menus or dialog boxes appear in the text like this. Here is an example: "To create a table, click on the **Create table** button. This will take you to the **Create table** screen."

Warnings or important notes appear like this.

Tips and tricks appear like this.

# Get in touch

Feedback from our readers is always welcome.

**General feedback**: Email `feedback@packtpub.com` and mention the book title in the subject of your message. If you have questions about any aspect of this book, please email us at `questions@packtpub.com`.

**Errata**: Although we have taken every care to ensure the accuracy of our content, mistakes do happen. If you have found a mistake in this book, we would be grateful if you would report this to us. Please visit `www.packtpub.com/submit-errata`, selecting your book, clicking on the Errata Submission Form link, and entering the details.

**Piracy**: If you come across any illegal copies of our works in any form on the Internet, we would be grateful if you would provide us with the location address or website name. Please contact us at `copyright@packtpub.com` with a link to the material.

**If you are interested in becoming an author**: If there is a topic that you have expertise in and you are interested in either writing or contributing to a book, please visit `authors.packtpub.com`.

# Reviews

Please leave a review. Once you have read and used this book, why not leave a review on the site that you purchased it from? Potential readers can then see and use your unbiased opinion to make purchase decisions, we at Packt can understand what you think about our products, and our authors can see your feedback on their book. Thank you!

For more information about Packt, please visit packtpub.com.

# Introduction to NoSQL Databases 1

Over the last decade, the volume and velocity with which data is generated within organizations has grown exponentially. Consequently, there has been an explosion of database technologies that have been developed to address these growing data needs. These databases have typically had distributed implementations, since the volume of data being managed far exceeds the storage capacity of a single node. In order to support the massive scale of data, these databases have provided fewer of the features that we've come to expect from relational databases.

The first generation of these so-called NoSQL databases only provided rudimentary key-value get/put APIs. They were largely schema-free and didn't require well-defined types to be associated with the values being stored in the database. Over the last decade, however, a number of features that we've come to expect from standard databases—such as type systems and SQL, secondary indices, materialized views, and some kind of concept of transactions—have come to be incorporated and overlaid over those rudimentary key-value interfaces.

Today, there are hundreds of NoSQL databases available in the world, with a few popular ones, such as MongoDB, HBase, and Cassandra, having the lion's share of the market, followed by a long list of other, less popular databases.

These databases have different data models, ranging from the document model of MongoDB, to the column-family model of HBase and Cassandra, to the columnar model of Kudu. These databases are widely deployed in hundreds of organizations and at this point are considered mainstream and commonplace.

This book covers some of the most popular and widely deployed NoSQL databases. Each chapter covers a different NoSQL database, how it is architected, how to model your data, and how to interact with the database. Before we jump into each of the NoSQL databases covered in this book, let's look at some of the design choices that should be considered when one is setting out to build a distributed database.

Knowing about some of these database principles will give us insight into why different databases have been designed with different architectural choices in mind, based on the use cases and workloads they were originally designed for.

# Consistency versus availability

A database's **consistency** refers to the reliability of its functions' performance. A consistent system is one in which reads return the value of the last write, and reads at a given time epoch return the same value regardless of where they were initiated.

NoSQL databases support a range of consistency models, such as the following:

- **Strong consistency**: A system that is strongly consistent ensures that updates to a given key are ordered and reads reflect the latest update that has been accepted by the system
- **Timeline consistency**: A system that is timeline consistent ensures that updates to a given key are ordered in all the replicants, but reads at a given replicant might be stale and may not reflect the latest update that has been accepted by the system
- **Eventual consistency**: A system that is eventually consistent makes no guarantees about whether updates will be applied in order in all the replicants, nor does it make guarantees about when a read would reflect a prior update accepted by the system

A database's **availability** refers to the system's ability to complete a certain operation. Like consistency, availability is a spectrum. A system can be unavailable for writes while being available for reads. A system can be unavailable for admin operations while being available for data operations.

As is well known at this point, there's tension between consistency and availability. A system that is highly available needs to allow operations to succeed even if some nodes in the system are unreachable (either dead or partitioned off by the network). However, since it is unknown as to whether those nodes are still alive and are reachable by some clients or are dead and reachable by no one, there are no guarantees about whether those operations left the system in a consistent state or not.

So, a system that guarantees consistency must make sure that all of the nodes that contain data for a given key must be reachable and participate in the operation. The degenerate case is that a single node is responsible for operations on a given key. Since there is just a single node, there is no chance of inconsistency of the sort we've been discussing. The downside is that when a node goes down, there is a complete loss of availability for operations on that key.

# ACID guarantees

Relational databases have provided the traditional properties of **ACID**: **atomicity**, **consistency**, **isolation**, and **durability**:

- **Atomicity** is self-explanatory and refers to the all-or-nothing nature of a set of operations.
- **Consistency** in ACID and **consistency** in the CAP theorem refer to different things. Consistency in ACID refers to the principle that the system must be left in a consistent state while processing transactions, it either reflects the state after successful completion of the transaction or must roll back to a state prior to the start of the transaction.
- **Isolation** refers to the interaction effects between transactions. Under what conditions is the state modified by one transaction visible to other active transactions in the system? It ranges from weak isolation levels, such as read-committed, and goes all the way to linearizable.
- **Durability** indicates that once a transaction has committed, the effects of the transaction remain despite events such as errors and crashes.

NoSQL databases vary widely in their support for these guarantees, with most of them not approaching the level of strong guarantees provided by relational databases (since these are hard to support in a distributed setting).

# Hash versus range partition

Once you've decided to distribute data, how should the data be distributed?

Firstly, data needs to be distributed using a partitioning key in the data. The partitioning key can be the primary key or any other unique key. Once you've identified the partitioning key, we need to decide how to assign a key to a given shard.

One way to do this would be to take a key and apply a hash function. Based on the hash bucket and the number of shards to map keys into, the key would be assigned to a shard. There's a bit of nuance here in the sense that an assignment scheme based on a modulo by the number of nodes currently in the cluster will result in a lot of data movement when nodes join or leave the cluster (since all of the assignments need to be recalculated). This is addressed by something called consistent hashing, a detailed description of which is outside the scope of this chapter.

Another way to do assignments would be to take the entire keyspace and break it up into a set of ranges. Each range corresponds to a shard and is assigned to a given node in the cluster. Given a key, you would then do a binary search to find out the node it is meant to be assigned to. A range partition doesn't have the churn issue that a naive hashing scheme would have. When a node joins, shards from existing nodes will migrate onto the new node. When a node leaves, the shards on the node will migrate to one or more of the existing nodes.

What impact do the hash and range partitions have on the system design? A hash-based assignment can be built in a decentralized manner, where all nodes are peers of each other and there are no special master-slave relationships between nodes. Ceph and Cassandra both do hash-based partition assignment.

On the other hand, a range-based partitioning scheme requires that range assignments be kept in some special service. Hence, databases that do range-based partitioning, such as Bigtable and HBase, tend to be centralized and peer to peer, but instead have nodes with special roles and responsibilities.

# In-place updates versus appends

Another key difference between database systems is how they handle updates to the physical records stored on disk.

Relational databases, such as MySQL, maintain a variety of structures in both the memory and disk, where writes from in-flight transactions and writes from completed transactions are persisted. Once the transaction has been committed, the physical record on disk for a given key is updated to reflect that. On the other hand, many NoSQL databases, such as HBase and Cassandra, are variants of what is called a **log-structured merge (LSM)** database.

In such an LSM database, updates aren't applied to the record at transaction commit. Instead, updates are applied in memory. Once the memory structure gets full, the contents of the memory are flushed to the disk. This means that updates to a single record can be fragmented and located within separate flush files that are created over time. This means that when there is a read for that record, you need to read in fragments of the record from the different flush files and merge the fragments in reverse time order in order to construct the latest snapshot of the given record. We will discuss the mechanics of how an LSM database works in the Chapter 6, *HBase*.

# Row versus column versus column-family storage models

When you have a logical table with a bunch of rows and columns, there are multiple ways in which they can be stored physically on a disk.

You can store the contents of entire rows together so that all of the columns of a given row would be stored together. This works really well if the access pattern accesses a lot of the columns for a given set of rows. MySQL uses such a row-oriented storage model.

On the other hand, you could store the contents of entire columns together. In this scheme, all of the values from all of the rows for a given column can be stored together. This is really optimized for analytic use cases where you might need to scan through the entire table for a small set of columns. Storing data as column vectors allows for better compression (since there is less entropy between values within a column than there is between the values across a column). Also, these column vectors can be retrieved from a disk and processed quickly in a vectorized fashion through the SIMD capabilities of modern processors. SIMD processing on column vectors can approach throughputs of a billion data points/sec on a personal laptop.

Hybrid schemes are possible as well. Rather than storing an entire column vector together, it is possible to first break up all of the rows in a table into distinct row groups, and then, within a row group, you could store all of the column vectors together. Parquet and ORC use such a data placement strategy.

Another variant is that data is stored row-wise, but the rows are divided into row groups such that a row group is assigned to a shard. Within a row group, groups of columns that are often queried together, called column families, are then stored physically together on the disk. This storage model is used by HBase and is discussed in more detail in `Chapter 6,` *HBase*.

# Strongly versus loosely enforced schemas

Databases can decide up-front how prescriptive they want to be about specifying a schema for the data.

When NoSQL databases came to the fore a decade ago, a key point was that they didn't require a schema. The schema could be encoded and enforced in the application rather than in the database. It was thought that schemas were a hindrance in dealing with all of the semi structured data that was getting produced in modern enterprise. So because the early NoSQL systems didn't have a type system, they didn't enforce the standard that all rows in the table have the same structure, they didn't enforce a whole lot.

However, today, most of these NoSQL databases have acquired an SQL interface. Most of them have acquired a rich type system. One of the reasons for this has been the realization that SQL is widely known and reduces the on-board friction in working with a new database. Getting started is easier with an SQL interface than it is with an obscure key-value API. More importantly, having a type system frees application developers from having to remember how a particular value was encoded and to decode it appropriately.

Hence, Cassandra deprecated the Thrift API and made CQL the default. HBase still doesn't support SQL access natively, but use of HBase is increasingly pivoting towards SQL interfaces over HBase, such as Phoenix.

# Summary

In this chapter, we introduced the notion of a NoSQL database and considered some of the principles that go into the design of such a database. We now understand that there are many trade-offs to be considered in database design based on the specific use cases and types of workloads the database is being designed for. In the following chapters, we are going to be looking in detail at seven popular NoSQL databases. We will look at their architecture, data, and query models, as well as some practical tips on how you can get started using these databases, if they are a fit for your use case.

# 2
# MongoDB

MongoDB is an open source, document-oriented, and cross-platform database. It is primarily written in C++. It is also the leading NoSQL database and tied with the SQL database in fifth position after PostgreSQL. It provides high performance, high availability, and easy scalability. MongoDB uses JSON-like documents with schema. MongoDB, developed by MongoDB Inc., is free to use. It is published under a combination of the GNU Affero General Public License and the Apache License.

Let's go through the MongoDB features:

- **Rich query support**: We can query the database as we do with SQL databases. It has a large query set that supports insert, update, delete and select operations. MongoDB supports fields, range queries, and regular expressions. Queries also support the projection where they return a value for specific keys.

- **Indexing**: MongoDB supports primary and secondary indices in its fields.

- **Replication**: Replication means providing more than one copy of data. MongoDB provides multiple copies of data with multiple servers. It provides fault tolerance, if one database server goes down, the application uses other database servers.

- **Load balancing**: Replica sets provide multiple copies of data. MongoDB can scale read operation by client request directly to the secondary node. This divides loads across multiple servers.

- **File storage**: We can store documents up to 6 MB directly to the MongoDB JSON field. For documents exceeding the size limit of 16 MB, MongoDB provides GridFS to store in chunks.

- **Aggregation**: The aggregate function takes a number of records and calculates single results like sum, min, and max. MongoDB provides a data pipeline and multistage pipeline to move large data to the aggregate function which improves performance.

# Installing of MongoDB

You can download the latest version of MongoDB
here: `https://www.mongodb.com/download-center#community`. Follow the setup
instructions to install it.

Once MongoDB is installed on your Windows PC, you have to create the following
directory:

**Data directory C:\data\db**

Once you have successfully installed MongoDB, you will be able to see the following
executable:

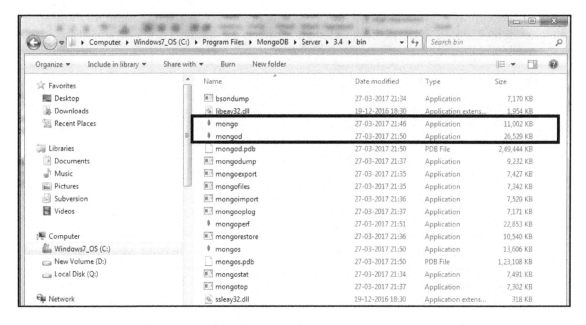

We have to start the `mongod` instances to begin working with MongoDB. To start
the `mongod` instance, execute it from the command prompt, as shown in the following
screenshot:

```
C:\Users\devramk>cd C:\Program Files\MongoDB\Server\3.4\bin

C:\Program Files\MongoDB\Server\3.4\bin>mongod
2017-07-24T17:09:54.750+0530 I CONTROL   [initandlisten] MongoDB starting : pid=12128
ath=C:\data\db\ 64-bit host=PPG-DEVRAM
2017-07-24T17:09:54.751+0530 I CONTROL   [initandlisten] targetMinOS: Windows 7/Windo
R2
2017-07-24T17:09:54.751+0530 I CONTROL   [initandlisten] db version v3.4.3
2017-07-24T17:09:54.751+0530 I CONTROL   [initandlisten] git version: f07437fb5a6cca0
6eb1d6d5e1
2017-07-24T17:09:54.751+0530 I CONTROL   [initandlisten] OpenSSL version: OpenSSL 1.0
p 2016
2017-07-24T17:09:54.751+0530 I CONTROL   [initandlisten] allocator: tcmalloc
2017-07-24T17:09:54.751+0530 I CONTROL   [initandlisten] modules: none
2017-07-24T17:09:54.751+0530 I CONTROL   [initandlisten] build environment:
2017-07-24T17:09:54.751+0530 I CONTROL   [initandlisten]     distmod: 2008plus-ssl
2017-07-24T17:09:54.751+0530 I CONTROL   [initandlisten]     distarch: x86_64
2017-07-24T17:09:54.751+0530 I CONTROL   [initandlisten]     target_arch: x86_64
2017-07-24T17:09:54.751+0530 I CONTROL   [initandlisten] options: {}
2017-07-24T17:09:54.770+0530 I -         [initandlisten] Detected data files in C:\da
by the 'wiredTiger' storage engine, so setting the active storage engine to 'wiredTi
2017-07-24T17:09:54.770+0530 I STORAGE   [initandlisten] wiredtiger_open config: crea
495M,session_max=20000,eviction=(threads_min=4,threads_max=4),config_base=false,stat
og=(enabled=true,archive=true,path=journal,compressor=snappy),file_manager=(close_id
,checkpoint=(wait=60,log_size=2GB),statistics_log=(wait=0),
2017-07-24T17:09:56.461+0530 I CONTROL   [initandlisten]
2017-07-24T17:09:56.461+0530 I CONTROL   [initandlisten] ** WARNING: Access control i
or the database.
2017-07-24T17:09:56.461+0530 I CONTROL   [initandlisten] **          Read and write a
nd configuration is unrestricted.
2017-07-24T17:09:56.461+0530 I CONTROL   [initandlisten]
2017-07-24T17:09:56.461+0530 I CONTROL   [initandlisten] Hotfix KB2731284 or later up
talled, will zero-out data files.
2017-07-24T17:09:56.462+0530 I CONTROL   [initandlisten]
2017-07-24T17:09:58.860+0530 I FTDC      [initandlisten] Initializing full-time diagn
ure with directory 'C:/data/db/diagnostic.data'
2017-07-24T17:09:58.894+0530 I NETWORK   [thread1] waiting for connections on port 27
```

Once mongod has started, we have to connect this instance using the **mongo** client with the mongo executable:

```
C:\Users\devramk>cd C:\Program Files\MongoDB\Server\3.4\bin

C:\Program Files\MongoDB\Server\3.4\bin>mongo
MongoDB shell version v3.4.3
connecting to: mongodb://127.0.0.1:27017
MongoDB server version: 3.4.3
Server has startup warnings:
2017-07-24T17:09:56.461+0530 I CONTROL   [initandlisten]
2017-07-24T17:09:56.461+0530 I CONTROL   [initandlisten] ** WARNING: Access control i
or the database.
2017-07-24T17:09:56.461+0530 I CONTROL   [initandlisten] **          Read and write a
nd configuration is unrestricted.
2017-07-24T17:09:56.461+0530 I CONTROL   [initandlisten]
2017-07-24T17:09:56.461+0530 I CONTROL   [initandlisten] Hotfix KB2731284 or later up
talled, will zero-out data files.
2017-07-24T17:09:56.462+0530 I CONTROL   [initandlisten]
>
```

Once we are connected to the database, we can start working on the database operations.

# MongoDB data types

Documents in MongoDB are *JSON-like* objects. JSON is a simple representation of data. It supports the following data types:

- `null`: The `null` data type is used to represent the `null` value as well as a value that does not exist:

```
{ "firstName": null }
```

- `boolean`: The `boolean` type is used to represent `true` and `false` values:

```
{ "isEditable": true }
```

- `number`: In MongoDB, the shell default supports 64-bit floating-point numbers. To process long and integer numbers, MongoDB provides `NumberLong` and `NumberInt`, which represent 4 bytes and 8 bytes, respectively.
- `string`: The `string` data type represents the collection of characters. The MongoDB default supports UTF-* character encoding:

```
{ "city": "london" }
```

- `date`: MongoDB stores dates in milliseconds since the epoch. The time zone information is not saved:

```
{
    "birthDate" : new Date(1501086866059)
}
```

- After inserting a date using the preceding way in the document, when we query using `find` it returns a document with a date in the following format:

```
{
    "_id" : ObjectId("5978c5ca24de39c8f206196b"),
    "birthDate" : ISODate("2017-07-26T16:34:26.059Z")
}
```

- array: A set or list of values represents arrays. Also, multiple JSON objects represent an array of elements. The following example shows an array of city values:

```
{
    "cities" : ["London", "Delhi", "New York"]
}
```

- Embedded document: Another MongoDB document-like structure, which can also be used as a key. In the following screenshot, we are storing address fields as an array of addresses, instead of creating a separate collection of addresses:

```
{
    "_id" : ObjectId("59769440c5160d8a42a02358"),
    "firstName" : "John",
    "lastName" : "Cent",
    "age" : 45,
    "email" : "john.cent@abc.com",
    "address" : [
        {
            "city" : "NY",
            "state" : "NY",
            "country" : "USA"
        }
    ]
}
>
```

# The MongoDB database

Data is stored in a database in the form of collections. It is a container for collection, just like in SQL databases where the database is a container for tables.

To create a database in MongoDB, we use the following command:

```
> use sample_db;
switched to db sample_db
```

This command creates a database called sample_db, which can be used as a container for storing collections.

The default database for `mongo` is `test`. If we do not specify a database before storing our collection, MongoDB will store the collection in the `test` database.

Each database has its own set of files on the filesystem. A MongoDB server can have multiple databases. We can see the list of all the databases using the following command:

```
> show databases;
local       0.000GB
mongo_lam   0.063GB
test        0.000GB
```

## MongoDB collections

The collection is a container for MongoDB documents. It is equivalent to SQL tables, which store the data in rows. The collection should only store related documents. For example, the `user_profiles` collection should only store data related to user profiles. It should not contain a user's friend list as this should not be a part of a user's profile; instead, this should fall under the `users_friend` collection.

To create a new collection, you can use the following command:

```
> db.createCollection("users_profile");
{ "ok" : 1 }
```

Here, `db` represents the database in which we are storing a collection and `users_profile` is the new collection we are creating.

Documents in a collection should have a similar or related purpose. A database cannot have multiple collections with the same name, they are unique in the given database.

Collections do not force the user to define a schema and are thus known as schemaless. Documents within the collection have different fields. For example, in one document, we can have `user_address`, but in another document, it is not mandatory to have the `user_address` field.

This is suitable for an agile approach.

# MongoDB documents

Data in MongoDB is actually stored in the form of documents. The document is a collection of key-value pairs. The key is also known as an **attribute**.

Documents have a dynamic schema and documents in the same collection may vary in field set.

Here is the structure of a MongoDB document:

```
{
    "_id" : ObjectId("596ce40ceafa9cc9cf097a41"),
    "title" : "MongoDB Overview",
    "description" : "MongoDB is no sql database",
    "by" : "tutorials point",
    "url" : "http://www.tutorialspoint.com",
    "tags" : [
        "MongoDB",
        "database",
        "NoSQL"
    ],
    "likes" : 100.0,
    "comments" : [
        {
            "user" : "user1",
            "message" : "My first comment",
            "dateCreated" : ISODate("2011-02-19T20:45:00.000Z"),
            "like" : 0.0
        },
        {
            "user" : "user2",
            "message" : "My second comments",
            "dateCreated" : ISODate("2011-02-25T02:15:00.000Z"),
            "like" : 5.0
        }
    ]
}
```

MongoDB documents have a special field called _id._id is a 12-byte hexadecimal number that ensures the uniqueness of the document. It is generated by MongoDB if not provided by the developer.

Of these 12 bytes, the first 4 bytes represent the current time stamp, the next 3 bytes represent the machine ID, the next 2 bytes represent the process ID on the MongoDB server, and the remaining 3 bytes are simple auto-increment values, as shown in the following diagram:

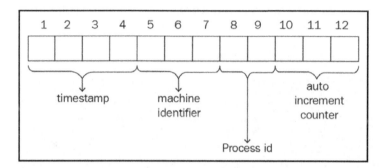

_id also represents the primary key for MongoDB documents.

Let's look at a quick comparison between SQL and MongoDB:

| SQL | MongoDB |
| --- | --- |
| Database | Database |
| Table | Collection |
| Row | Document |
| Column | Field |

Here are some of MongoDB's advantages over RDBMS:

- Collections in the MongoDB database are schemaless. Documents inserted in collections can have different sets of fields.
- The structure of a single-document object is simple and clear.
- Complex joins are not required as the MongoDB database supports an embedded document structure.
- MongoDB has rich query support. MongoDB supports dynamic queries on a database.
- MongoDB is easy to scale.
- Conversion or mapping between database objects and application objects is simple as most of the application supports JSON mapping with database objects.
- Integrated memory support allows the user to access data in a much faster way.

The following are the uses of MongoDB:

- Document-oriented storage
- Index on any attribute
- Replication and high availability
- Auto-sharding
- Rich query support
- Professional support from MongoDB

The applications of MongoDB are:

- **User profiles**: Authentication tools and LDAP are good for authentication and authorization, but data, such as rewards, criminal records, promotions, phone numbers, and addresses are added day by day. Other databases are not able to adopt such quick-changing data. We can use MongoDB dynamic documents to store such data over time in the document.
- **Product and catalog data**: In e-commerce companies or chemical companies, many new products are getting added every day. Each time a new product is added, it is not easy to change schema quickly. In these scenarios, using a document-based database is easier than using any other traditional database.
- **Metadata**: We often require metadata that describes our data. In such scenarios, a graph-based database is a good choice, but we can also use MongoDB for these applications.
- **Content**: MongoDB is mainly a document database. It is great for serving text as well as HTML documents. Also, it provides fine control over storing and indexing contents.

The limitations of MongoDB are:

- The maximum document size supported by MongoDB is 16 MB.
- The maximum document-nesting level supported by MongoDB is 100.
- The maximum namespace (*database + collection name*) supported by MongoDB is 123 characters.
- The database name is limited to 64 characters.
- If we apply an index on any field, that field value cannot contain more than 1024 bytes.
- A maximum of 64 indexes are allowed per collection and a maximum of 34 fields are allowed in compound indexes.

- A hashed index cannot be unique.
- A maximum of 12 nodes are allowed in a replica set.
- A maximum of 512 bytes are allowed for shard keys.
- You cannot rollback automatically if data is more than 300 MB. Manual intervention is needed in such cases.

Now we will go through the MongoDB CRUD operations.

# The create operation

The create operation inserts the new document into the collection. If a collection does not exist, MongoDB will create a new collection and insert a document in it. MongoDB provides the following methods to insert a document into the database:

- db.collection.insertOne();
- db.collection.insertMany();

The MongoDB insert operation will target single collections. Also, mongo preserves atomicity at the document level:

```
db.users_profile.insertOne({
        userId : 1,
        firstName : "John",
        lastName : "Richard",
        age : 26,
        email : "john2992@mail.com"
})
```

This method returns a document that contains the newly added documents _id value:

```
/* 1 */
{
    "acknowledged" : true,
    "insertedId" : ObjectId("596ce72cbc5266c2c9c44e8d")
}
```

The method `insertMany()`, can insert multiple documents into the collection at a time. We have to pass an array of documents to the method:

```
db.users_profile.insertMany([
    {
        userId : 1, firstName : "John", lastName : "Rcihard",
        age : 26, email : "john2992@mail.com"
    },
    {
        userId : 2, firstName : "Kedar", lastName : "Sans",
        age : 29, email : "kedar.sans@mail.com"
    },
    {
        userId : 3, firstName : "Chan", lastName : "Kuli",
        age : 27, email : "chann.k@mail.com"
    }
]);
```

In MongoDB, each document requires an `_id` field that uniquely identifies the document that acts as a **primary key**. If a user does not insert the `_id` field during the insert operation, MongoDB will automatically generate and insert an ID for each document:

```
/* 1 */
{
    "acknowledged" : true,
    "insertedIds" : [
        ObjectId("596ce893bc5266c2c9c44e8e"),
        ObjectId("596ce893bc5266c2c9c44e8f"),
        ObjectId("596ce893bc5266c2c9c44e90")
    ]
}
```

The following is the list of methods that can also be used to insert documents into the collection:

- `db.collection.update();`
- `db.collection.updateOne();`
- `db.collection.updateMany();`
- `db.collection.findAndModify();`
- `db.collection.findOneAndUpdate();`
- `db.collection.findOneAndReplace();`
- `db.collection.save();`
- `db.collection.bulkWrite();`

# The read operation

The read operation retrieves documents or data from documents in the collection. To retrieve all documents from a given collection, pass an empty document as a filter. We have to pass the query filter parameter in order to apply our criteria for the selection of documents:

```
db.users_profile.find({})
```

The preceding code returns all the documents in the given collection:

```
/* 1 */
{
    "_id" : ObjectId("596ce72cbc5266c2c9c44e8d"),
    "userId" : 1.0,
    "firstName" : "John",
    "lastName" : "Rcihard",
    "age" : 26.0,
    "email" : "john2992@mail.com"
}

/* 2 */
{
    "_id" : ObjectId("596ce893bc5266c2c9c44e8e"),
    "userId" : 1.0,
    "firstName" : "John",
    "lastName" : "Rcihard",
    "age" : 26.0,
    "email" : "john2992@mail.com"
}
```

This operation will return all the documents from the user_profiles collection. It is also equivalent to the following SQL operation, where user_profiles is the table, and the query will return all the rows from the table:

```
SELECT * FROM user_profiles;
```

# Applying filters on fields

To apply equal conditions, we use the following filter expression:

```
<field>:<value>
```

For example, to select the user profile with `John` as the user's first name, we have to apply the query as:

```
db.users_profile.find({
        firstName : "John"
    });
```

This gives us all the documents where we have the `firstName` as `John`:

```
/* 1 */
{
    "_id" : ObjectId("596ce72cbc5266c2c9c44e8d"),
    "userId" : 1.0,
    "firstName" : "John",
    "lastName" : "Rcihard",
    "age" : 26.0,
    "email" : "john2992@mail.com"
}

/* 2 */
{
    "_id" : ObjectId("596ce893bc5266c2c9c44e8e"),
    "userId" : 1.0,
    "firstName" : "John",
    "lastName" : "Rcihard",
    "age" : 26.0,
    "email" : "john2992@mail.com"
}]
```

This query will return all the documents where the first name is `John`. This operation is equivalent to the following SQL operation:

```
SELECT * FROM user_profiles WHERE firstName='John';
```

# Applying conditional and logical operators on the filter parameter

We can apply conditional parameters while retrieving data from collections, such as `IN`, `AND`, and `OR` with less than and greater than conditions:

- Apply the `IN` condition: We can set filter parameters so the query can match values from a given set and retrieve values from collections where documents match values from a given set. The syntax for the `in` parameter is the following:

```
{<field 1> : {<operator 1> : <value 1>},....}
```

The following query will return all the documents from `user_profiles` where the first name is John or Kedar:

```
db.users_profile.find({
    firstName : {
        $in :["John", "Kedar"]
    }
});
```

Here, we get all the documents with a `firstName` of either John or Kedar:

```
/* 2 */
{
    "_id" : ObjectId("596ce893bc5266c2c9c44e8e"),
    "userId" : 1.0,
    "firstName" : "John",
    "lastName" : "Rcihard",
    "age" : 26.0,
    "email" : "john2992@mail.com"
}

/* 3 */
{
    "_id" : ObjectId("596ce893bc5266c2c9c44e8f"),
    "userId" : 2.0,
    "firstName" : "Kedar",
    "lastName" : "Sans",
    "age" : 29.0,
    "email" : "kedar.sans@mail.com"
}
```

The preceding operation corresponds to the following SQL operation query:

```
SELECT * FROM user_profiles WHERE firstName in ('John',
'Kedar');
```

- Apply the AND condition: If the implicit query applies to more than two fields, it covers the AND condition and does not need to apply it separately. This compound query matches all the conditions specified and returns documents where all these conditions are met.

For example, the following query returns the result where the `firstname` matches `John` and the age of the user is less than `29`:

```
db.users_profile.find({
        firstName : "John",
        age : { $lt : 29 }
});
```

This corresponds to the following SQL query:

```
SELECT * FROM user_profiles WHERE firstName='John' AND age<30;
```

- Apply the OR condition: Using the $or operator, we can specify the compound query that can apply to two or more fields. The following is the query example where we retrieve any user's profile that has either the first name of John or an age value of less than 30:

```
db.users_profile.find({
        $or : [
                { "firstName" : "John" },
                { "age" : { $lt : 30 } }
        ]
});
```

This corresponds to the following SQL query:

```
SELECT * FROM user_profiles WHERE firstName='John' or age<30;
```

- Apply the AND/OR condition in the combine. The following is a query example where we apply both the AND and OR operators in the combine to retrieve documents. This query returns user's profiles where the `firstName` is `John` and the age is less than `30` or the `lastName` starts with `s`:

```
db.users_profile.find({
        "firstName" : "John",
        $or : [
                { "age" : { $lt : 30 } },
                { "lastName" : /^s/ },
        ]
});
```

This operation corresponds to the following SQL operation:

```
SELECT * FROM user_profiles WHERE firstName='John'
AND age<30 OR lastName like 's%';
```

MongoDB also supports $regex to perform string-pattern matching. Here is a list of the comparison query operators:

| Operator | Description |
|---|---|
| $eq | Matches values that equals a specified value |
| $gt | Matches values that are greater than a specified value |
| $gte | Matches values that are greater than or equal to a specified value |
| $lt | Matches values that are less than a specified value |
| $lte | Matches values that are less than or equal to a specified value |
| $ne | Matches values that are not equal to a specified value |
| $in | Matches values that are specified in a set of values |
| $nin | Matches values that are not specified in a set of values |

Here is a list of logical operators:

| Operator | Description |
|---|---|
| $or | Joins query clauses with the OR operator and returns all the documents that match any condition of the clause. |
| $and | Joins query clauses with the AND operator and returns documents that match all the conditions of all the clauses. |
| $not | Inverts the effects of the query expression and returns all the documents that do not match the given criteria. |
| $nor | Joins query clauses with the logical NOR operator and returns all the documents that match the criteria specified in the clauses. |

MongoDB also uses the findOne method to retrieve documents from the mongo collection. It internally calls the find method with a limit of 1. findOne matches all the documents with the filter criteria and returns the first document from the result set.

# The update operation

The following is a list of methods MongoDB uses to update the document information:

```
* db.collection.updateOne(<filter>, <update>, <options>);
* db.collection.updateMany(<filter>, <update>, <options>);
* db.collection.replaceOne(<filter>, <update>, <options>);
```

If the update operation increases the size of the document while updating, the update operation relocates the document on the disk:

- **Update single document**: The following example uses the db.collection.updateOne() method to update a single document. The following query finds the userId 1 document in user_profiles and updates the age to 30:

```
db.users_profile.updateOne(
    { userId : 1 },
    { $set : {
        age : 30
    }
});
```

Here, the query uses the $set operator to update the value of the age field, where the userId matches 1:

```
/* 1 */
{
    "acknowledged" : true,
    "matchedCount" : 1.0,
    "modifiedCount" : 1.0
}
```

- **Update multiple documents**: The following example uses the `db.collection.updateMany()` method to update multiple documents where the condition matches.

  The following example updates the age of all users between the ages of 30 to 35:

```
db.users_profile.updateMany(
        { age : 20 },
        { $set : {age : 35}
}) ;
```

  The output gives us acknowledgement of how many documents have been updated:

```
/* 1 */
{
    "acknowledged" : true,
    "matchedCount" : 0.0,
    "modifiedCount" : 0.0
}
```

- **Replace document**: The `db.collection.replaceOne()` method replaces an entire document with a new document, except for the _id field. The _id field has the same value as the current document. The following example replaces a user's document with that of `userId : 1`:

```
db.users_profile.replaceOne(
        { userId : 1 },
        {
        userId : 1,
        firstName : "Sam",
        lastName : "Billings",
        age : 26,
        email : "sam2992@mail.com"
        });
```

The following are additional methods that can be used for the update operation:

- db.collection.findOneAndReplace();
- db.collection.findOneAndUpdate();
- db.collection.findAndModify();
- db.collection.save();
- db.collection.bulkWrite();

# The delete operation

MongoDB provides the following methods to remove documents from the collection:

- db.collection.deleteOne();
- db.collection.deleteMany();

The db.collection.deleteMany() method is used to delete all the documents that match the given criteria. If you want to delete all the documents, you can pass an empty document criterion:

```
db.users_profile.deleteMany({});
```

This query will delete all the documents contained in the user_profiles collection.

To delete the single most document which matched the given criteria, we use the db.collection.deleteOne() method. The following query deletes the record where the userId is equal to 1:

```
db.users_profile.deleteOne({
        userId : 1
});
```

The following methods can also delete documents from the collection:

- db.collection.findOneAndDelete()
- db.collection.findAndModify()
- db.collection.bulkWrite()

# Data models in MongoDB

The MongoDB collection does not enforce structure on the document. This allows the document to map to objects or entities easily. Each document can match a data field of the entity. In practice, documents in collections share the same structure.

When deciding on data modeling, we have to consider the requirements of the application, the performance characteristics of the database's design, and data retrieval patterns. When designing data models, we have to focus on the application's usage of data and the inherent structure of the data.

While deciding the data model, we have to consider the structure of the document and how documents relate to each other. There are two key data models that show these relationships:

- The reference document data model
- The embedded data model

# The references document data model

In this model, the relationship is maintained using links between documents. References from one document is stored in another document. This process is also called normalization; it establishes the relationship between different collections and defines collections for a more specific purpose:

We use the normalized data approach in the following scenarios:

- When embedding data, it will create duplicate data but not provide significant read performance
- To represent more complex many-to-many relationships
- To model large hierarchical data

# The embedded data model

In this document model, the relationships between data are maintained by storing data in a single document. Here, we do not create a separate document to define a relationship. We can embed the document structure in a field or array within the document. These documents are denormalized. This allows us to retrieve data in a single operation, but it unnecessarily increases the size of the document.

The embedded document structure allows us to store related pieces of data in the same document. This also allows us to update a single document without worrying about data consistency.

The embedded document structure is used in two cases:

- When there is a **one-to-one relationship** with the embedded document. We can store the embedded document as an object field.
- When there is a **one-to-many relationship** with the embedded document. Here we can store the embedded document as an array of the object field.

The embedded structure provides better performance for read operations, requests and retrieves related data in a single database operation, and updates the data in a single atomic operation. But this approach can lead to an increase in the size of the document, and MongoDB will store such documents in a fragment, which leads to poor write performance.

Modeling the application data for MongoDB depends on the data as well as the characteristics of MongoDB itself. When creating data models for applications, analyze all of the read and write operations with the following operations and MongoDB features:

- **Document size**: The update operation on a document may increase the size of the document as MongoBD documents are schemaless. An update may include adding more elements to an array or adding new elements to the document. If the document size exceeds the maximum limit, MongoDB automatically relocates the document on to the disk.

- **Atomicity**: In MongoDB, each operation is atomic at the document level. A single operation can change only one document at a time. So, the operation that modified more than one document needed multiple write operations. The embedded document structure is more suitable in such a scenario where all related data is stored in a single document.
- **Sharding**: Sharding provides horizontal scaling in MongoDB. This enables deployment with a large dataset and high throughput for operations. Sharding allows us to partition a collection and store documents from collections across multiple instances of `mongod` or clusters. MongoDB uses shard keys to select data. The sharding key has an effect on performance and can prevent query isolation and increased write capacity. So be careful when choosing the shard key.
- **Indexes**: We use indexes to improve performance for common queries. Normally, we build indexes on a field that is often used in filter criteria and can be in sorted order so that searching will use effective algorithms, such as mid-search. MongoDB will automatically create an index on the `_id` field. While creating indexes, consider the following points:
    - Each index requires at least 8 KB of space.
    - Indexes have a negative impact on write operations. For collection with a high write-to-read ratio, indexes are much more expensive as each insert operation leads to some update operations.
    - Collections with a high read-to-write ratio often benefit from indexes. Indexes do not affect read operations on non-index fields.
    - Active indexes use disk space and memory. This usage can be significant and we should analyze it for performance considerations.
- **Large numbers of collections**: In some use cases, we may decide to store data over multiple collections instead of a single one. If the number of documents in the collection is low, then we can group the documents by type. For example, by maintaining a separate collection for the dev, prod, and debug logs, instead of using three collections named `dev_log`, `prod_log`, and `deug_log`, we can maintain a single collection called **log**. Having a large number of collections decreases the performance of operations. When adding collections, consider the following points:
    - Each collection has an overhead of a few kilobytes.
    - Each index on `_id` requires at least 8 KB of data space.
    - Each database single namespace stores the metadata. And each index and collection have an entry in the namespace file.

- **Data lifecycle management**: The **Time to live** (**TTL**) feature of a collection expires documents after a certain period of time. We can consider using the TTL feature if certain data in the collection is not useful after a specific period of time. If an application used only recently-inserted documents, use **capped collections**. The capped collection provides **first in, first out** (**FIFO**) management of documents that supports insert and read operations based on insertion order.

# Introduction to MongoDB indexing

Indexes allow efficient execution of MongoDB queries. If we don't have indexes, MongoDB has to scan all the documents in the collection to select those documents that match the criteria. If proper indexing is used, MongoDB can limit the scanning of documents and select documents efficiently. Indexes are a special data structure that store some field values of documents in an easy-to-traverse way.

Indexes store the values of specific fields or sets of fields, ordered by the values of fields. The ordering of field values allows us to apply effective algorithms of traversing, such as the mid-search algorithm, and also supports range-based operations effectively. In addition, MongoDB can return sorted results easily.

Indexes in MongoDB are the same as indexes in other database systems. MongoDB defines indexes at the collection level and supports indexes on fields and sub-fields of documents.

# The default _id index

MongoDB creates the `default` `_id` index when creating a document. The `_id` index prevents users from inserting two documents with the same `_id` value. You cannot drop an index on an `_id` field.

The following syntax is used to create an index in MongoDB:

```
>db.collection.createIndex(<key and index type specification>, <options>);
```

The preceding method creates an index only if an index with the same specification does not exist. MongoDB indexes use the B-tree data structure.

The following are the different types of indexes:

- **Single field**: In addition to the _id field index, MongoDB allows the creation of an index on any single field in ascending or descending order. For a single field index, the order of the index does not matter as MongoDB can traverse indexes in any order. The following is an example of creating an index on the single field where we are creating an index on the firstName field of the user_profiles collection:

```
db.user_profiles.createIndex({ "firstName" : 1 });
```

  The query gives acknowledgment after creating the index:

```
{
    "createdCollectionAutomatically" : false,
    "numIndexesBefore" : 1,
    "numIndexesAfter" : 2,
    "ok" : 1.0
}
```

  This will create an ascending index on the firstName field. To create a descending index, we have to provide -1 instead of 1.

- **Compound index**: MongoDB also supports user-defined indexes on multiple fields. The order of fields defined while creating an index has a significant effect. For example, a compound index defined as {firstName:1, age:-1} will sort data by firstName first and then each firstName with age.

- **Multikey index**: MongoDB uses multi-key indexes to index the content in the array. If you index the field that contains the array values, MongoDB creates an index for each field in the object of an array. These indexes allow queries to select the document by matching the element or set of elements of the array. MongoDB automatically decides whether to create multi-key indexes or not.

- **Text indexes**: MongoDB provides text indexes that support the searching of string contents in the MongoDB collection. To create text indexes, we have to use the db.collection.createIndex() method, but we need to pass a *text* string literal in the query:

```
db.reviews.createIndex({"comments" : "text"})
```

You can also create text indexes on multiple fields, for example:

```
db.reviews.createIndex({
        "comments" : "text",
        "subject" : "text"
});
```

Once the index is created, we get an acknowledgment:

```
{
    "createdCollectionAutomatically" : false,
    "numIndexesBefore" : 1,
    "numIndexesAfter" : 2,
    "ok" : 1.0
}
```

Compound indexes can be used with text indexes to define an ascending or descending order of the index.

- **Hashed index**: To support hash-based sharding, MongoDB supports hashed indexes. In this approach, indexes store the hash value and query, and the select operation checks the hashed indexes. Hashed indexes can support only equality-based operations. They are limited in their performance of range-based operations.

Indexes have the following properties:

- **Unique indexes**: Indexes should maintain uniqueness. This makes MongoDB drop the duplicate value from indexes.
- **Partial Indexes**: Partial indexes apply the index on documents of a collection that match a specified condition. By applying an index on the subset of documents in the collection, partial indexes have a lower storage requirement as well as a reduced performance cost.
- **Sparse index**: In the sparse index, MongoDB includes only those documents in the index in which the index field is present, other documents are discarded. We can combine unique indexes with a sparse index to reject documents that have duplicate values but ignore documents that have an indexed key.

- **TTL index**: TTL indexes are a special type of indexes where MongoDB will automatically remove the document from the collection after a certain amount of time. Such indexes are ideal to remove machine-generated data, logs, and session information that we need for a finite duration. The following TTL index will automatically delete data from the log table after 3000 seconds:

```
db.log.createIndex(
    {
        "createdAt" : 1
    },{
        "expireAfterSeconds":3000
    });
```

Once the index is created, we get an acknowledgment message:

```
{
    "createdCollectionAutomatically" : false,
    "numIndexesBefore" : 1,
    "numIndexesAfter" : 2,
    "ok" : 1.0
}
```

The limitations of indexes:

- A single collection can have up to 64 indexes only.
- The qualified index name is `<database-name>.<collection-name>.$<index-name>` and cannot have more than 128 characters. By default, the index name is a combination of index type and field name. You can specify an index name while using the `createIndex()` method to ensure that the fully-qualified name does not exceed the limit.
- There can be no more than 31 fields in the compound index.
- The query cannot use both text and geospatial indexes. You cannot combine the $text operator, which requires text indexes, with some other query operator required for special indexes. For example, you cannot combine the $text operator with the $near operator.
- Fields with 2d sphere indexes can only hold geometry data. 2d sphere indexes are specially provided for geometric data operations. For example, to perform operations on co-ordinate, we have to provide data as points on a planer co-ordinate system, [x, y]. For non-geometries, the data query operation will fail.

The limitation on data:

- The maximum number of documents in a capped collection must be less than 2^32. We should define it by the max parameter while creating it. If you do not specify, the capped collection can have any number of documents, which will slow down the queries.
- The MMAPv1 storage engine will allow 16,000 data files per database, which means it provides the maximum size of 32 TB.
  We can set the `storage.mmapv1.smallfile` parameter to reduce the size of the database to 8 TB only.
- Replica sets can have up to 50 members.
- Shard keys cannot exceed 512 bytes.

# Replication

A replica set is a group of MongoDB instances that store the same set of data. Replicas are basically used in production to ensure a high availability of data.

**Redundancy and data availability**: because of replication, we have redundant data across the MongoDB instances. We are using replication to provide a high availability of data to the application. If one instance of MongoDB is unavailable, we can serve data from another instance. Replication also increases the read capacity of applications as reading operations can be sent to different servers and retrieve data faster. By maintaining data on different servers, we can increase the locality of data and increase the availability of data for distributed applications. We can use the replica copy for backup, reporting, as well as disaster recovery.

# Replication in MongoDB

A replica set is a group of MongoDB instances that have the same dataset. A replica set has one arbiter node and multiple data-bearing nodes. In data-bearing nodes, one node is considered the primary node while the other nodes are considered the secondary nodes.

All write operations happen at the primary node. Once a write occurs at the primary node, the data is replicated across the secondary nodes internally to make copies of the data available to all nodes and to avoid data inconsistency.

If a primary node is not available for the operation, secondary nodes use election algorithms to select one of their nodes as a primary node.

A special node, called an arbiter node, is added in the replica set. This arbiter node does not store any data. The arbiter is used to maintain a quorum in the replica set by responding to a heartbeat and election request sent by the secondary nodes in replica sets. As an arbiter does not store data, it is a cost-effective resource used in the election process. If votes in the election process are even, the arbiter adds a voice to choose a primary node. The arbiter node is always the arbiter, it will not change its behavior, unlike a primary or secondary node. The primary node can step down and work as secondary node, while secondary nodes can be elected to perform as primary nodes.

Secondary nodes apply read/write operations from a primary node to secondary nodes asynchronously.

# Automatic failover in replication

Primary nodes always communicate with other members every 10 seconds. If it fails to communicate with the others in 10 seconds, other eligible secondary nodes hold an election to choose a primary-acting node among them. The first secondary node that holds the election and receives the majority of votes is elected as a primary node. If there is an arbiter node, its vote is taken into consideration while choosing primary nodes.

# Read operations

Basically, the read operation happens at the primary node only, but we can specify the read operation to be carried out from secondary nodes also. A read from a secondary node does not affect data at the primary node. Reading from secondary nodes can also give inconsistent data.

# Sharding

Sharding is a methodology to distribute data across multiple machines. Sharding is basically used for deployment with a large dataset and high throughput operations. The single database cannot handle a database with large datasets as it requires larger storage, and bulk query operations can use most of the CPU cycles, which slows down processing. For such scenarios, we need more powerful systems.

One approach is to add more capacity to a single server, such as adding more memory and processing units or adding more RAM on the single server, this is also called vertical scaling. Another approach is to divide a large dataset across multiple systems and serve a data application to query data from multiple servers. This approach is called horizontal scaling. MongoDB handles horizontal scaling through sharding.

# Sharded clusters

MongoDB's sharding consists of the following components:

- **Shard**: Each shard stores a subset of sharded data. Also, each shard can be deployed as a replica set.
- **Mongos**: Mongos provide an interface between a client application and sharded cluster to route the query.
- **Config server**: The configuration server stores the metadata and configuration settings for the cluster. The MongoDB data is sharded at the collection level and distributed across sharded clusters.
- **Shard keys**: To distribute documents in collections, MongoDB partitions the collection using the shard key. MongoDB shards data into chunks. These chunks are distributed across shards in sharded clusters.

# Advantages of sharding

Here are some of the advantages of sharding:

- When we use sharding, the load of the read/write operations gets distributed across sharded clusters.
- As sharding is used to distribute data across a shard cluster, we can increase the storage capacity by adding shards horizontally.
- MongoDB allows continuing the read/write operation even if one of the shards is unavailable. In the production environment, shards should deploy with a replication mechanism to maintain high availability and add fault tolerance in a system.

# Storing large data in MongoDB

MongoDB is document-based database, data is stored in JSON and XML documents. MongoDB has a document size limit of 16 MB. If the size of a JSON document exceeds 16 MB, instead of storing data as a single file, MongoDB divides the file into chunks and each chunk is stored as a document in the system. MongoDB creates a chunk of 255 KB to divide files and only the last chuck can have less than 255 KB.

MongoDB uses two collections to work with `gridfs`. One collection is used to store the chunk data and another collection is used to store the metadata. When you query MongoDB for the operation of the `gridfs` file, MongoDB uses the metadata collection to perform the query and collect data from different chunks. GridFS stores data in two collections:

- `chunks`: Stores binary chunks.
- `files::` Stores the file's metadata.

# Summary

In this chapter, we learned about MongoDB, which is one of the most popular NoSQL databases. It is widely used in projects where requirements change frequently and is suitable for agile projects. It is a highly fault-tolerant and robust database.

# 3
# Neo4j

Some application use cases or data models may place as much (or more) importance on the relationships between entities as the entities themselves. When this is the case, a graph database may be the optimal choice for data storage. In this chapter, we will look at **Neo4j**, one of the most commonly used graph databases.

Over the course of this chapter, we will discuss several aspects of Neo4j:

- Useful features
- Appropriate use cases
- Anti-patterns and pitfalls
- Ways of using Neo4j with languages such as:
    - Cypher
    - Python
    - Java

Once you have completed this chapter, you will begin to understand the significance of graph databases. You will have worked through installing and configuring Neo4j as you build up your own server. You will have employed simple scripts and code to interact with and utilize Neo4j, allowing you to further explore ideas around modeling interconnected data.

We'll start with a quick introduction to Neo4j. From there, we will move on to the appropriate graph database use cases, and begin to learn more about the types of problems that can be solved with Neo4j.

# What is Neo4j?

Neo4j is an open source, distributed data store used to model graph problems. It was released in 2007 and is sponsored by Neo4j, Inc., which also offers enterprise licensing and support for Neo4j. It departs from the traditional nomenclature of database technologies, in which entities are stored in schema-less, entity-like structures called **nodes**. Nodes are connected to other nodes via relationships or edges. Nodes can also be grouped together with optional structures called **labels**.

This relationship-centric approach to data modeling is known as the **property graph model**. Under the property graph model, both nodes and edges can have properties to store values. Neo4j embraces this approach. It is designed to ensure that nodes and edges are stored efficiently, and that nodes can *share any number or type of relationships without sacrificing performance.*[8]

# How does Neo4j work?

Neo4j stores nodes, edges, and properties on disks in stores that are specific to each type—for example, nodes are stored in the node store.[5, s.11] They are also stored in two types of caches—the **file system (FS)** and the **node/relationship** caches. The FS cache is divided into regions for each type of store, and data is evicted on a **least-frequently-used (LFU)** policy.

Data is written in transactions assembled from commands and sorted to obtain a predictable update order. Commands are sorted at the time of creation, with the aim of preserving consistency. Writes are added to the transaction log and either marked as committed or rolled back (in the event of a failure). Changes are then applied (in sorted order) to the store files on disk.

It is important to note that transactions in Neo4j dictate the state and are therefore idempotent by nature.[5, s.34] They do not directly modify the data. Reapplying transactions for a recovery event simply replays the transactions as of a given safe point.

In a **high-availability (HA)**, clustered scenario, Neo4j embraces a master/slave architecture. Transaction logs are then shared between all Neo4j instances, regardless of their current role. Unlike most master/slave implementations, slave nodes can handle both reads and writes.[5, s.37] On a write transaction, the slave coordinates a lock with the master and buffers the transaction while it is applied to the master. Once complete, the buffered transaction is then applied to the slave.

Another important aspect of Neo4j's HA architecture is that each node/edge has its own unique identifier (ID). To accomplish this, the master instance allocates the IDs for each slave instance in blocks. The blocks are then sent to each instance so that IDs for new nodes/edges can be applied locally, preserving consistency, as shown in the following diagram:

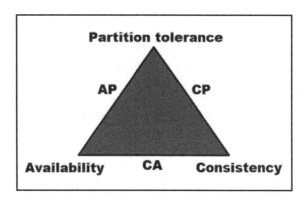

A graphical representation of the CAP theorem, using the corners of a triangle to denote the design aspects of consistency, availability, and partition tolerance

When looking at Neo4j within the context of Brewer's CAP theorem (formerly known as both *Brewer's CAP principle* and *Brewer's CAP conjecture*), its designation would be as a CP system.[3, p.1] It earns this designation because of its use of locking mechanisms to support **Consistency** (**C**) over multiple, horizontally-scaled instances in a cluster. Its support for clustering multiple nodes together indicates that Neo4j is also **Partition tolerant** (**P**).

While the Enterprise Edition of Neo4j does offer high-availability clustering as an option, there are a limited number of nodes that can accept write operations. Despite the name, this configuration limits its ability to be considered highly-available within the bounds of the CAP theorem.

# Features of Neo4j

Aside from its support of the property graph model, Neo4j has several other features that make it a desirable data store. Here, we will examine some of those features and discuss how they can be utilized in a successful Neo4j cluster.

# Clustering

Enterprise Neo4j offers horizontal scaling through two types of clustering. The first is the typical **high-availability clustering**, in which several slave servers process data overseen by an elected master. In the event that one of the instances should fail, a new master is chosen.

The second type of clustering is known as **causal clustering**. This option provides additional features, such as disposable read replicas and built-in load balancing, that help abstract the distributed nature of the clustered database from the developer. It also supports causal consistency, which aims to support **Atomicity Consistency Isolation and Durability (ACID)** compliant consistency in use cases where eventual consistency becomes problematic. Essentially, causal consistency is delivered with a distributed transaction algorithm that ensures that a user will be able to immediately read their own write, regardless of which instance handles the request.

# Neo4j Browser

Neo4j ships with Neo4j Browser, a web-based application that can be used for database management, operations, and the execution of Cypher queries. In addition to, monitoring the instance on which it runs, Neo4j Browser also comes with a few built-in learning tools designed to help new users acclimate themselves to Neo4j and graph databases. Neo4j Browser is a huge step up from the command-line tools that dominate the NoSQL landscape.

# Cache sharding

In most clustered Neo4j configurations, a single instance contains a complete copy of the data. At the moment, true sharding is not available, but Neo4j does have a feature known as **cache sharding**. This feature involves directing queries to instances that only have certain parts of the cache preloaded, so that read requests for extremely large data sets can be adequately served.

# Help for beginners

One of the things that Neo4j does better than most NoSQL data stores is the amount of documentation and tutorials that it has made available for new users. The Neo4j website provides a few links to get started with in-person or online training, as well as meetups and conferences to become acclimated to the community. The Neo4j documentation is very well-done and kept up to date, complete with well-written manuals on development, operations, and data modeling. The blogs and videos by the Neo4j, Inc. engineers are also quite helpful in getting beginners started on the right path.

Additionally, when first connecting to your instance/cluster with Neo4j Browser, the first thing that is shown is a list of links directed at beginners. These links direct the user to information about the Neo4j product, graph modeling and use cases, and interactive examples. In fact, executing the `play movies` command brings up a tutorial that loads a database of movies. This database consists of various nodes and edges that are designed to illustrate the relationships between actors and their roles in various films.

# Evaluating your use case

Because of Neo4j's focus on node/edge traversal, it is a good fit for use cases requiring analysis and examination of relationships. The property graph model helps to define those relationships in meaningful ways, enabling the user to make informed decisions. Bearing that in mind, there are several use cases for Neo4j (and other graph databases) that seem to fit naturally.

# Social networks

Social networks seem to be a natural fit for graph databases. Individuals have friends, attend events, check in to geographical locations, create posts, and send messages. All of these different aspects can be tracked and managed with a graph database such as Neo4j.

Who can see a certain person's posts? Friends? Friends of friends? Who will be attending a certain event? How is a person connected to others attending the same event? In small numbers, these problems could be solved with a number of data stores. But what about an event with several thousands of people attending, where each person has a network of 500 friends? Neo4j can help to solve a multitude of problems in this domain, and appropriately scale to meet increasing levels of operational complexity.

# Matchmaking

Like social networks, Neo4j is also a good fit for solving problems presented by matchmaking or dating sites. In this way, a person's interests, goals, and other properties can be traversed and matched to profiles that share certain levels of equality. Additionally, the underlying model can also be applied to prevent certain matches or block specific contacts, which can be useful for this type of application.

# Network management

Working with an enterprise-grade network can be quite complicated. Devices are typically broken up into different domains, sometimes have physical and logical layers, and tend to share a delicate relationship of dependencies with each other. In addition, networks might be very dynamic because of hardware failure/replacement, organization, and personnel changes.

The property graph model can be applied to adequately work with the complexity of such networks. In a use case study with **Enterprise Management Associates (EMA)**, this type of problem was reported as *an excellent format for capturing and modeling the inter dependencies that can help to diagnose failures.*[4]

For instance, if a particular device needs to be shut down for maintenance, you would need to be aware of other devices and domains that are dependent on it, in a multitude of directions. Neo4j allows you to *capture that easily and naturally without having to define a whole mess of linear relationships between each device.*[4] The path of relationships can then be easily traversed at query time to provide the necessary results.

# Analytics

Many scalable data store technologies are not particularly suitable for business analysis or **online analytical processing (OLAP)** uses. When working with large amounts of data, coalescing desired data can be tricky with **relational database management systems (RDBMS)**. Some enterprises will even duplicate their RDBMS into a separate system for OLAP so as not to interfere with their **online transaction processing (OLTP)** workloads.

Neo4j can scale to present meaningful data about relationships between different enterprise-marketing entities. In his graduate thesis titled *GraphAware: Towards Online Analytical Processing in Graph Databases*, researcher *Michal Bachman* illustrates this difference in a simple comparison of traversing relationships in both RDBMS and **graph database management systems** (**GDBMS**). Bachman observes that *What might be a straightforward shallow breadth-first search in a GDBMS (hence considered OLTP) could be a very expensive multi-join operation in RDBMS (thus qualifying as OLAP).*[2]

However, Bachman also urges caution with analytical workloads on graph databases, stating that *graph databases lack native OLAP support.*[2] This implies that additional tools may need to be built to suit specific business analysis needs.

# Recommendation engines

Many brick-and-mortar and online retailers collect data about their customers' shopping habits. However, many of them fail to properly utilize this data to their advantage. Graph databases, such as Neo4j, can help assemble the bigger picture of customer habits for searching and purchasing, and even take trends in geographic areas into consideration.

For example, purchasing data may contain patterns indicating that certain customers tend to buy certain beverages on Friday evenings. Based on the relationships of other customers to products in that area, the engine could also suggest things such as cups, mugs, or glassware. Is the customer also a male in his thirties from a sports-obsessed area? Perhaps suggesting a mug supporting the local football team may spark an additional sale. An engine backed by Neo4j may be able to help a retailer uncover these small troves of insight.

# Neo4j anti-patterns

Relative to other NoSQL databases, Neo4j does not have a lot of anti-patterns. However, there are some common troubles that seem to befall new users, and we will try to detail them here.

## Applying relational modeling techniques in Neo4j

Using relational modeling techniques can lead to trouble with almost every NoSQL database, and Neo4j is no exception to that rule. Similar to other NoSQL databases, building efficient models in Neo4j involves appropriately modeling the required queries. Relational modeling requires you to focus on how your data is stored, and not as much on how it is queried or returned.

Whereas modeling for Neo4j requires you to focus on what your nodes are, and how they are related to each other. Additionally, the relationships should be dependent on the types of questions (queries) that your model will be answering. Failure to apply the proper amount of focus on your data model can lead to performance and operational troubles later.

## Using Neo4j for the first time on something mission-critical

In a talk at GraphConnect, San Francisco, Stefan Armbruster (field engineer for Neo4j, Inc.) described this as one of the main ways new users can get into trouble. Starting with a mission-critical use case for your first Neo4j project will probably not end well. Developers new to Neo4j need to make sure that they have an appropriate level of experience with it before attempting to build something important and complicated and move it into production. The best idea is to start with something small and expand your Neo4j footprint over time.

One possible way to avoid this pitfall is to make sure that you have someone on your team with graph database experience. Failing to recruit someone with that experience and knowledge, avoiding training, and ignoring the graph learning curve are surefire ways to *make sure you really mess up your project on the very first day*.[1] The bottom line is that there is no substitute for experience, if you want to get your graph database project done right.

## Storing entities and relationships within entities

While it might seem like a good idea to define entities as properties inside other entities, this can quickly get out of control. Remember that each property on an entity should directly relate to that entity, otherwise you will find your nodes getting big and queries becoming limited.

For example, it might be tempting to store things, such as drivers and cars, together, storing attributes about the car as properties on the driver. Querying will become difficult to solve if new requirements to query properties about the cars are introduced. But querying will become near impossible once the system needs to account for drivers with multiple cars. The bottom line is that if you need to store properties for an entity, it should have its own node and there should be a relationship to it.

 Don't forget that relationships can store properties too.

# Improper use of relationship types

Be sure to build your edges with meaningful relationship types. Do not use a single, general type such as CONNECTED_TO for different types of relationships.[1] Be specific. On the other end of that spectrum, it is also important not to make every relationship unique. Neo4j caps the number of relationship types at 65,000, and your model should not approach that number. Following either of those extremes will create trouble later with queries that traverse relationships. Problems with relationship type usage usually stem from a lack of understanding of the property graph model.

# Storing binary large object data

While Neo4j does offer primitive storage types, resist the urge to store **binary large object (BLOB)** data. BLOB data storage leads to large property values. Neo4j stores property values in a single file.[1] Large property values take a while to read, which can slow down all queries seeking property data (not just the BLOBs). To suit projects with requirements to store BLOB data, a more appropriate data store should be selected.

# Indexing everything

Indexes can be a helpful tool to improve the performance of certain queries. The current release of Neo4j offers two types of indexes: **schema indexes** and **legacy indexes**. Schema indexes should be used as your *go-to* index for new development, but legacy indexes are still required for things such as full-text indexing.[1] However, beware of creating indexes for every property of a node or label. This can cause your disk footprint to increase by a few orders of magnitude because of the extra write activity.

# Neo4j hardware selection, installation, and configuration

Building your Neo4j instance(s) with the right hardware is essential to running a successful cluster. Neo4j runs best when there is plenty of RAM at its disposal.

## Random access memory

One aspect to consider is that Neo4j runs on a **Java virtual machine** (**JVM**). This means that you need to have at least enough **random-access memory** (**RAM**) to hold the JVM heap, plus extra for other operating system processes. While Neo4j can be made to run on as little as 2 GB of RAM, a memory size of 32 GB of RAM (or more) is recommended for production workloads. This will allow you to configure your instances to map as much data into memory as possible, leading to optimal performance.

## CPU

Neo4j supports both x86 and OpenPOWER architectures. It requires at least an Intel Core i3, while an Intel Core i7 or IBM POWER8 is recommended for production.

## Disk

As with most data store technologies, disk I/O is a potential performance bottleneck. Therefore, it is recommended to use solid-state drives with either the ZFS or ext4 file systems. To get an idea of the amount of required disk space, the Neo4j documentation offers the following approximations (Neo4j Team 2017d):

- **Nodes**: 15 bytes
- **Edges**: 33 bytes
- **Properties**: 41 bytes

For example, assume that my data model consists of 400,000 nodes, 1.2 million relationships, and 3 million properties. I can then calculate my estimated disk usage with Neo4j as:

$$400000\ nodes \ \times\ 15\ bytes \to 6\ MB$$
$$1200000\ edges \ \times\ 33\ bytes \to 39.6\ MB$$
$$3000000\ properties \ \times\ 41\ bytes \to 123\ MB$$

---

$$Approximate\ disk\ space\ used \to 168.6\ MB$$

 Neo4j, Inc. offers a hardware calculator on their website, which can be found at
`https://neo4j.com/developer/guide-sizing-and-hardware-calculator/`.

# Operating system

For development, Neo4j should run fine on Windows and most flavors of Linux or BSD. A DMG installer is also available for OS X. When going to production, however, Linux is the best choice for a successful cluster. With Neo4j version 2.1 and earlier, one of the cache layers was off heap in the Linux releases, but on heap for Windows. This essentially made it impossible to cache a large amount of graph data while running on Windows.[1]

On Linux, Neo4j requires more than the default number of maximum open file handles. Increase that to 40,000 by adjusting the following line in the `/etc/security/limits.conf` file:

```
* - nofile 40000
```

# Network/firewall

Neo4j requires the following (TCP) ports to be accessible:

- `2003`: Graphite outbound
- `3637`: JMX (not enabled by default)
- `6362`: Backups
- `7687`: Neo4j's binary Bolt protocol
- `7474`: HTTP Neo4j Browser and Bolt

- `7473`: REST API
- `5001, 6001`: High-availability cluster communication
- `5000, 6000, 7000`: Causal cluster communication via the Raft protocol

# Installation

Here, we will install a single Neo4j instance running on one server. We will start by downloading the latest edition of the Neo4j Community Edition from `https://neo4j.com/download/other-releases/#releases`. There are downloads with nice, GUI-based installers available for most operating systems. We will select the Linux tarball install and download it. Then, we will copy the tarball to the directory from which we intend to run it. For this example, we will use the Neo4j 3.3.3 Community Edition:

```
sudo mkdir /local
sudo chown $USER:$USER /local
cd /local
mv ~/Downloads/neo4j-community-3.3.3-unix.tar.gz .
```

Now we can untar it, and it should create a directory and expand the files into it:

```
tar -zxvf neo4j-community-3.3.3-unix.tar.gz
```

Many people find it more convenient to rename this directory:

```
mv neo4j-community-3.3.3/ neo4j/
```

## Installing JVM

Be sure to use the most recent version of Java 8 from either Oracle or OpenJDK with Neo4j. Note that at the time of writing, Java 9 is *not* yet compatible with Neo4j.

# Configuration

For the purposes of the following examples, no additional configuration is necessary. But for deploying a production Neo4j server, there are settings within the `conf/neo4j.conf` file that are desirable or necessary to be altered.

The underlying database filename can be changed from its default setting of `graph.db`:

```
# The name of the database to mount
  dbms.active_database=graph.db
```

The section after the database name configuration is where things such as the data, certificates, and log directories can be defined. Remember that all locations defined here are relative, so make sure to explicitly define any paths that may be required to be located somewhere other than the Neo4j home directory:

```
# Paths of directories in the installation.
#dbms.directories.data=data
#dbms.directories.plugins=plugins
#dbms.directories.certificates=certificates
#dbms.directories.logs=logs
#dbms.directories.lib=lib
#dbms.directories.run=run
```

 The configuration properties in the preceding example are all prefaced with a hash sign (#) or commented out. To change them, first remove the hash sign, and then alter the value. If you're changing these properties on an already-running instance, be sure to restart the Neo4j process as well.

For instance, if we wanted to put the data or log location on a different directory or mount point (`data0` off of `root` and `/var/log`, respectively), we could define them like this:

```
dbms.directories.data=/data0
dbms.directories.logs=/var/log/neo4j
```

Our instance should be able to accept connections from machines other than the localhost (`127.0.0.1`), so we'll also set the `default_listen_address` and `default_advertised_address`. These settings can be modified in the network connector configuration section of the `neo4j.conf` file:

```
dbms.connectors.default_listen_address=192.168.0.100
dbms.connectors.default_advertised_address=192.168.0.100
```

The default connector ports can be changed as well. Client connections will need the Bolt protocol enabled. By default, it is defined to connect on port 7687:

```
#Bolt connector
dbms.connector.bolt.enabled=true
dbms.connector.bolt.listen_address=:7687
```

Note that if you disable the `bolt` connector, then client applications will only be able to connect to Neo4j using the REST API. The web management interface and REST API use HTTP/HTTPS, so they connect (by default) on ports `7474` and `7473`, respectively. These ports can also be altered:

```
# HTTP Connector. There must be exactly one HTTP connector.
dbms.connector.http.enabled=true
dbms.connector.http.listen_address=:7474
# HTTPS Connector. There can be zero or one HTTPS connectors.
dbms.connector.https.enabled=true
dbms.connector.https.listen_address=:7473
```

Now is also a good time to change the initial password. Neo4j installs with a single default admin username and password of `neo4j/neo4j`. To change the password, we can use the following command:

**`bin/neo4j-admin set-initial-password flynnLives`**

This command only works if you have not yet started Neo4j for the first time.

By default, Neo4j installs with the **Usage Data Collector** (UDC) enabled.[7] The UDC collects data concerning your usage and installation, tars it up and sends it to `udc.neo4j.org`. A full description of the data collected can be found at `http://neo4j.com/docs/operations-manual/current/configuration/usage-data-collector/`.

To disable this feature, simply add this line to the bottom of your `neo4j.conf` file:

```
dbms.udc.enabled=false
```

While the default JVM settings should be fine for most single-instance Neo4j clusters, larger operational workloads may require the tuning of various settings. Some bulk-load operations may not complete successfully if the JVM stack size is too small. To adjust it (say, to 1 MB), add the following line to the end of the `neo4j.conf` file:

```
dbms.jvm.additional=-Xss1M
```

The default garbage collector for Neo4j is the **Concurrent Mark and Sweep (CMS)** garbage collector. As Neo4j typically recommends larger heap sizes for production (20 GB+), performance can be improved by using the garbage-first garbage collector (G1GC). For example, to enable G1GC with a 24 GB heap and a target pause time of 200 ms, add the following settings to your neo4j.conf file:

```
dbms.memory.heap.max_size=24G
dbms.memory.heap.initial_size=24G
dbms.jvm.additional=-XX:+UseG1GC
dbms.jvm.additional=-XX:MaxGCPauseMillis=200
```

Note that regardless of the choice of the garbage collector and its settings, Neo4j should be tested under the production load to ensure that performance is within desirable levels. Be sure to keep track of GC behaviors and trends, and make adjustments as necessary.

# High-availability clustering

Neo4j supports **high-availability** (HA) master/slave clustering. To set up an HA Neo4j cluster, build the desired number of instances as if they were single-server installs. Then, adjust or add the following properties in the conf/neo4j.conf file:

```
ha.server_id=1
ha.initial_hosts=192.168.0.100:5001,192.168.0.101:5001,192.168.0.102:5001
dbms.mode=HA
```

Each Neo4j instance in your cluster must have a unique ha.server_id. It must be a positive number. List each IP address with its HA port (5001 by default) in the ha.initial_hosts property. Host names can also be used here. The property defaults to single, and should be set to HA for an HA cluster.

Each instance of Neo4j can now be started in any order.

# Causal clustering

Neo4j 3.1 introduced support for a new type of clustering known as **causal clustering**. With causal clustering, a few core servers will be configured, along with many read replicas. The configuration for causal clustering is similar to HA clustering:

```
causal_clustering.initial_discovery_members=192.168.0.100:5000,192.168.0.10
1:5000,192.168.0.102:5000
causal_clustering.expected_core_cluster_size=3
dbms.mode=CORE
```

This will define the `192.168.0.100-102` instances as core servers. Note that `dbms.mode` is set to `CORE`. The `ha.initial_hosts` property is replaced with the `causal_clustering.initial_discovery_members` property. The expected number of core servers is defined with the `causal_clustering.expected_core_cluster_size` property.

Configuring a read replica requires the same three lines in the configuration file, except that the `dbms.mode` is specified differently:

```
dbms.mode=READ_REPLICA
```

 Clustering (high-availability or causal) is not available in the Community Edition of Neo4j. If your application requires either HA or causal clustering, please reach out to Neo4j, Inc. for assistance with licensing and installing the Enterprise Edition.

# Using Neo4j

You should now be able to start your Neo4j server process in the foreground:

```
bin/neo4j console
```

This yields the following output:

```
Active database: graph.db
Directories in use:
  home:         /local/neo4j
  config:       /local/neo4j/conf
  logs:         /local/neo4j/logs
  plugins:      /local/neo4j/plugins
  import:       /local/neo4j/import
  data:         /local/neo4j/data
  certificates: /local/neo4j/certificates
  run:          /local/neo4j/run
Starting Neo4j.
2017-07-09 17:10:05.300+0000 INFO  ======== Neo4j 3.2.2 ========
2017-07-09 17:10:05.342+0000 INFO  Starting...
2017-07-09 17:10:06.464+0000 INFO  Bolt enabled on 192.168.0.100:7687.
2017-07-09 17:10:09.576+0000 INFO  Started.
2017-07-09 17:10:10.982+0000 INFO  Remote interface available at
http://192.168.0.100:7474/
```

Alternatively, Neo4j can be started with the `start` command (instead of `console`) to run the process in the background. For this, current logs for the server process can be obtained by tailing the `log/debug.log` file:

```
tail -f /local/neo4j/log/debug.log
```

If Neo4j is running as a service, it will respond to the service `start`/`stop` commands as well:

```
sudo service neo4j start
```

Similarly, the Neo4j process can be stopped in the following ways:

- **Foreground process**: *Ctrl + C* (key combination)
- **Background process**: `bin/neo4j stop`
- **Service**: `sudo service neo4j stop`

When the Neo4j process is started, it returns output describing the on-disk locations of various server components. This information is helpful for operators to apply changes to the configuration quickly. It also clearly lists the addresses and ports that it is listening on for Bolt and HTTP connections.

# Neo4j Browser

To run Neo4j Browser, navigate to the URL mentioned in your server output (or in your `neo4j.log` file) as the `Remote interface`:

```
INFO  Remote interface available at http://192.168.0.100:7474/
```

If you did not set the initial password from the preceding command line, Neo4j Browser will prompt you to do so immediately.

 While additional users can be created, role-based security and Kerberos integration is only available in the Enterprise Edition of Neo4j.

Once you have successfully logged in, you should see a screen similar to this:

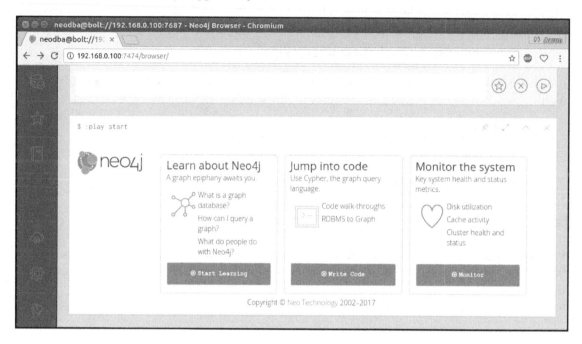

Neo4j Browser after login

This initial screen gives you several links to get started with, including an introduction to Neo4j, walkthroughs with the code, and ways to monitor the current server's resources.

# Cypher

The underlying query language used in Neo4j is called **Cypher**. It comes with an intuitive set of pattern-matching tools to allow you to model and query nodes and relationships. The top section, located above the **play start** section in the previous screenshot, is a command panel that accepts Cypher queries.

Let's click the command panel and create a new node:

```
CREATE (:Message { title:"Welcome",text:"Hello world!" });
```

With the preceding command, I have created a new node of the `Message` type. The `Message` node has two properties, `title` and `text`. The `title` property has the value of `Welcome`, and the `text` property has the value of `Hello world!`.

In the following screenshot, in the left-hand portion of Neo4j Browser, I can see that I now have a node label named **Message**. Click the **Message** label:

Neo4j Browser with result panes after creating the Welcome message node, and clicking the message node label

Once you do that, Neo4j Browser sends the server process a Cypher query of its own:

```
MATCH (n:Message) RETURN n LIMIT 25;
```

The results of this query appear in a new pane, and the default view is one that shows a graphical representation of your node, which right now is only a blue **Message** node, as shown in the previous screenshot. If you hover over the **Welcome** message node, you should see its properties displayed at the bottom of the pane:

```
<id>: 0 text: Hello world! Title: Welcome
```

Of course, this lone node doesn't really help us do very much. So let's create a new node representing the new query language that we're learning, Cypher:

```
CREATE (:Language { name:"Cypher",version:"Cypher w/ Neo4j 3.2.2" });
```

Now, our node labels section contains types for both Message and Language. Feel free to click around for the different node types. But this still doesn't give us much that we can be productive with.

Next, we'll create a relationship or edge. Edges can be one-way or two-way, but we'll just create a one-way edge (from Message to Language) for now:

```
MATCH (m:Message),(c:Language)
WHERE m.title = 'Welcome' AND c.name = 'Cypher'
CREATE (m)-[:ACCESSED_FROM]->(c);
```

When running the previous query, you may be presented with a warning stating **This query builds a cartesian product between disconnected patterns**. Essentially, this is saying that the current query is inefficient, as Neo4j will have to check all Message nodes and all Language nodes to build the result set for the matching property values. The concept of a Cartesian product in Neo4j is similar to its counterpart in the relational database world (all rows) and should be avoided. This could be solved by adding an index on both the Message.title and Language.name properties, but for the small amount of data used in this example, it is ok to run.

We now have an entry in the left-hand navigation menu under **Relationships Types,** as shown in the following screenshot. Click the **ACCESSED_FROM** relationship to see a graphical view of the `Welcome` message and the Cypher language connected by the new edge:

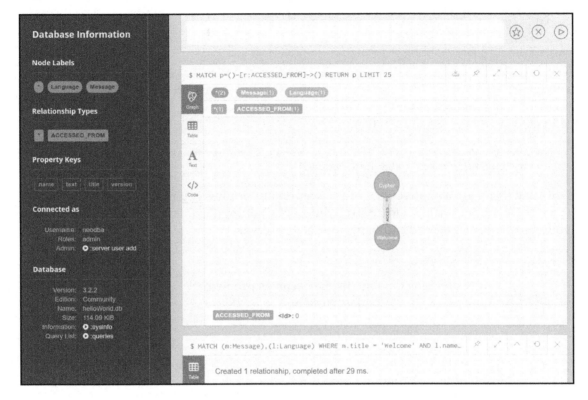

A result pane after the creation of two different types of nodes and a relationship

Next, we will load a file of NASA astronaut data[6] into our local Neo4j instance. Download the following files (or clone the repository) from `https://github.com/aploetz/packt/`:

- `astronaut_data.neo`
- `neoCmdFile.py`

If it is not present, install the Neo4j Python driver:

```
pip install neo4j-driver
```

For this and some of the following exercises, you will need a version of Python installed, along with the pip tool for Python package management.

The `neoCmdFile.py` is a Python script designed to load files that consist of Cypher commands. The `astronaut_data.neo` file is a Cypher command file that will build a series of nodes and edges for the following examples. Run the `neoCmdFile.py` script to load the `astronaut_data.neo` file:

```
python neoCmdFile.py 192.168.0.100 neo4j flynnLives astronaut_data.neo
Data from astronaut_data.neo loaded!
```

Note that if you get a `TransientError` exception informing you that your JVM stack size is too small, try increasing it to 2 MBs (or more) by adding the following line to the end of your `neo4j.conf` file (and bouncing your Neo4j server):

```
dbms.jvm.additional=-Xss2M
```

If loading the data in this file becomes problematic, try using the `LazyWebCypher` loader found at http://www.lyonwj.com/LazyWebCypher/.

With the astronaut data now loaded, we can return to Neo4j Browser and run Cypher queries against it. Run this query for NASA astronauts who were recruited in `group 1`:

```
MATCH p=()-[r:RECRUITED_IN_CLASS]->(g {group:"1"}) RETURN p;
```

The output for the preceding query would look like this:

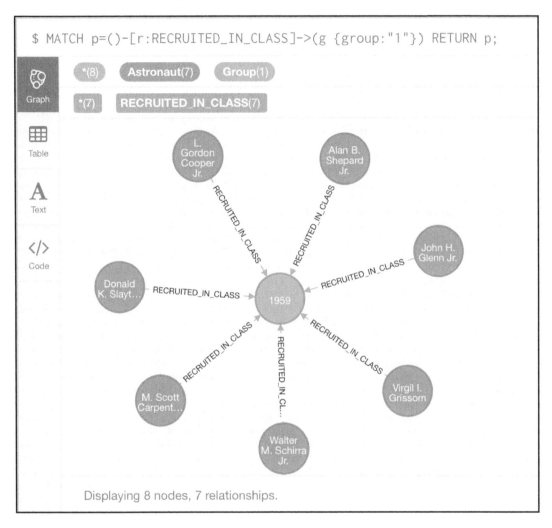

Data for the NASA astronauts recruited in group 1 (1959)

This particular query, in the preceding screenshot, returns data for the famous Mercury Seven astronauts.

In addition to querying astronauts by group, we can also query by other things, such as a specific mission. If we wanted data for the astronauts who flew on the *successful failure* of Apollo 13, the query would look like this:

```
MATCH (a:Astronaut)-[:FLEW_ON]->(m:Mission {name:'Apollo 13'})
RETURN a, m;
```

If we view astronaut as the criterion, we can easily modify the query to return data for other entities based on relationships. Here, we can prepend an edge of EDUCATED_AT to the School node on the previous query:

```
MATCH (s:School)<-[:EDUCATED_AT]-
(a:Astronaut)-[:FLEW_ON]->(m:Mission {name:'Apollo 13'})
RETURN a, m, s;
```

The output for the preceding query would look like this:

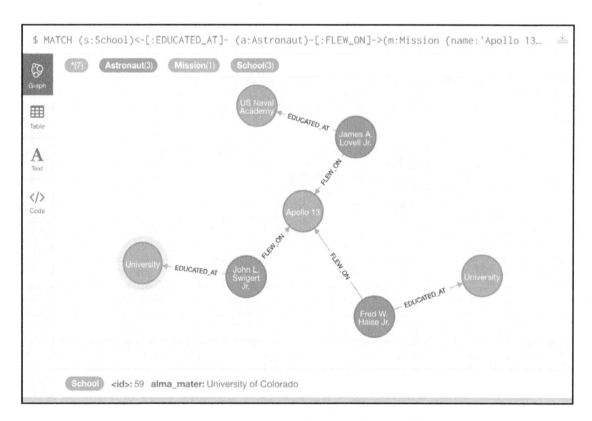

Data for the NASA astronauts who flew on Apollo 13, including the university (School) where they were educated

In addition to the entities for the `Apollo 13` mission and the three astronauts, we can also see where each of the astronauts received their education. Feel free to further explore and experiment with the astronaut data. In doing so, we will begin to realize the potential of graph database modeling and the problems that it can help us to solve.

# Python

Now let's try using Neo4j with Python. If it wasn't installed before, make sure to install the (officially supported) Neo4j Python driver:

```
sudo pip install neo4j-driver
```

Now we will write a simple Python script (named `neo4jHelloWorld.py`) to accomplish three tasks:

- Create a node representing the Python language entity
- Create an `ACCESSED_FROM` edge connecting Python with the `Welcome` message
- Query the `Welcome` message via the `ACCESSED_FROM` Python edge

We will start with our imports and our system arguments to handle `hostname`, `username`, and `password` from the command line:

```
from neo4j.v1 import GraphDatabase, basic_auth import sys

hostname=sys.argv[1]
username=sys.argv[2]
password=sys.argv[3]
```

Next, we will connect to our local Neo4j instance using the `bolt` protocol:

```
driver=GraphDatabase.driver("bolt://" + hostname +
   ":7687",auth=basic_auth(username,password))
session=driver.session()
```

With our session established, we will create the Python language node:

```
createLanguage="CREATE (:Language {name:{name},version:{ver}});"
session.run(createLanguage, {"name":"Python","ver":"2.7.13"})
```

Next, we will create the `ACCESSED_FROM` edge:

```
createRelationship="""MATCH (m:Message),(l:Language)
  WHERE m.title='Welcome' AND l.name='Python'
  CREATE (m)-[:ACCESSED_FROM]->(l);"""
session.run(createRelationship)
```

Then, we will query for the Python node via the `ACCESSED_FROM` edge to the `Welcome` message and process the result set as output:

```
queryRelationship="""MATCH (m:Message)-[:ACCESSED_FROM]->
  (l:Language {name:'Python'})
  RETURN m,l;"""
resultSet = session.run(queryRelationship)

for result in resultSet:
  print("%s from %s" % (result["m"]["text"], result["l"]["name"]))
```

Finally, we will close our connection to Neo4j:

```
session.close()
```

Running this script from the command line yields the following output:

```
python neo4jHelloWorld.py 192.168.0.100 neo4j flynnLives
Hello world! from Python
```

Going back to Neo4j Browser, if we click the **ACCESSED_FROM** edge, as shown in the screenshot provided previously in the chapter, two language nodes should now be connected to the `Welcome` message.

Now let's move to a more complicated example. The current data set stops at the `ISS Expedition 50/51` mission. We will write a Python script to add data for the `ISS Expedition 51/52`. The name of the script will be `neo4jISS52.py`. The beginning will be very similar to the previous Python script, with our imports, parsing command-line arguments, and building the session connection object to our Neo4j instance:

```
from neo4j.v1 import GraphDatabase, basic_auth
import sys

hostname=sys.argv[1]
username=sys.argv[2]
password=sys.argv[3]

driver=GraphDatabase.driver("bolt://" + hostname + ":7687",
auth=basic_auth(username,password))
session=driver.session()
```

With our session established, we will create the new `Mission` node:

```
createMission="CREATE (:Mission {name:{name}});"
session.run(createMission,{"name":"ISS-51/52 (Soyuz)"})
```

With the `Mission` node created, we can now create our `FLEW_ON` edges to it from the three NASA astronauts who were assigned to it:

```
createRelationship="""MATCH (m:Mission),(a:Astronaut)
    WHERE m.name={mname} AND a.name={aname}
    CREATE (a)-[:FLEW_ON]->(m);"""
session.run(createRelationship,{"mname":"ISS-51/52 (Soyuz)",
  "aname":"Jack D. Fischer"})
session.run(createRelationship,{"mname":"ISS-51/52 (Soyuz)",
  "aname":"Peggy A. Whitson"})
session.run(createRelationship,{"mname":"ISS-51/52 (Soyuz)",
  "aname":"Randolph J. Bresnik"})
```

With the mission and required edges created, we can now query the mission for all astronauts who flew on it, print out the results to the console, and close our connection:

```
queryRelationship="""MATCH (m:Mission {name:'ISS-51/52 (Soyuz)'})
  <-[:FLEW_ON]-(a:Astronaut) RETURN m,a;"""
resultSet=session.run(queryRelationship)

for result in resultSet:
  print("%s flew on %s" % (result["a"]["name"],result["m"]["name"]))

session.close()
```

Running this script from the command line yields the following output:

```
python neo4jISS52.py 192.168.0.100 neo4j flynnLives
Randolph J. Bresnik flew on ISS-51/52 (Soyuz)
Peggy A. Whitson flew on ISS-51/52 (Soyuz)
Jack D. Fischer flew on ISS-51/52 (Soyuz)
```

# Java

Similarly, we can write client applications using Java to interact and work with Neo4j. One way to do this is with the official Neo4j Java driver, via Apache Maven. To accomplish this, we will create a new Maven project with the following dependency in `pom.xml`:

```
<dependencies>
  <dependency>
      <groupId>org.neo4j.driver</groupId>
```

```
        <artifactId>neo4j-java-driver</artifactId>
        <version>1.2.1</version>
    </dependency>
</dependencies>
```

Once that is done, we will write our Java code (similar to the first Python example) to create a new language with an edge to the Welcome message node and print out the results to the console. We will start by writing a Java class to handle all of our interactions with Neo4j and name it Neo4jConnection. To start this class, we will give it four Neo4j-specific imports and then create two constructors:

```java
import org.neo4j.driver.v1.AuthTokens;
import org.neo4j.driver.v1.Driver;
import org.neo4j.driver.v1.GraphDatabase;
import org.neo4j.driver.v1.Session;

public class Neo4jConnection {
  private Driver driver;
  private Session session;
  public Neo4jConnection() {
  }
  public Neo4jConnection(String node, String user, String pwd) {
    connect(node,user,pwd);
  }
```

Next, we will create a public method to connect to our Neo4j instance:

```java
public void connect(String node, String user, String pwd) {
  driver = GraphDatabase.driver( "bolt://"
    + node + ":7687", AuthTokens.basic( user, pwd ) );
  session = driver.session();
}
```

Additionally, we will expose a public getter for the Session object:

```java
public Session getSession() {
  return session;
}
```

Finally, we will add a public method to close the connection to Neo4j by invoking the close methods on the driver and session objects:

```java
public void close() {
  session.close();
  driver.close();
}
}
```

Lastly, we will create a short main class `Neo4jHelloWorld` to connect to our instance. This class will connect to Neo4j using our `Neo4jConnection` class. It will then query the message node and its edge to the Java language node and print the results to the console. First, we will define our imports and establish our connection to Neo4j:

```
import org.neo4j.driver.v1.Session;
import org.neo4j.driver.v1.StatementResult;
import org.neo4j.driver.v1.Record;
import static org.neo4j.driver.v1.Values.parameters;

public class Neo4jHelloWorld {
  public static void main(String[] args) {
    Neo4jConnection conn = new Neo4jConnection(
      "192.168.0.100","neodba","flynnLives");
    Session session = conn.getSession();
```

To start out, we will create the Java language node:

```
session.run( "CREATE (:Language {name:{name},version:{ver}})",
  parameters("name", "Java", "ver", "1.8.0_74"));
```

Next, we will create the `ACCESSED_FROM` relationship edge from the Java language node to the `Welcome` message node:

```
String createRelationship = "MATCH (m:Message),(l:Language) "
  + "WHERE m.title = {title} AND l.name={language} "
  + "CREATE (m)-[:ACCESSED_FROM]->(l);";
session.run(createRelationship,
  parameters("title", "Welcome", "language", "Java"));
```

Here, we will query the message node(s) accessed from Java and build a result set:

```
String queryRelationship = "MATCH (m:Message)-[:ACCESSED_FROM]->"
  + "(l:Language {name:{language}}) "
  + "RETURN m.title,l.name;";
StatementResultresultSet = session.run(queryRelationship,
  parameters("language", "Java"));
```

Finally, we will process the result set, print the output to the console, and close our connection to Neo4j:

```
while (resultSet.hasNext()) {
  Record result = resultSet.next();
  System.out.println( result.get("m.title")
    + " from " + result.get("l.name"));
}
```

```
      session.close();
   }
 }
```

Running this code yields the following output:

```
"Welcome" from "Java"
```

Similar to our second Python script, we will now write a Java class to account for the proposed `ISS Expedition 52/53` mission. We'll use the same `Neo4jConnection` class to handle the connection to our Neo4j instance. Our new main class, `Neo4jISS53`, will use the same imports that our last Java main class did. It will start similarly, where we connect it to our instance:

```
public class Neo4jISS53 {
  public static void main(String[] args) {
    Neo4jConnection conn = new
      Neo4jConnection("192.168.0.100","neodba","flynnLives");
    Session session = conn.getSession();
```

Next, we'll start by creating a node for the `ISS-52/53 (Soyuz)` mission:

```
String createMission = "CREATE (:Mission {name:{name}})";
session.run(createMission,parameters("name","ISS-52/53 (Soyuz)"));
```

With the `Mission` node in place, we will create edges to the three NASA astronauts who are scheduled to serve on that mission:

```
String createRelationship = "MATCH (m:Mission),(a:Astronaut) "
  + "WHERE m.name={mname} AND a.name={aname} "
  + "CREATE (a)-[:FLEW_ON]->(m)";
session.run(createRelationship, parameters("mname","ISS-52/53
(Soyuz)",
    "aname","Joseph M. Acaba"));
session.run(createRelationship, parameters("mname","ISS-52/53
(Soyuz)",
    "aname","Mark T. VandeHei"));
session.run(createRelationship, parameters("mname","ISS-52/53
(Soyuz)",
    "aname","Randolph J. Bresnik"));
```

With the node and edges built, we can then query the mission for astronauts who flew on it and process the result set:

```
String queryRelationship = "MATCH (m:Mission {name:{name}})"
  + "<-[:FLEW_ON]-"
  + "(a:Astronaut) RETURN m.name,a.name;";
```

```
StatementResult resultSet = session.run(queryRelationship,
    parameters("name", "ISS-52/53 (Soyuz)"));

while (resultSet.hasNext()) {
  Record result = resultSet.next();
  System.out.println( result.get("a.name")
    + " flew on " + result.get("m.name"));
}
```

Finally, we can close the connection to our Neo4j instance:

```
    session.close();
  }
}
```

Running this code yields the following output:

```
"Randolph J. Bresnik" flew on "ISS-52/53 (Soyuz)"
"Mark T. VandeHei" flew on "ISS-52/53 (Soyuz)"
"Joseph M. Acaba" flew on "ISS-52/53 (Soyuz)"
```

The complete code for all classes can be found at
https://github.com/aploetz/packt/.

# Taking a backup with Neo4j

The exact steps for backing up and restoring a Neo4j instance depend largely on the edition used. Neo4j Enterprise comes with full-fledged backup and restoration tools. Neo4j Community delivers similar functionality (albeit minus some features) via the dump/load functions that are a part of the Neo4j Admin tool.

## Backup/restore with Neo4j Enterprise

First of all, backups for Neo4j Enterprise need to be enabled in the neo4j.conf file:

```
dbms.backup.enabled=true
dbms.backup.address=192.168.0.100:6362
```

Performing a full backup involves running the `backup` command with the Neo4j admin tool:

```
bin/neo4j-admin backup --from=192.168.0.100 --backup-dir=/backups/ --
name=astronaut.db-backup
Doing full backup...
```

This should create a new `astronaut.db-backup` file in the `/backups/` directory.

The same command will invoke an incremental backup if the following conditions are met:

- The backup location exists
- All transaction logs from the time of the prior backup to the present exist

```
bin/neo4j-admin backup --from=192.168.0.100 --backup-dir=/backups/ --
name=astronaut.db-backup --fallback-to-full=true
Destination is not empty, doing incremental backup...
```

Using the `fallback-to-full=true` option ensures that a full backup will be taken, should the incremental backup fail.

 It is a good idea to ensure that backup files are moved off the database instance to ensure survivability in the event of a disk or other hardware failure.

Restoring from a backup is done in a similar manner. Before restoring from a prior backup, the Neo4j instance must first be shut down:

```
neo4j stop
```

 If you are running in a causal or HA cluster configuration, be sure to shut down all clustered Neo4j instances.

Once the instance has been shut down, the database can be restored with the following command:

```
bin/neo4j-admin restore -from=/backups/astronaut.db-backup --
database=graph.db --force
```

The `-force` option is necessary here to ensure that the current database is overwritten in favor of the one contained in the backup. Once the restore command is completed, restart Neo4j on the instance to bring the restored database online.

# Backup/restore with Neo4j Community

An important difference between the dump and backup commands is that backup can be run while the Neo4j instance is live. For dump to run, the instance must be stopped. Therefore, the first step to taking a backup with the Neo4j Community Edition is to stop Neo4j:

```
bin/neo4j stop
Stopping Neo4j.. stopped
```

Next, we will run the following commands from the neo4j-admin tool:

```
mkdir /backups/astronaut.db-backup/
bin/neo4j-admin dump --database=graph.db --to=backups/astronaut.db-
backup/2017-09-11.dump
bin/neo4j start
```

 The backup directory must exist before the dump command is run.

Before getting into the load functionality, let's create a new node for the ISS-53/54 (Soyuz) mission. From within Neo4j Browser, we'll execute this CREATE Cypher statement:

```
CREATE (m:Mission {name: 'ISS-53/54 (Soyuz)'});
```

Now, let's run two MATCH/CREATE queries that will find two existing astronauts (Joeseph M. Acaba and Mark T. VandeHei) and tie them to the ISS-53/54 (Soyuz) mission node:

```
MATCH (m:Mission),(a:Astronaut) WHERE m.name='ISS-53/54 (Soyuz)' AND
    a.name='Joseph M. Acaba' CREATE (a)-[:FLEW_ON]->(m);
MATCH (m:Mission),(a:Astronaut) WHERE m.name='ISS-53/54 (Soyuz)' AND
    a.name='Mark T. VandeHei' CREATE (a)-[:FLEW_ON]->(m);
```

Querying for that mission and the astronauts that flew on it should yield results similar to this:

```
MATCH (m:Mission {name:"ISS-53/54 (Soyuz)"})<-[:FLEW_ON]-(a:Astronaut)
RETURN m,a;
```

The output for the preceding query would look like this:

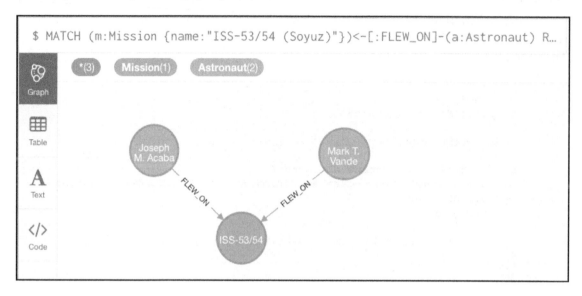

Query showing the NASA astronauts on the ISS-53/54 (Soyuz) mission

Now that we have altered the data (created a new node with two new relationships), let's restore from our backup to revert to the original state. As with the `restore` command, the Neo4j instance must be stopped before a `load` command will function. Therefore, we will stop our instance and then run the `load` command:

```
bin/neo4j stop
Stopping Neo4j.. stopped
bin/neo4j-admin load --from=backups/astronaut.db-backup/2017-9-11.dump
--database=graph.db -force
```

With that complete, we will restart our instance:

```
bin/neo4j start
```

Now, we'll jump back over to our Neo4j Browser and rerun our Cypher query to check for the `ISS-53/54 (Soyuz)` mission and its astronauts:

```
MATCH (m:Mission {name:"ISS-53/54 (Soyuz)"})<-[:FLEW_ON]-(a:Astronaut)
RETURN m,a;
```

Or, if we simply query for only the mission node itself (no relationships), we are presented with a similar result:

```
MATCH (m:Mission {name:"ISS-53/54 (Soyuz)"})RETURN m;
```

The output for the preceding query would look like this:

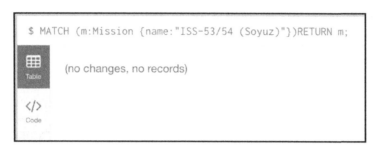

Both our original query (for the mission and its astronauts) and this one for the mission itself should return an empty result set once the load operation is complete

As the query results show, running the `load` command to restore our database to its state prior to the addition of the `ISS-53/54 (Soyuz)` mission was indeed successful.

# Differences between the Neo4j Community and Enterprise Editions

| Feature | Neo4j Community | Neo4j Enterprise |
|---|---|---|
| *Hot* backups | No | Yes |
| Data dump/load | Yes | Yes |
| HA clustering | No | Yes |
| Causal clustering | No | Yes |
| User-based security | Yes | Yes |
| Role-based security | No | Yes |
| Kerberos-based security | No | Yes |
| Support from Neo4j, Inc. | No | Yes |

# Tips for success

- Run Neo4j on Linux or BSD
- Take advantage of the training options offered by Neo4j, Inc.
- Talk to others in the community
- Don't use Neo4j for the first time on something mission-critical
- Recruit someone to your team who has graph database experience
- Once in production, continue to monitor your instances' JVMs for GC performance and tune as necessary

As with all NoSQL data stores, it is important to remember that Neo4j is not a general-purpose database. It works well with specific use cases. Usually such cases are where the relationship is as (or more) important as the entities that it connects. To that end, Neo4j makes a great fit for things such as social networks, matchmaking sites, network management systems, and recommendation engines.

Equally as important as applying Neo4j to a proper use case is knowing what Neo4j antipatterns look like. Be sure to avoid using Neo4j with a full relational model (it is not a RDBMS). Try to avoid improper use of relationship types, as well as storing entities and relationships within other entities. Neo4j doesn't handle BLOB data particularly well, nor does it perform optimally when too many properties have been indexed.

Finally, it is a good idea to have a **proof-of-concept** (POC) project as your first foray into Neo4j. Using it for the first time on something mission-critical without an appropriately-experienced development team is a recipe for failure.

In summary, it should be apparent as to why Neo4j is the most widely-adopted NoSQL database used to solve graph problems. It supports interaction with drivers from several different languages and offers Cypher as its own graph-based query language. Newer users can get a feel for solving smaller graph problems on the Community Edition, while the Neo4j Enterprise Edition is capable of scaling to meet larger operational workloads. For more information, check out `http://www.neo4j.com/` today.

# Summary

In this chapter, we have introduced the Neo4j database and how to use it with relationship-based modeling problems. One of the main advantages of Neo4j is the robust tutorial and help system that can be used with Neo4j Browser. It is the author's opinion that more databases should follow Neo4j's example, intrinsically providing intuitive examples and ways to get started. This can certainly improve both the adoption of the technology and proper use case selection.

One aspect of Neo4j that this chapter has spent some time discussing are the subtle differences between the Community and Enterprise Editions. The Community Edition may contain enough of a feature set to develop a prototype or demonstrate a use case. However, if features such as hot backups, security integration, and clustering for heavy operational workloads are required, the Enterprise Edition should be given serious consideration. Also, if your team is new to Neo4j or graph databases in general, an enterprise support contract could prove to be valuable.

# References

1. Armbruster S (San Francisco,CA, 2016) *Welcome to the Dark Side: Neo4j Worst Practices (& How to Avoid Them)*, Neo4j Blog-Originally presented at GraphConnect San Francisco. Retrieved on 20170723 from: `https://neo4j.com/blog/dark-side-neo4j-worst-practices/`

2. Bachman M (London, 2013) *GraphAware: Towards Online Analytical Processing in Graph Databases. Imperial College London*, section 2.5, pp 13-14. Retrieved on 20170722 from: `https://graphaware.com/assets/bachman-msc-thesis.pdf`

3. Brewer E., Fox, A (Berkeley, CA, 1999) *Harvest, Yield, and Scalable Tolerant Systems.* University of California at Berkeley, Doi: 10.1.1.24.3690. Retrieved on 20170530 from: `http://citeseerx.ist.psu.edu/viewdoc/download?doi=10.1.1.24.3690rep=rep1type=pdf`

4. EMA (2015) *Interview: Solve Network Management Problems with Neo4j.* Enterprise Management Associates, Retrieved on 20170722 from: `https://neo4j.com/blog/solve-network-management-problems-with-neo4j/`

5. Lindaaker T (2012) *An overview of Neo4j Internals.* Tobias Lindaaker [SlideShare], Retrieved on 20170721 from: `https://www.slideshare.net/thobe/an-overview-of-neo4j-internals`

6. NASA (2017) *NASA Astronauts, 1959-Present, QA.*, NASA profile on Kaggle. Released under CC0: Public Domain License, Retrieved on 20170611 from: https://www.kaggle.com/nasa/astronaut-yearbook

7. Neo4j Team (2017) *The Neo4j Operations Manual v3.2 - Usage Data Collector*. Neo4j, Inc., Retrieved on 20170709 from: http://neo4j.com/docs/operations-manual/current/configuration/usage-data-collector/

8. Neo4j Team (2017) *What is a Graph Database?* Neo4j, Inc., Retrieved on 20170720 from: https://neo4j.com/developer/graph-database/

9. Neo4j Team (2017c) *How to set up a Neo4j Cluster*. Neo4j, Inc., Retrieved on 20170723 from: https://neo4j.com/developer/guide-clustering-neo4j/

10. Neo4j Team (2017d) *Neo4j's Hardware Requirements*. Neo4j, Inc., . Retrieved on 20170724 from: https://neo4j.com/developer/guide-sizing-and-hardware-calculator/

# 4
## Redis

Redis is a popular data store utilized by businesses of all sizes, from start-ups to large enterprises. It can function as a data store, cache layer, and a message broker. Redis mainly holds its data in memory, making operations lightning fast.

In this chapter, we will explore and learn about several aspects of Redis, including:

- Key features
- Appropriate use cases
- Data modeling
- Anti-patterns
- How to leverage Redis with different tools and languages such as:
  - redis-cli
  - Lua
  - Python
  - Java

After reading through this chapter, you will gain an insight into how Redis works, and how to leverage it to solve interesting problems. You will learn how to install and configure Redis, as well as how to back up and restore its persistence layer. Application examples will help you to round out your approach to Redis. These will provide demonstrations on several topics, including querying Redis from the application layer and utilizing the publish/subscribe features.

Let's start with a quick introduction to Redis. We'll take a look at how it works and discuss the types of problems that it can solve.

# Introduction to Redis

**REmote DIctionary Server (Redis)** is an open source, key-value, single-threaded, in-memory data store that is commonly referred to as a **data structure server**.[9] It is capable of functioning as a NoSQL database, key/value store, a cache layer, and a message broker (among other things). Redis is known for its speed, as it can store complex data structures in memory, and serve them to multiple users or applications.

Redis was primarily designed to serve as an in-memory cache, intended to support atomic operations on a single server. It was written (in C) by Salvatore Sanfilippo, who used it to replace the MySQL instance running at his start-up. Clustering options are available (as of Redis 3.0) with the advent of Redis Cluster. It is important to note that in terms of distributed systems, these two configurations do behave differently:

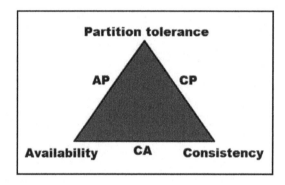

A diagrammatic representation of the CAP theorem, using corners of a triangle to denote the design aspects of consistency, availability, and partition tolerance.

When looking at Redis within the context of Brewer's CAP theorem (formerly known as both **Brewer's CAP principle** and **Brewer's CAP conjecture**), its designation would be as a **CA** system (Brewer, Fox, 1999, p.1). It earns this designation by being able to support both consistency (**C**) and availability (**A**), while partition tolerance for a single instance configuration is not a concern.

However, when Redis Cluster is used, this designation becomes harder to pinpoint. Redis's creator Salvatore Sanfilippo states that Redis Cluster[10] is *more biased toward consistency than availability*. That being said, there are times (however small) when acknowledged writes may be lost during re-hashing or election periods.[4] It is also possible that *slave nodes* can be configured to serve *dirty reads*, with the client potentially reading stale data during a small window of time. This (like many NoSQL databases) allows Redis to continue to serve its data during periods of server or (partial) network outages. These factors make it difficult for Redis to fully support strong consistency, despite its intent.

Given the available data, this author can only conclude that Redis Cluster would earn an **AP** CAP designation. While the possibility of reading stale data does not sound desirable, the alternatives of returning an error or making a client application wait for consistency to be achieved can be even more undesirable. For instance, in a high-performance web client environment, the possibility of returning stale data (say, for a small window of double-digit milliseconds) is preferable to returning nothing.

In any case, Redis aims to provide high-performance, in-memory data storage. With multiple nodes working together using Redis Cluster, it is also capable of scaling linearly to meet operational workloads of increasing throughput. Application architects should perform adequate testing while observing both consistency and availability, to ensure that the tenant application's requirements are being met.

# What are the key features of Redis?

Redis has many features that make it an attractive option for an application data store. Its penchant for performance makes it a favorite of developers. But there are several other additional points of functionality that make Redis unique.

## Performance

The underlying idea behind Redis is very straightforward: to read and write as much data as possible in RAM. As the majority of the operations do not include disk or network I/O, Redis is able to serve data very quickly.

# Tunable data durability

The underlying architecture that allows Redis to perform so well is that data is both stored and read from RAM. The contents of RAM can be persisted to disk with two different options:

- Via a forked snapshot process which creates an RDB file
- Using **Append-only Files (AOF)**, which saves each write individually

While using the AOF option has a direct impact on performance, it is a trade-off that can be made depending on the use case and the amount of data durability that an application requires. Redis allows you to use either AOF, snapshots, or both. Using both is the recommended approach, and the two features are designed so as not to interfere with each other.

Snapshots produce RDB files, providing an option for point-in-time recovery. They are written based on the number of keys updated over a specified amount of time. By default, Redis writes snapshots under the following conditions:

- Every 15 minutes, assuming that at least one key has been updated
- Every 5 minutes, assuming that at least 10 keys have been updated
- Every minute, assuming that at least 10,000 keys have been updated

With AOF, each write operation to Redis is logged and written immediately. The problem with the *immediate* write is that it has simply been written to the kernel's output buffer, and not actually written to disk.[11] Writing the contents from the output buffers to disk happens only on a (POSIX) `fsync` call. With RDB snapshots representing a point-in-time of Redis' data, the 30 seconds to wait for `fsync` isn't as much of a concern. But for AOF, that 30 seconds could equate to 30 seconds of unrecoverable writes. To control this behavior, you can modify the `appendfsync` setting in the configuration file to one of three options:

- `always`: This calls `fsync` with every write operation, forcing the kernel to write to disk
- `everysec`: This calls `fsync` once per second to invoke a write to disk
- `no`: This lets the operating system decide when to call `fsync`; it is usually within 30 seconds

A graphical representation of this functionality can be seen in the following figure:

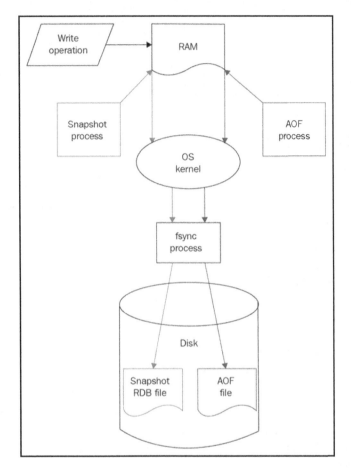

A diagram representing the persistence path in Redis.

The preceding diagram is a very simplified representation of the path of persistence for both Redis and a POSIX-based operating system. It is intended to demonstrate the layers and steps required for Redis to persist data from RAM to disk, as well as a high-level view of what is controlled by the OS.

Obviously, the less Redis has to block for disk I/O, the faster it will be. Always calling `fsync` will be slow. Letting the operating system decide may not provide an acceptable level of durability. Forcing `fsync` once per second may be an acceptable middle ground.

Also, `fsync` simply forces data from the OS cache to the drive controller, which may also (read: probably does) use a cache. So our writes are not even committed at that point. Even Sanfilippo illustrates how hard it is to be sure of your data durability at this point when he later states:[11]

> *There is no guarantee because of the possible disk controller caching, but we'll not consider this aspect because this is an invariant among all the common database systems.*

# Publish/Subscribe

Better known as **Pub/Sub**, this allows users to be alerted to updates on channels. When a message is *published* to a channel, Redis sends the message to all of the *subscribers*. This functionality has many uses for multi-user or social websites, mainly around notifications for chat messages, tweets, emails, and other events.

# Useful data types

Redis provides several useful data types for developers to model their use cases with:

- **Strings**: This stores string values up to a maximum size of 512 MB
- **Lists**: A collection of string values, sequenced by the insertion order
- **Sets**: A unique collection of string values
- **Sorted Sets**: A unique collection of string values, sorted by a score
- **Hashes**: Allows for the storing of object data by mapping string properties and values
- **Bitmaps**: Still a string at its core, but allows for storage of bitmasks or bit operations
- **HyperLogLogs**: Probabilistic type used to estimate collection cardinality

# Expiring data over time

Developers can set the expire time (also known as the **time to live**) on keys stored on a Redis server. This is a useful tool when data is only valid for a certain period of time. Periodically (every 100 ms) Redis performs a sampling of its dataset and deletes a percentage of the keys that are determined to have expired.

# Counters

While the main data type used in Redis is a string, string values can be incremented and decremented if they are numeric. This can be useful for counting things like page views and access totals. An operation performed on a counter is an atomic operation, and (when complete) the new, current value is returned.

# Server-side Lua scripting

Redis allows you to write server-side Lua scripts, essentially embedding scripts in your Redis instance to execute more complex operations. Redis maintains a script cache, so that you don't have to reload your scripts for each use.

 It is important to note that Lua scripts have a 5-second time limit (by default) before being terminated. This limit exists to protect your Redis instance from long-running scripts, as Lua scripts are blocking due to Redis' single-threaded nature.

# Appropriate use cases for Redis

Redis is known for being a *very* fast data store. And as developers, who doesn't want the fastest data store? The far more complicated question is: when is Redis the *right* choice for a data store? Let's take a look at some project aspects that could help determine when a use case might work well with Redis.

# Data fits into RAM

If your entire dataset can fit into memory, then Redis may be a good choice. Using Redis in this scenario should drastically limit (or possibly eliminate) latency due to disk I/O.

# Data durability is not a concern

In looking at your intended dataset objectively, what would happen if it was lost? If your tenant application is simply caching data that is helpful, but not necessarily mission-critical, then Redis might be a good solution. Or if you can reload data for your Redis instance from another source of truth system quickly, then Redis may also be a good fit for your application.

For example, if your application is simply using Redis as an in-memory session cache for a website, you can probably disable snapshotting and AOF for maximum performance. In this scenario, if the Redis server crashes, nothing of grave importance will have been lost.

 While Redis is certainly capable of supporting and providing persistent data durability (as previously described), that feature is not something it was originally designed to be good at. If your application does require data durability, make sure to test your Redis instance extensively with a variety of usage and failure scenarios to ensure that it meets the project requirements.

# Data at scale

Using Redis Cluster, Redis can scale data across multiple machines. This can allow it to serve your dataset from a clustered server approach, whether scaling for RAM or throughput. If your dataset is slightly larger than the amount of RAM on your server, then perhaps a clustered or sharded approach might be beneficial.

# Simple data model

Redis works best with simple key-value oriented data. It is good at storing data in different data types, ranging from the primitive to the fairly complex. If your application can query by a specific key, and retrieve useful data in a string, set, list, or hashmap, then Redis may be a good fit. On the other hand, if your plan is to pull data from separate keysets and put them together with an application-side join, then Redis may not be the best choice.

# Features of Redis matching part of your use case

Redis was developed by programmers for programmers, which means that it has several useful tools or building blocks that programmers tend to use. If your application requires things such as the storage or computation of counters, a queue, leaderboard, or sorted set, or even in-app notifications, Redis may be able to help. Utilizing a feature inherent to Redis can save development time spent building such features on your own.

# Data modeling and application design with Redis

Redis performs quite well without a whole lot of configuration or tuning. However, there are things that can be done on the application side to ensure that your instance will continue to perform well.

## Taking advantage of Redis' data structures

Redis ships with tools and types that are intended to make development easier. It has structures to simplify tasks, such as maintaining a queue of sequential events, or lists of unique items (ordered or unordered). Chances are that one of Redis' delivered types will suit how your application needs to store or manage data.

## Queues

Unlike many data stores, Redis can easily support queue-like functionality. Updates and deletes can be performed with minimal overhead, and it has data types available to work with **Last In First Out (LIFO)** and **First In First Out (FIFO)** queuing scenarios. Redis can also keep the number of items in a queue at the desired size, as well as provide methods for adding an item to the top or to the bottom of a list structure.

## Sets

Sometimes applications may require the ability to keep track of not just the frequency or log of events, but a list of unique items. For these scenarios, Redis has the `set` data structure. Sets in Redis are essentially unique lists of items.

For those times when a set of unique items needs to be presented in a specific order, Redis offers the *sorted set* structure. In this way, unique items are added to a set and ordered by a score. Check the *Using Redis* section for an example of using a sorted set from the `redis-cli`.

# Notifications

Sometimes an application may require notifications for certain events. Let's assume that a message board is being developed, and a user needs to be notified if someone responds to one of their posts. In this case, the Redis Publish/Subscribe functionality could be used. Each user could be written to *subscribe* to their own *channel,* and then certain events could trigger a *publish* to that channel.

# Counters

Often, an application is required to count and store counts of things. Redis comes with counters as a tool to help solve requirements like this. A common scenario is to count views of a page, article, or post. Redis counters are capable of solving problems like this. Especially in a web environment, where multiple users could be viewing the same element, Redis has safeguards in place which help to ensure that simultaneous hits to the same counter will not be lost.

# Caching

One use case which Redis is quite suited for is that of web caching. Often users on a website generate temporary data, such as session information or abandoned shopping carts that can manifest as residual bloat on other types of data stores. By using Redis as a web cache, those extra trips to the main database can be eliminated. Things like the commonly searched product or page data can be cached in Redis, shielding the database from additional calls and simultaneously improving the web experience for the user.

# Redis anti-patterns

Redis is a favorite data store of many developers due to its raw performance. However, it is important to make sure that it is being used properly, otherwise, problems can and will occur.

# Dataset cannot fit into RAM

Redis' greatest asset is its speed, due to the fact that data is written to and read from RAM. If your dataset cannot fit into RAM, then disk I/O begins to enter the picture (as memory is swapped to disk) and performance can quickly degrade.

 Larger-than-RAM datasets were previously managed in Redis by a feature known as disk store, but it has since been deprecated.

# Modeling relational data

Several good tools exist for storing, serving, and managing relational data; Redis is not one of them. As Redis requires a query-based modeling approach, reading relational data may require multiple operations and potentially application-side joins. Additionally, Redis is not an ACID-compliant database, which can further complicate write operations if the relational-like behavior is expected.

 **ACID** is an acronym for **Atomicity, Consistency, Integrity,** and **Durability**. Typically, only relational databases are considered to be ACID-compliant databases.

# Improper connection management

Many web languages offer developers tool sets with which they can quickly build and deploy stateless applications. However, it is still important to ensure that all connections from the application are being appropriately closed. While it is generally considered good practice to close all open connections, failing to do so in Redis can[1] lead to problems like stale connections or memory leaks.

Many newer Redis drivers will implement connection pooling and close connections for you (behind the scenes) once they go out of scope. It is recommended to thoroughly read through your driver's documentation on connection management, just to be clear on how connections to Redis are handled and closed.

# Security

Redis is designed to be run on a network that is secured behind an enterprise-grade firewall. That being said, Redis does come with features designed to help you tighten up security. It is important to remember that not using those security features, as well as doing things like exposing Redis IP addresses to the internet is dangerous and can have disastrous consequences.

Salvatore Sanfilippo caused quite a stir in November 2015, when he detailed a 5-minute hack[12] that demonstrated how to compromise SSH on a Linux server via an unsecured Redis instance. While Redis' security tools are robust, care needs to be taken to ensure that the server on which it runs is locked down and not exposed to the internet. Additionally, you can (and should) try to enable things such as protected mode and `requirepass` authentication.

# Using the KEYS command

In Redis, the `KEYS` command can be used to perform exhaustive pattern matching on **all stored keys**. This is not advisable, as running this on an instance with a large number of keys could take a long time to complete, and will slow down the Redis instance in the process. In the relational world, this is equivalent to running an unbound query (`SELECT...FROM` without a `WHERE` clause). Execute this type of operation with care, and take necessary measures to ensure that your tenants are not performing a `KEYS` operation from within their application code.

# Unnecessary trips over the network

Reduce network time by following some simple guidelines in your application:

- Reuse connection objects; avoid constantly creating/destroying connections to Redis
- Execute multiple commands together in transaction blocks (Thalla, et-al 2015), instead of running them individually
- Use aggregation commands to perform operations with multiple keys

# Not disabling THP

When building your Redis server, be sure to disable **transparent huge pages** (THP) by running this command as a privileged user:

```
sudo echo never > /sys/kernel/mm/transparent_hugepage/enabled
```

If it is not disabled, THP can cause latency issues once Redis forks a background process to persist data to disk. If your server is multi-purpose (for example, a web server also running Redis), the increase in latency could be exponentially worse. The bottom line is that disabling THP on Linux for Redis is the best approach.

# Redis setup, installation, and configuration

Redis is designed to run with a small footprint and provide quick access to its in-memory data. This allows it to be an effective data store on commodity hardware, cloud instances, and containers. Bearing these aspects in mind, there are a few hardware recommendations that make sense to follow.

# Virtualization versus on-the-metal

As Redis IO indicates in its documentation,[6] it is preferable to deploy Redis on a physical machine over a VM. This is because a VM will have a higher intrinsic latency, or rather latency that we cannot improve upon with any amount of server or application configuration.

The `redis-cli` does have a means by which to measure intrinsic latency. Simply run the following on your Redis server (not the client), from the `redis` directory. It will measure latency on the machine (Redis does not need to be running) for a period of 30 seconds:

```
src/redis-cli --intrinsic-latency 30
```

Running this command (after installing Redis) will return output similar to this:

```
Max latency so far: 1 microseconds.
Max latency so far: 2 microseconds.
Max latency so far: 44 microseconds.
Max latency so far: 54 microseconds.
Max latency so far: 59 microseconds.
284459835 total runs (avg latency: 0.1055 microseconds / 105.46 nanoseconds
per run).
Worst run took 559x longer than the average latency.
```

We'll run this test on a few different implementations (checking intrinsic latency for a period of 30 seconds), and receive the following results:

```
Machine #1: AMD A8-5500, quad core, 8GB RAM, Ubuntu 16.04
Machine #2: Intel i7-4870, quad core, 16GB RAM, OSX 10.12
Machine #3: VM hosted on OpenStack cloud, dual core, 16GB RAM, CentOS 7.3
```

The following table shows intrinsic latencies for various implementations, measured in microseconds (μs):

|  | M1 (metal) | M2 (metal) | M3 (OpenStack) |
|---|---|---|---|
| **Max Latency** | 59 μs | 96 μs | 100 μs |
| **Avg Latency** | 0.1055 μs | 0.0738 μs | 0.1114 μs |
| **Worst run relative to Avg Latency** | 559x | 1300x | 898x |

 The VM results for Machine M3 in the preceding table do not take *noisy neighbors* into account.

This test measures how much CPU time the `redis-cli` process is getting (or not getting). It is important for application architects to run this test on their target platforms to gain an understanding of the latencies, which they may be subject to.

# RAM

As Redis aims to serve its complete dataset in memory, having a sufficient amount of RAM is paramount to achieving high levels of performance. The Redis FAQ offers some estimates on how the RAM footprint is affected by differing levels of data length and width:[5]

- Empty instance — about 1 MB of RAM
- 1 million small key/value (string) pairs — about 100 MB of RAM
- 1 million key/hash pairs (object with five fields) — about 200 MB of RAM

 These are estimates and should only be used as guidelines. Always thoroughly test and estimate with a sample of your own data to accurately predict the RAM footprint prior to deploying in a production environment.

# CPU

As Redis is single-threaded and based on a simple architecture, CPU usage is not much of a concern. It can become more of a factor when running Redis on a multi-function server. But when following good usage patterns and practices, processing power typically does not become a bottleneck. For a single server running Redis, a four-core CPU should be plenty.

# Disk

Because Redis is designed to function in memory, it should not require excessive amounts of an additional disk at runtime. However, Redis should have enough storage space available to accommodate the configured persistence settings for durability. Using AOF will consume more disk than using snapshots, and using both will consume the most. Be sure to run Redis thoroughly in a lower environment for a period of time to accurately gauge how much disk space will be consumed by normal operations.

# Operating system

Redis is capable of running on most flavors of Linux, **BSD (Berkley Software Distribution)**, and macOS X. It is **not** recommended to run Redis on Windows. Microsoft has been supported a 64-bit port (still open source) of Redis. But at the time of writing this (February 2018), it has been several months since the last pull request and more than a year since the last release. In short, the Windows port does not appear to be actively maintained, so use it with caution.

# Network/firewall

Redis requires the following TCP port to be accessible:

- 6379: Client-server connections
- 16379: Node-to-node cluster bus protocol

Redis in a single node setup will only use port 6379 (by default). On the other hand, Redis Cluster will use a port offset of + 10000 from its client port for node-to-node communication. Assuming the default configuration, this would also require the opening of port 16379. In a non-default port configuration for Redis Cluster, be sure to open both the client port as well as client port + 10000.

# Installation

Here we will install a single Redis instance running on one server. To get Redis, we will perform the following steps:

1. First navigate your way out to the Redis IO download page: https://redis.io/download. Unless you are an advanced user of Redis, you will want the stable release (Redis 4.0.8 as of the time of writing).

2. Download Redis, create a `local` directory, and move it there:

```
sudo mkdir /local
sudo chown $USER:$USER /local
cd /local
mv ~/Downloads/redis-4.0.8.tar.gz .
```

3. Now we can `untar` it, and it should create a directory and expand the files into it:

```
tar -zxvf redis-4.0.8.tar.gz
```

4. Many people find it more convenient to rename this directory:

```
mv redis-4.0.8/ redis
```

5. The browser interaction can be skipped entirely, by hitting `redis.io` download site for the latest, stable release with either `wget` or `curl` from the command line:

```
curl -O http://download.redis.io/redis-stable.tar.gz
```

6. And for the purposes of this example, it will also be untarred and renamed to `redis`:

```
tar -zxvf redis-stable.tar.gz
mv redis-stable/ redis
```

7. At this point, all that has been downloaded is the source code:

```
sudo apt-get update
sudo apt-get install gcc make tcl build-essential
```

 Be sure you have up-to-date versions of the `gcc`, `make`, `tcl`, and `build-essential` packages.

8. Next, `cd` into the Redis directory, and build it:

```
cd redis
make
```

It's also a good idea to run `make test`.

If all of the tests passed, you should see a message similar to the following:

```
\o/ All tests passed without errors!
```

Depending on the version of Redis, it may need a specific version of `tcl` to successfully run the tests. If you see an error relating to a specific version of `tcl`, install it, and re-run `make test`.

# Configuration files

At this point, you can make use of a delivered, interactive utility to configure Redis as a service (it generates an `init.d` script) and to generate a Redis configuration file. This step can be bypassed if the installation is done solely for local development. To run the setup utility, execute the following command (with `sudo`):

```
sudo utils/install_server.sh
```

The `install_server.sh` utility will prompt for a few specific settings. Leaving the defaults and providing the path to the server executable returns a summary similar to this:

```
Selected config:
Port : 6379
Config file : /etc/redis/6379.conf
Log file : /var/log/redis_6379.log
Data dir : /var/lib/redis/6379
Executable : /local/redis/src/redis-server
Cli Executable : /local/redis/src/redis-cli
Is this ok? Then press ENTER to go on or Ctrl-C to abort.
Copied /tmp/6379.conf => /etc/init.d/redis_6379
Installing service...
Success!
Starting Redis server...
Installation successful!
```

The `init.d` entry reads as `redis_6379`, which will also be the name of the service. This is the port number, which will also be a part of many of the underlying configuration, log, and data file locations.

To `start`/`stop`/`restart` the service, provide the entire service name. Example:

```
sudo service redis_6379 stop
```

Like many other NoSQL databases, Redis treats security as a bit of an afterthought. While it does not provide robust user or role-based security features, you can enable authentication by setting a password in the `config` file. By default, this feature is disabled. To enable it, simply uncomment the `requirepass` line, and provide a good, long password:

```
requirepass currentHorseBatteryStaple
```

It is important to remember that this password will be stored in clear text in your configuration file. While it will be owned by the root user, it is recommended to make this password long and difficult to remember (the preceding example notwithstanding).

Additionally, Redis defaults to **protected mode** as of version 3.2. This setting is also present in the `config` file:

```
protected-mode yes
```

What this setting does is it forces Redis to only accept client requests from the following loopback addresses:

- IPv4: `127.0.0.1`
- IPv6: `::1`

If you require your Redis instance to serve requests from remote clients, you will need to disable the protected mode: `protected-mode no`.

You should also bind Redis to a specific (preferably internal) IP address. By default, it binds to the IPv4 loopback IP:

```
bind 127.0.0.1
```

If you are intending your Redis node to serve remote clients, you will need to alter that line to an IP address that is accessible by the client application(s). It is not advisable to comment out that line, which would cause Redis to listen for connections on all network interfaces.

 A common mistake is to edit the `redis.conf` configuration file if you have run the `install_server` script. Remember that installing/configuring Redis via that script copies `redis.conf` from your installation directory, and places it with all configuration changes in `/etc/redis/6379.conf` (assuming the default port). To edit your configuration going forward, you will need to modify that file.

As mentioned earlier, it is also recommended to disable THP to avoid latency issues as a privileged user:

```
sudo echo never > /sys/kernel/mm/transparent_hugepage/enabled
```

Additionally, add that line to the end of your `/etc/rc.local` file to persist that change after a reboot of the server.

 All changes to the Redis configuration file (as well as the THP change) require a restart of the `redis-server` process to take effect.

If you have skipped the `install_server` step, you can run Redis with this command (specifying your redis.conf file):

```
src/redis-server redis.conf
```

To ensure that Redis is running, try to connect and authenticate with the `redis-cli`:

```
src/redis-cli
127.0.0.1:6379> ping
(error) NOAUTH Authentication required.
127.0.0.1:6379>auth currentHorseBatteryStaple
OK
127.0.0.1:6379> ping
PONG
127.0.0.1:6379> exit
```

Of course, you can always verify that Redis is running by checking the process scheduler for `redis`:

```
ps -ef | grep redis
```

# Using Redis

Now that we have a running server, we will cover some simple examples to explore some of Redis' basic functionality. This section will introduce tools such as redis-cli, as well as examples for interacting with Redis via Python and Java.

## redis-cli

Redis comes with the redis-cli command-line tool. This is a simple, yet powerful tool that allows you to write, query, and otherwise manage the key/values stored in your Redis instance. To run redis-cli (as demonstrated in the previous section), you can invoke it from the command line. To avoid the extra step of authentication, I'll send the password along with the -a flag:

```
src/redis-cli -a currentHorseBatteryStaple -n 0
```

You can also specify the database number with the -n flag. If you do not specify it, redis-cli will connect to the database 0 (zero) by default. Additionally, you can change databases with the SELECT command:

```
127.0.0.1:6379> SELECT 0
```

To start with, let's set a simple message in database 0. We will name the key packt:welcome and set it to the value of Hello world!:

```
127.0.0.1:6379> set packt:welcome "Hello world!"
```

Similarly, we can query the value for the packt:welcome key like this:

```
127.0.0.1:6379> get packt:welcome
"Hello world!"
```

Redis also allows you to get and set the value of a key in the same command using getset. When complete, it returns the original value held by the key, before the set was applied:

```
127.0.0.1:6379> getset packt:welcome "Hello world from getset!"
"Hello world!"
127.0.0.1:6379> get packt:welcome
"Hello world from getset!"
```

Now, let's assume we wanted to store a leaderboard for video game scores. We can add some scores (via the `redis-cli`) to a set type, and display them like this:

```
127.0.0.1:6379>zadd games:joust 48850 Connor
(integer) 1
127.0.0.1:6379>zadd games:joust 58150 Dad
(integer) 1
127.0.0.1:6379>zadd games:joust 49910 Toria
(integer) 1
127.0.0.1:6379>zadd games:joust 29910 Toria
(integer) 0
127.0.0.1:6379>zrange games:joust 0 -1 WITHSCORES
1) "Toria"
2) "29910"
3) "Connor"
4) "48850"
5) "Dad"
6) "58150"
```

 I added an entry for `Toria` twice. The last score entered (of `29910`) is the one that persists.

Redis stores items in sorted sets by a score in ascending order. It is also possible to return the set in descending order, which makes more sense for a video game leaderboard:

```
127.0.0.1:6379>zrevrange games:joust 0 -1 WITHSCORES
1) "Dad"
2) "58150"
3) "Connor"
4) "48850"
5) "Toria"
6) "29910"
```

This shows how easy it is to manage sets, as well as how Redis handles uniqueness and sort order. Note that the `zrange` and `zrevrange` commands return items in a set starting and ending with specific indexes. For this example, we are specifying a starting index of `0` (the first position) and an ending index of `-1` to return the entire list.

Now let's switch gears a little bit, and use Redis to keep track of our logins. A very useful datatype in Redis is the list type. The list type allows you to *push* new items into the list, from either the right side or the left side (`rpush` versus `lpush`). Similarly, you can *pop* existing elements off of the list, from either the right or left side (`rpop` versus `lpop`).

Let's assume that we want to use Redis to keep track of the most recently logged-in users for our application. Here, we will add a new user to the `packt:logins`:

```
127.0.0.1:6379>lpush packt:logins "aploetz 10.0.0.4 2017-06-24
16:22:04.144998"
(integer) 1
```

If the list key does not exist at the time a new item is added to it, it is created. Additionally, the current size of the list is returned after the command completes. Here we will add another item to the list, and then query it using the `lrange` command:

```
127.0.0.1:6379>lpush packt:logins "aploetz 10.0.0.4 2017-06-24
16:31:58.171875"
(integer) 2
127.0.0.1:6379>lrange packt:logins 0 -1
1) "aploetz 10.0.0.4 2017-06-24 16:31:58.171875"
2) "aploetz 10.0.0.4 2017-06-24 16:22:04.144998"
```

Note that `lrange` allows you to query a specified range of items from a list, starting at the left side. It takes integers for the start and stop indexes of the list. Like we saw with `zrange` and `zrevrange`, passing it a start of 0 (zero) and stop off -1 returns all contents of the list as output.

Next, let's look at utilizing Redis' Publish/Subscribe feature. The way this works is that one command is used to create messages and push them to a *channel*. At the same time, additional commands can be used to listen to the channel and display the messages as they come in.

To properly demonstrate this, we will need two terminal windows. On one terminal window, we will set up our subscriber:

```
src/redis-cli -a currentHorseBatteryStaple -n 0
127.0.0.1:6379> subscribe greeting
Reading messages... (press Ctrl-C to quit)
1) "subscribe"
2) "greeting"
3) (integer) 1
```

In this case, we have used the `subscribe` command to listen for messages posted to the `greeting` channel. After executing the command, we are presented with text informing us that we are currently *Reading messages...* and that we can quit this phase by pressing *Ctrl* + *C*.

Additionally, we see three (numbered) lines of text. This is because each message is an[7] *array reply with three elements.* The first element tells us that we have succeeded in subscribing to a channel. The second is informing us that we are listening to the greeting channel. The third element is providing us with the total number of channels that we are currently subscribing to; in our case, that is only one (1).

 Messages published to a channel in Redis are *not* persisted. They are sent to the subscribers and then discarded. Message persistence should be handled on the application side.

Now, let's switch over to our other terminal window, and also run redis-cli to our local instance:

```
src/redis-cli -a currentHorseBatteryStaple -n 0
```

Once we're in, let's go ahead and publish two messages to the greeting channel:

```
127.0.0.1:6379> publish greeting "Hello world!"
(integer) 1
127.0.0.1:6379> publish greeting "Hello world from pub/sub"
(integer) 1
```

The output from each publish command informs us that our message was received by one (1) subscriber.

Now, if we look at our first terminal window (which we have set up as our subscriber), here is what is displayed:

```
1) "message"
2) "greeting"
3) "Hello world!"
1) "message"
2) "greeting"
3) "Hello world from pub/sub!"
```

To get out of subscribe mode we can simply hit *Ctrl + C*. Unfortunately, that also exits us out of the redis-cli. Additionally, we can also use the unsubscribe command. The unsubscribe command can be used to unsubscribe a client from a specific channel. Without specifying a channel, the client is unsubscribed from all channels:

```
127.0.0.1:6379> unsubscribe
1) "unsubscribe"
2) (nil)
3) (integer) 0
```

In this case, our output is telling us that we have successfully unsubscribed and that we are currently subscribed to zero (0) channels.

# Lua

Earlier in this chapter, server-side Lua scripting was identified as a feature of Redis. This feature allows you to[2] create scripted extensions to the Redis database. In this section, we'll explore this functionality along with some short and simple scripts.

Let's start by expanding on our *hello world* example and write a short script to query that message. Lua code can be invoked with the EVAL command from the redis-cli:

```
127.0.0.1:6379> EVAL 'local text="Hello world!" return text' 0
"Hello world!"
```

The zero 0 on the end of the EVAL command tells Redis that we are not passing any keys to be used by Lua (more on that in a moment).

Lua scripts can invoke commands typically used in the redis-cli. This can be done with the redis.call() command. Let's use this command to return the value of our packt:welcome key:

```
127.0.0.1:6379> EVAL 'local text=redis.call("get","packt:welcome") return text' 0
"Hello world from getset!"
```

Of course, our last command really didn't have anything to do with getset. That's just the current value stored for the packt:welcome key (set in the prior section on *redis-cli*). Let's change that quickly:

```
127.0.0.1:6379> set packt:welcome "Hello world from Lua!"
```

Now, re-running our last Lua script makes a little more sense:

```
127.0.0.1:6379> EVAL 'local text=redis.call("get","packt:welcome") return text' 0
"Hello world from Lua!"
```

Data can be passed into Lua scripts in either keys or arguments. These values are stored in Lua as associative arrays called **tables**. There is one table available for the keys, and another for arguments. The values within can be referenced by a one-based, cardinal index.

This can be confusing to some, as most programming languages use zero-based indexes for their array structures.

Let's pass in `packt:welcome` as a key so that it doesn't have to be hardcoded into the script:

```
127.0.0.1:6379> EVAL 'local text=redis.call("get",KEYS[1]) return text' 1
packt:welcome
"Hello world from Lua!"
```

This works, because we're telling Lua that we are passing one (1) key, which we are specifying after the 1. Then, our `get` command is altered to pull this key from the `KEYS` table.

Now, let's personalize this script by passing in a name as a parameter. This command will invoke the script to return a personalized welcome message for a user named `Coriene`:

```
127.0.0.1:6379> EVAL 'local text=redis.call("get",KEYS[1]) return "Dear "
.. ARGV[1] .. ", " .. text' 1 packt:welcome Coriene
"Dear Coriene, Hello world from Lua!"
```

As our script is starting to get more complex, we can put our Lua code into its own file, and save it as `welcomeName.lua`:

```
local msg=redis.call("get",KEYS[1])
local name=ARGV[1]
local output="Dear "..name..", "..msg
return output
```

That script can now be invoked from the command line, via the `redis-cli`, like this:

```
src/redis-cli -a currentHorseBatteryStaple --eval welcomeName.lua
packt:welcome , Coriene
"Dear Coriene, Hello world from Lua!"
```

 When invoking a Lua script from the command line, you separate the keys and arguments with a comma. This is done in lieu of specifying the number of keys as you would from within the `redis-cli`.

Now that we have done a couple of simple examples, let's write something useful. In one of the earlier examples, we used the zrevrange command to return the values in a sorted set. This allowed us to get a list of players on the high score list for a particular video game, sorted by score:

```
127.0.0.1:6379> zrevrange games:joust 0 -1 WITHSCORES
```

We could write a one-line Lua script to abstract away the zrevrange command and save it as getHighScores.lua, like this:

```
return redis.call("zrevrange", KEYS[1], 0, -1,"WITHSCORES")
```

Here we can quickly return the contents of the games:joust sorted set by invoking the script from the command line:

```
src/redis-cli -a currentHorseBatteryStaple --eval getHighScores.lua
games:joust
1) "Dad"
2) "58150"
3) "Connor"
4) "48850"
5) "Toria"
6) "29910"
```

Similarly, we could take it a step further, and create a script designed to look up scores for Joust. The following one-line script would be saved as getJoustScores.lua:

```
return redis.call("zrevrange", "games:joust", 0, -1, "WITHSCORES")
```

Then the high scores for Joust could be quickly returned:

```
src/redis-cli -a currentHorseBatteryStaple --eval getJoustScores.lua
1) "Dad"
2) "58150"
3) "Connor"
4) "48850"
5) "Toria"
6) "29910"
```

In another example, we used a list called packt:logins to keep track of the most recently logged-in users. Returning the contents of that list required the following command:

```
127.0.0.1:6379> lrange packt:logins 0 -1
```

One way in which we could leverage Lua scripting to our advantage would be to abstract the `lrange` command and its parameters. Let's create a simple Lua script as its own file, named `getList.lua`. That script file would contain a single line:

```
return redis.call("lrange", KEYS[1], 0, -1)
```

Returning the contents of the `packt:logins` list (or any list in our database, for that matter) is a simple matter of invoking the script:

```
src/redis-cli -a currentHorseBatteryStaple --eval getList.lua packt:logins
1) "aploetz 10.0.0.4 2017-06-24 16:31:58.171875"
2) "aploetz 10.0.0.4 2017-06-24 16:22:04.144998"
```

Remember to keep your Lua scripts as short and simple as possible. Due to Redis' single-threaded nature,[3] nothing else can run during script execution. Use with caution!

# Python

Now let's try working with Redis from Python. First, make sure to install the redis-py driver:

```
pip install redis
```

It is also recommended to install Hiredis along with `redis-py`. Hiredis is a parsing class written by the core Redis team, and `redis-py` will use Hiredis if it is present. Its use can provide a significant performance gain over the default `PythonParser`. The `hiredis` parser can be installed similarly via `pip`:

```
pip install hiredis
```

Let's write a simple script to `set`, `get`, and output a simple welcome message. Create a new Python script and call it `redisHelloWorld.py`.

First, we will add our imports. We will need `StrictRedis`, as well as the `sys` module to pull in command-line arguments:

```
from redis import StrictRedis
import sys
```

Now we will pull in our `hostname` and `password` from the command-line arguments:

```
hostname = sys.argv[1]
password = sys.argv[2]
```

Next, we will pass along the `hostname` and `password` to a local object to hold our `StrictRedis` connection data. Since the port won't be changing much, we'll hardcode that to be the default port of `6379`. Additionally, we'll make sure we're sticking to database 0 (zero) by hardcoding that as well. But both `port` and `db` could very well be converted to command-line parameters as well:

```
r = StrictRedis(host=hostname,port=6379,password=password,db=0)
```

Here we will create a method to set the key `packt:welcome` to our message of `Hello world from Python!`:

```
def setPacktWelcome():
    #SET new value packt:welcome
    print("Writing \"Hello world from Python!\" to Redis...")
    r.set('packt:welcome','Hello world from Python!')
```

Next, we will create a method to query that message and print it as output:

```
def getPacktWelcome():
    #GET value stored in packt:welcome
    print("Displaying current welcome message...")
    value = r.get('packt:welcome')
    print("message = " + str(value))
```

Finally, we will call the `get`, `set`, and then `get` once more. In this way, we are querying the `packt:welcome` key for its value, setting it to a new value, and then querying it again and posting the value as output:

```
getPacktWelcome()
setPacktWelcome()
getPacktWelcome()
```

Running this from the command line yields the following output:

```
python redisHelloWorld.py 127.0.0.1 currentHorseBatteryStaple
Displaying current welcome message...
message = Hello world!
Writing "Hello world from Python!" to Redis...
Displaying current welcome message...
message = Hello world from Python!
```

As you can see, querying the key `packt:welcome` shows our initial value that we set in the `redis-cli` example. Next, we're setting the value to `Hello world from Python!` Finally, we query the same key and see our new message.

Now we'll try something a little different. Let's write a script to manage our entries into the packt:logins list that we have created, and keep the list to a size of three. We'll call this script redisQueryUser.py.

Our imports will be similar to the previous script, except that we'll include the datetime.datetime item:

```
from redis import StrictRedis
from datetime import datetime
import sys
```

In addition to passing the hostname and password for our Redis instance, we will also pass the userid and ip address. Additionally, we will connect to Redis the same way that we did in the previous script:

```
hostname=sys.argv[1]
password=sys.argv[2]
userid=sys.argv[3]
ip=sys.argv[4]
r = StrictRedis(host=hostname,port=6379,password=password,db=0)
```

Next, we will create a new method to log entries for the userid and ip address. This method will also log the current time, concatenate them all into a string, and execute a lpush onto the packt:logins list structure:

```
def addNewLogin(user,ipaddress):
    print("Logging entry for " + user + " from " + ipaddress)
    time = str(datetime.now())
    r.lpush('packt:logins',user + " " + ipaddress + " " + time)
```

For the final command of that method, I'll execute a ltrim on the list. We only want to keep track of the last three user logins into our system. So, trimming the list (again from the left) from items zero to two ensures that there will only ever be three items in the list and that they will always be the three most recent entries:

```
r.ltrim('packt:logins',0,2)
```

Next, we'll write a simple method to query the complete list, and output it to the screen:

```
def getList():
    list = r.lrange('packt:logins',0,-1)
    print(list)
```

Finally, we will call both methods. This will add a new entry to the list, and query the list output:

```
addNewLogin(userid,ip)
getList()
```

Running the script yields this output:

```
python redisQueryUser.py 127.0.0.1 currentHorseBatteryStaple aploetz
10.0.0.6
Logging entry for aploetz from 10.0.0.6
['aploetz 10.0.0.6 2017-06-24 16:43:29.228135', 'aploetz 10.0.0.4
2017-06-24 16:31:58.171875', 'aploetz 10.0.0.4 2017-06-24 16:22:04.144998']
```

After running the script one more time, I can query it from within redis-cli to see its current contents:

```
127.0.0.1:6379> lrange packt:logins 0 -1
1) "aploetz 10.0.0.9 2017-06-24 16:43:49.958260"
2) "aploetz 10.0.0.6 2017-06-24 16:43:29.228135"
3) "aploetz 10.0.0.4 2017-06-24 16:31:58.171875"
```

As you can see, of the original two entries (done from the command line), only one remains. This affirms that our code to keep the list to a size of three is working correctly.

Next, let's write two scripts to demonstrate the Publish/Subscribe functionality of Redis. Let's assume that we are building a messaging application for baseball games. We'll start by creating our script (named redisPub.py) with our normal imports and argument processing statements:

```
#!/usr/bin/python
from redis import StrictRedis
import sys

if len(sys.argv) < 4:
    print "Please enter a valid hostname, password, and channel."
    exit(len(sys.argv))

hostname=sys.argv[1]
password=sys.argv[2]
channel=sys.argv[3]
```

Next, we'll set up our connection to Redis, and instantiate a local object named publisher to manage our message publishing:

```
r = StrictRedis(host=hostname,port=6379,password=password,db=0)
publisher = r.pubsub()
```

With that complete, let's build a `while` loop to show a prompt, process our input, and publish the messages:

```
while True:
    message=raw_input("Describe play, or press [Enter] to quit: ")

    if not message:
        break
    else:
        r.publish(channel,message)

print "Publish program ended."
```

Now let's shift gears to our subscriber script. We will name it `redisSub.py`. It will start with the same imports and argument processing statements as the previous script did:

```
#!/usr/bin/python
from redis import StrictRedis
import sys

if len(sys.argv) < 4:
    print "Please enter a valid hostname, password, and channel."
    exit(len(sys.argv))

hostname=sys.argv[1]
password=sys.argv[2]
channel=sys.argv[3]
```

Next, we'll set up our connection to Redis, and instantiate a local object for our `channels`. Additionally, we'll issue a command to subscribe to the provided channel:

```
r = StrictRedis(host=hostname,port=6379,password=password,db=0)
channels = r.pubsub()
channels.subscribe(channel)
```

With that complete, we can now build a `for` loop to listen for messages. We will use an `if` construct to see if the message consists of the uppercase word END. If it does, we'll break from the loop. Otherwise, we will print the message contents:

```
for message in channels.listen():
    if message['data']=='END':
        break
    else:
        print message['data']

channels.unsubscribe(channel)
print "Unsubscribed"
```

Now let's see these scripts in action! As with our `redis-cli` Publish/Subscribe example, we'll need to open two terminal windows: one for the subscriber and one for the publisher. Starting with the subscriber, let's invoke it with our localhost (`127.0.0.1`), our password, and `OMG15UBaseball` as our channel:

```
python redisSub.py 127.0.0.1 currentHorseBatteryStaple OMG15UBaseball
1
```

After running that command, Redis returns a 1 as our first message, indicating that we are listening on a single channel. Next, let's run the publisher in another terminal window:

```
python redisPub.py 127.0.0.1 currentHorseBatteryStaple OMG15UBaseball

Describe play; [Enter] to quit: Henry strikes out swinging (Out 1).
Describe play; [Enter] to quit: Avery singles to RF.

Describe play; [Enter] to quit: Avery steals 2b.

Describe play; [Enter] to quit: Gareth doubles to LF, Avery scores.

Describe play; [Enter] to quit: Gareth steals 3b.

Describe play; [Enter] to quit: Leighton grounds out to SS, Gareth scores
(Out 2).

Describe play; [Enter] to quit: Aaron grounds out to SS (Out 3).

Describe play; [Enter] to quit: END

Describe play; [Enter] to quit:
Publish program ended.
```

When we look at the terminal running our subscriber, the following output is displayed:

```
1
Henry strikes out swinging (Out 1).

Avery singles to RF.

Avery steals 2b.

Gareth doubles to LF, Avery scores.

Gareth steals 3b.

Leighton grounds out to SS, Gareth scores (Out 2).
```

```
Aaron grounds out to SS (Out 3).
Unsubscribed
```

Complete code for all scripts can be found at: `https://github.com/aploetz/packt/`.

# Java

Similarly, we can write client applications using Java to interact and work with Redis. The easiest way to do so is with the Jedis Java driver for Redis, via Apache Maven. To accomplish this, I'll create a new Maven project with the following entries in the `pom.xml`:

```
<dependencies>
    <dependency>
        <groupId>redis.clients</groupId>
        <artifactId>jedis</artifactId>
        <version>2.9.0</version>
        <type>jar</type>
        <scope>compile</scope>
    </dependency>
</dependencies>
```

Look for the most recent version of Jedis at: `https://github.com/xetorthio/jedis`.

Once that is done, we will write our Java code (similar to the previous Python example) to get, set, and output a welcome message from the Redis server. We will start by writing a Java class to handle all of our interactions with Redis, and name it `RedisConnection`:

```
import redis.clients.jedis.Jedis;

public class RedisConnection {
    private Jedis redisConn;
```

We will create two constructors: one without arguments, and one that accepts a node and a password:

```
public RedisConnection() {
    }
public RedisConnection(String node, String pwd) {
    connect(node,pwd);
    }
```

Then we'll create a `public void connect` method that takes an endpoint and our password and connects to our Redis server:

```
public void connect(String node, String pwd) {
    redisConn = new Jedis(node);
    redisConn.auth(pwd);
    }
```

We will also create methods to query and update the data, as well as to close the connection to Redis (returning it to the connection pool):

```
public String get(String strKey) {
    return redisConn.get(strKey);
    }

public void set(String strKey, String strValue) {
    redisConn.set(strKey, strValue);
    }

public void close() {
    redisConn.close();
    }
```

Finally, we will create a short main class to connect to our server, query the value stored at the `packt:welcome` key, change the message, and return the new message as output:

```
public class RedisHelloWorld {
    public static void main(String[] args) {
        RedisConnection conn = new RedisConnection("127.0.0.1",
            "currentHorseBatteryStaple");
        System.out.println("Connected to Redis");

        String key = "packt:welcome";
        String newMessage = "Hello world from Java!";
```

This section queries the current value stored at our `packt:welcome` key:

```
//GET value stored in packt:welcome
System.out.println("Displaying current welcome message...");
String message = conn.get("packt:welcome");
System.out.println(message);
```

Here, we set the key's value to store the new welcome message:

```
//SET new value packt:welcome
System.out.println("Writing \"" + newMessage + "\" to Redis...");
conn.set(key, newMessage);
```

Here, we will query the key's value one more time, and display the current welcome message. When finished, we will invoke our `RedisConnection`'s `close()` method:

```
//GET value stored in packt:welcome
    System.out.println("Displaying the new welcome message...");
    message = conn.get("packt:welcome");
    System.out.println(message);
    conn.close();
  }
}
```

When running this code in my **Integrated Developer Environment (IDE)**, I get the following results:

```
Connected to Redis
Displaying current welcome message...
Hello world from Python!
Writing "Hello world from Java!" to Redis...
Displaying the new welcome message...
Hello world from Java!
```

The preceding code was meant to show the basic `get`/`set` methods of Redis/Jedis. It could be further optimized (reducing a network trip) by implementing the use of the `getset` command in the `RedisConnection` class:

```
public String getSet(String strKey, String strValue) {
    return redisConn.getSet(strKey, strValue);
  }
```

Now that we have a simple `hello world` app working with Java and Redis, we will switch back to our recent login tracking use case. We will use the same `RedisConnection` class, with three new methods.

The first new method will be the `getList` method. Simply put, this will take a key as a parameter, and return the associated list of values as a `List<String>`. We are forcing a start index of `0` (zero) and an ending index of `-1`, to ensure that the list is returned in its entirety:

```
public List<String>getList(String strKey) {
    return redisConn.lrange(strKey, 0, -1);
}
```

Next, we need a method to add a new value to a list. This method will execute a `lpush` (left push) to add our new value to the left-most position in the list:

```
public void pushToList(String strKey, String strValue) {
    redisConn.lpush(strKey, strValue);
}
```

As with our previous implementation of this functionality in Python, our business requirements dictate that we only need to keep track of a finite number of user logins. This method will execute a `ltrim` (only keep N number of items, starting from the left) on the list, and allows us to specify the number of entries that we want it to contain:

```
public void capList(String strKey, intintLen) {
    redisConn.ltrim(strKey, 0, intLen - 1);
}
```

Now we will write a new main class to create our connection to Redis, insert a new entry to the `packt:logins` list, and then return the list as output. For this implementation, we will need a few more Java imports:

```
import java.util.List;
import java.text.SimpleDateFormat;
import java.util.Date;

public class RedisQueryUser {
  public static void main(String[] args) {
    RedisConnection conn = new
      RedisConnection("127.0.0.1","currentHorseBatteryStaple");
    System.out.println("Connected to Redis");
```

Here, we will pre-define local variables with their necessary values, and assemble the value that we want to push out to the `packt:logins` list:

```
String key = "packt:logins";
String userid = System.getProperty("user.name");
//get ip address as the lone command line argument
String ip = args[0];
```

```
String strTime = new SimpleDateFormat(
  "yyyy-MM-dd HH:mm:ss.SSS").format(new Date());
String value = userid + " " + ip + " " + strTime;
```

With that complete, we can push our new value to Redis:

```
//log user
conn.pushToList(key, value);
```

With the new item in the list, we will next want to ensure that it only tracks the three most recent logins:

```
//keep list to a max of 3
conn.capList(key, 3);
```

Next, we will read the `packt:logins` list and output its contents:

```
//read login list
List<String> logins = conn.getList(key);
//output login list
for (String user : logins) {
  System.out.println(user);
}
```

Finally, we will invoke our `RedisConnection close()` method:

```
    conn.close();
  }
}
```

When running the preceding code (passing in `10.0.0.4` as a parameter), I see the following output:

```
Connected to Redis
aploetz 10.0.0.4 2017-07-01 10:21:43.196
aploetz 10.0.0.9 2017-06-26 23:00:19.104434
aploetz 10.0.0.9 2017-06-24 16:43:49.958260
```

 Complete code for both classes can be found at: `https://github.com/aploetz/packt/`.

# Taking a backup with Redis

Taking a backup of the current state of a Redis instance is a fairly simple matter. It involves forcing the contents of RAM to be persisted to disk and copying the resulting dump.rdb file to another location.

First, let's check the last time the contents of our Redis instance were written to disk. We can do that with the lastsave command in the redis-cli:

```
127.0.0.1:6379> lastsave
(integer) 1501703515
```

This command returns the UNIX epoch timestamp of the last time the instance's data was persisted to disk.

The UNIX epoch time is the number of seconds that have elapsed since January 1, 1970.

Next, let's ensure that the contents of our Redis instance have been written to disk. We can do that with the bgsave command in the redis-cli:

```
127.0.0.1:6379> bgsave
Background saving started
```

This executes a background save against the current instance, persisting the contents of RAM to disk. It is important to note that this command does not affect the instance's ability to handle requests.

If the bgsave command errors out or does not complete, we can use the save command instead. save invokes an immediate point-in-time snapshot that blocks all other requests until its completion. Therefore, you should only use it in a production environment as the last resort.

To see if the bgsave command has completed, we can (again) run the lastsave command:

```
127.0.0.1:6379> lastsave
(integer) 1501703515
127.0.0.1:6379> lastsave
(integer) 1501703515
127.0.0.1:6379> lastsave
(integer) 1501790543
```

When the output of `lastsave` displays a new timestamp, then `bgsave` has completed. Next, we copy the `dump.rdb` file, and move it to another location. Before doing that, check to see where the `dump.rdb` file was written to:

```
127.0.0.1:6379> config get dir
1) "dir"
2) "/var/lib/redis/6379"
```

Now `exit` the `redis-cli`, and create a `backup` directory:

```
127.0.0.1:6379> exit
mkdir /local/redis/backup
```

We will then verify the location of the `dump.rdb` file, based on the result of the `config get dir` command:

```
ls -al /var/lib/redis/6379/
total 12
drwxr-xr-x 2 root root 4096 Aug  3 15:02 .
drwxr-xr-x 3 root root 4096 Jun 18 19:38 ..
-rw-r--r-- 1 root root  394 Aug  3 15:02 dump.rdb
```

Next, we will copy the `dump.rdb` file to the `/local/redis/backup` directory:

```
cp /var/lib/redis/6379/dump.rdb /local/redis/backup/dump_20170803.rdb
```

> Moving a dump file to another directory is not enough in the event of a catastrophic failure. The best plan is to ensure that the backups are copied to a remote, secure location.

# Restoring from a backup

Let's say that shortly after taking the backup, we are in the `redis-cli` and accidentally overwrite data that we need:

```
127.0.0.1:6379> set packt:welcome blahblahblahblah
OK
127.0.0.1:6379> get packt:welcome
"blahblahblahblah"
```

To get the prior data back, we will need to restore the latest backup file. First of all, we will need to exit the `redis-cli` and stop the Redis instance. Do note that this will result in an outage of your database:

```
sudo service redis_6379 stop
```

Next, either rename or remove the existing `dump.rdb` file:

```
sudo mv /var/lib/redis/6379/dump.rdb /var/lib/redis/6379/dump_bad.rdb
```

Check to see if AOF is enabled:

```
grep appendonly /etc/redis/6379.conf
appendonly no
# The name of the append only file (default: "appendonly.aof")
appendfilename "appendonly.aof"
```

If AOF is enabled, modify the value of `appendonly` to yes and rename any `*.aof` files in the Redis directory. Next, copy the most recent backup of the dump file to the data directory:

```
sudo cp /local/redis/backup/dump_20170803.rdb /var/lib/redis/6379/dump.rdb
```

Double-check the ownership of the `dump.rdb` file, and ensure that it is owned by the user that Redis runs as:

```
ls -al /var/lib/redis/6379/
total 16
drwxr-xr-x 2 root root 4096 Sep  2 15:50 .
drwxr-xr-x 3 root root 4096 Jun 18 19:38 ..
-rw-r--r-- 1 root root  388 Aug  3 15:02 dump_bad.rdb
-rw-r--r-- 1 root root  394 Aug  3 15:49 dump.rdb
```

To verify that the restore worked as expected, we can now restart Redis and query the `packt:welcome` key:

```
sudo service redis_6379 start
src/redis-cli -a currentHorseBatteryStaple
127.0.0.1:6379> get packt:welcome
"Hello world from Java!"
```

# Tips for success

- Run Redis on Linux or BSD
- Better performance on a physical machine, than on a VM
- Be sure to open port 6379
- If using Redis Cluster, then also open the cluster bus port, which has an offset of +10000 (default would be 16379)
- Enable security
- Enterprise support available from Redis Labs

# Summary

In this chapter, the Redis data store was presented and discussed, along with acceptable features and use cases. Simple cases for using Redis were also shown, along with a description of what the coded examples intended to accomplish. Redis has been shown to perform very well, with configuration options for data expiration, as well as several available data types to assist with storage. It also has additional features that can be used for message brokering, counter types, and server-side scripting.

It is important to note that there are some cases where Redis may not perform optimally. Care should be taken to properly configure things such as security and THP, as well as taking care to follow good practices in the application code, such as avoiding the use of the KEYS command and unnecessary trips over the network. The intended dataset should also be inspected, so as to be sure that it fits into RAM, and that it is not relational in nature.

Redis is flexible, lightweight, easy to use, and has drivers available for several different languages. It also has options for persistence which make it capable of offering levels of data durability similar to what is seen in other data stores.

There are plenty of features within Redis that make it a desirable fit for certain use cases, or applications that meet certain conditions. Evaluating it on[13] a feature-by-feature basis is certainly a worthwhile exercise. After all, Redis may be a fit for specific aspects of your application, but unsuitable for others. When it comes to choosing the right tool for the job, sometimes architecting a hybrid approach of Redis with another data store may be the best solution.

# References

1. Grunwald A. (2017). *Learn Redis the Hard Way (In production)*. Trivago Tech Blog. Retrieved on 20170617 from: `http://tech.trivago.com/2017/01/25/learn-redis-the-hard-way-in-production`

2. Morgan-Walker D. (2016). *A Speed Guide To Redis Lua Scripting*. Compose - An IBM Company. Retrieved on 20170923 from: `https://www.compose.com/articles/a-quick-guide-to-redis-lua-scripting/`

3. O'Rourke B.P. (2107). *Lua: A Guide for Redis Users*. Redis Green - Stovepipe Studios. Retrieved on 20170923 from: `https://www.redisgreen.net/blog/intro-to-lua-for-redis-programmers/`

4. Redis.IO (2017). *Redis Cluster Specification*. Redis documentation. Retrieved on 20170617 from: `https://redis.io/topics/cluster-spec`

5. Redis.IO (2017). *FAQ - Redis*. Redis documentation. Retrieved on 20170624 from: `https://redis.io/topics/faq`

6. Redis.IO (2017). *Redis latency problems troubleshooting*. Redis documentation. Retrieved on 20170701 from: `https://redis.io/topics/latency`

7. Redis.IO (2017). *Pub/Sub*. Redis documentation. Retrieved on 20171001 from: `https://redis.io/topics/pubsub`

8. Redis Labs (2017). *Hardware and software requirements*. Redis Labs. Retrieved on 20170624 from: `https://redislabs.com/redis-enterprise-documentation/installing-and-upgrading/hardware-software-requirements/`

9. Russo M. (2010). *Redis from the Ground Up*. Retrieved on 20170617 from: `http://blog.mjrusso.com/2010/10/17/redis-from-the-ground-up.html`

10. Sanfilippo S. (2012). *Redis data model and eventual consistency*. <antirez>. Retrieved on 20170624 from: `http://antirez.com/news/36`

11. Sanfilippo S. (2012). *Redis persistence demystified*. Retrieved on 20170702 from: `http://oldblog.antirez.com/post/redis-persistence-demystified.html`

12. Sanfilippo S. (2015). *A few things about Redis security*. Retrieved on 20170624 from: `http://antirez.com/news/96`

13. Seguin K. (2011). *Redis: Zero to Master in 30 minutes - Part 1*. Karl Seguin's Blog. Retrieved on 20170701 from: `http://openmymind.net/2011/11/8/Redis-Zero-To-Master-In-30-Minutes-Part-1/`

14. Thalla S., Mills C.D., m12m3r, charmander, theoretick, jedp (2015). *Redis Tips*. Mozilla Developer Network. Retrieved on 20170701 from: `https://developer.mozilla.org/en-US/docs/Mozilla/Redis_Tips`

# 5
# Cassandra

Apache Cassandra is one of the most widely used NoSQL databases. It is used by many enterprise organizations to store and serve data on a large scale. Cassandra is also designed to continue to function through partial node failure, remaining highly available to serve consistently high amounts of traffic.

In this chapter, we will discuss Cassandra at length, going into detail on several topics, including:

- Key features
- Appropriate use cases
- Anti-patterns
- How to leverage Cassandra with different tools and languages, such as:
  - Nodetool
  - CQLSH
  - Python
  - Java

By the end of this chapter, you will understand how to build and architect a Cassandra cluster from the ground up. You will find tips and best practices on hardware selection, installation, and configuration. You will also learn how to perform common operational tasks on a Cassandra cluster, such as adding or removing a node, and taking or restoring from a snapshot.

We will start with a quick introduction to Cassandra, and illustrate the types of problems that Cassandra is designed to solve.

# Introduction to Cassandra

Cassandra is an open source, distributed, non-relational, partitioned row store. Cassandra rows are organized into tables and indexed by a key. It uses an append-only, log-based storage engine. Data in Cassandra is distributed across multiple *masterless* nodes, with no single point of failure. It is a top-level Apache project, and its development is currently overseen by the **Apache Software Foundation (ASF)**.

Each individual machine running Cassandra is known as a **node**. Nodes configured to work together and support the same dataset are joined into a cluster (also called a **ring**). Cassandra clusters can be further subdivided based on geographic location, by being assigned to a logical data center (and potentially even further into logical racks.) Nodes within the same data center share the same *replication factor*, or configuration, that tells Cassandra how many copies of a piece of data to store on the nodes in that data center. Nodes within a cluster are kept informed of each other's status, by the **Gossiper**. All of these components work together to abstract Cassandra's distributed nature from the end user.

# What problems does Cassandra solve?

Cassandra is designed to solve problems associated with operating at a large (web) scale. It was designed under similar principles discussed in Amazon's Dynamo paper,[7, p.205] where in a large, complicated system of interconnected hardware, something is always in a state of failure. Given Cassandra's masterless architecture, it is able to continue to perform operations despite a small (albeit significant) number of hardware failures.

In addition to high availability, Cassandra also provides **network partition tolerance**. When using a traditional RDBMS, reaching the limits of a particular server's resources can only be solved by vertical scaling or **scaling up**. Essentially, the database server is augmented with additional memory, CPU cores, or disks in an attempt to meet the growing dataset or operational load. Cassandra, on the other hand, embraces the concept of horizontal scaling or **scaling out**. That is, instead of adding more hardware resources to a server, the additional server is added to the existing Cassandra cluster:

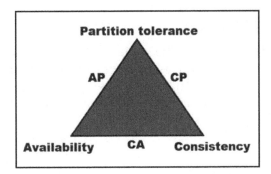

A diagrammatic representation of the CAP theorem, using corners of a triangle to denote the design aspects of consistency, availability, and partition tolerance.

Given this information, if you were to look at Cassandra within the context of Brewer's CAP theorem, Cassandra would be designated as an **AP** system[4, p.1]. It earns this designation by being able to support both high **Availability** (**A**) and **Partition tolerance** (**P**), at the expense of **Consistency** (**C**).

Essentially, Cassandra offers the ability to serve large amounts of data at web-scale. Its features of linear scalability and distributed masterless architecture allow it to achieve high performance in a fast-paced environment, with minimal downtime.

# What are the key features of Cassandra?

There are several features that make Cassandra a desirable data store. Some of its more intrinsic features may not be overtly apparent to application developers and end users. But their ability to abstract complexity and provide performance ultimately aims to improve the experience on the application side. Understanding these features is paramount to knowing when Cassandra can be a good fit on the backend.

# No single point of failure

In Cassandra, multiple copies of the data are stored on multiple nodes. This design allows the cluster (and the applications that it serves) to continue to function in the event of a loss of one or more nodes. This feature allows Cassandra to remain available during maintenance windows and even upgrades.

# Tunable consistency

Although Cassandra embraces the AP side of the CAP theorem triangle, it does allow the level of consistency to be adjusted. This especially becomes useful in multi-tenant clusters, where some applications may have different consistency requirements than others. Cassandra allows consistency to be configured on each operation, allowing for more granular control of reads and writes.

# Data center awareness

Cassandra offers best-in-class data center awareness for more finely tuned control over data replication and performance. This is quite useful for applications that serve large geographic regions, where setting up nodes in corresponding cloud regions (and availability zones) can help improve application performance.

# Linear scalability

Cassandra scales linearly to help you meet your operational workloads. For example, if your cluster of five nodes benchmarks at 5,000 operations per second, then doubling your cluster to 10 nodes should allow your cluster to handle 10,000 operations per second.

# Built on the JVM

Cassandra is written in Java and runs on a JVM. While managing a JVM can present its share of challenges, it also provides intrinsic benefits. Cassandra will respond to heap tuning for performance, and this also allows it to expose useful metrics and commands via **Java Management Extensions (JMX)**.

# Appropriate use cases for Cassandra

There are several known, good use cases for Cassandra. Understanding how Cassandra's write path works can help you in determining whether or not it will work well for your use case:

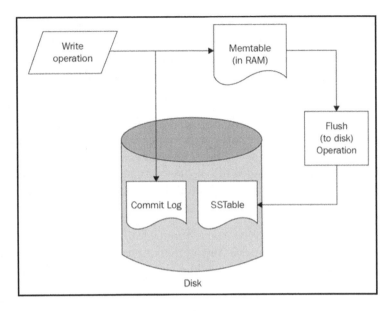

Cassandra applies writes both in memory and on disk.

 The commit log exists to provide durability. If a Cassandra node experiences a plug-out-of-the-wall event, the commit log is verified against what is stored on disk when the Cassandra process is restarted. If there was any data stored in memory that had not yet been persisted to disk, it is replayed from the commit log at that time.

# Overview of the internals

The preceding figure showed that write is stored both in memory and on disk. Periodically, the data is flushed from memory to disk:

 The main thing to remember is that Cassandra writes its sorted string data files (SSTable files) as immutable. That is, they are written once, and never modified. When an SSTable file reaches its maximum capacity, another is written. Therefore, if data for a specific key has been written several times, it may exist in multiple SSTable files, which will all have to be reconciled at read-time.

Additionally, deletes in Cassandra are written to disk in structures known as **tombstones**. A tombstone is essentially a timestamped placeholder for a delete. The tombstone gets replicated out to all of the other nodes responsible for the deleted data. This way, reads for that key will return consistent results, and prevent the problems associated with ghost data.

Eventually, SSTable files are merged together and tombstones are reclaimed in a process called **compaction**. While it takes a while to run, compaction is actually a good thing and ultimately helps to increase (mostly read) performance by reducing the number of files (and ultimately disk I/O) that need to be searched for a query. Different compaction strategies can be selected based on the use case. While it does impact performance, compaction throughput can be throttled (manually), so that it does not affect the node's ability to handle operations.

 SizeTieredCompactionStrategy (default) may require up to 50% of the available disk space to complete its operations. Therefore, it is a good idea to plan for an extra 50% when sizing the hardware for the nodes.

In a distributed database environment (especially one that spans geographic regions), it is entirely possible that write operations may occasionally fail to distribute the required amount of replicas. Because of this, Cassandra comes with a tool known as **repair**. Cassandra anti-entropy repairs have two distinct operations:

- Merkle trees are calculated for the current node (while communicating with other nodes) to determine replicas that need to be repaired (replicas that should exist, but do not)
- Data is streamed from nodes that contain the desired replicas to fix the damaged replicas on the current node

To maintain data consistency, repair of the primary token ranges must be run on each node within the gc_grace_seconds period (default is 10 days) for a table. The recommended practice is for repairs to be run on a weekly basis.

Read operations in Cassandra are slightly more complex in nature. Similar to writes, they are served by structures that reside both on disk and in memory:

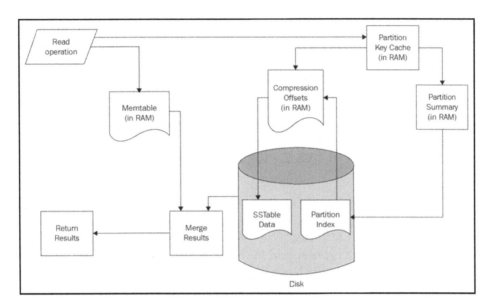

Cassandra reconciles read requests from structures both in memory and on disk.

A **Read operation** simultaneously checks structures in memory and on **Disk**. If the requested data is found in the **Memtable** structures of the current node, that data is merged with results obtained from the disk.

The read path from the disk also begins in memory. First, the **Bloom Filter** is checked. The Bloom Filter is a probability-based structure that speeds up reads from disk by determining which SSTables are likely to contain the requested data.

 While not shown in the preceding figure, the row cache is checked for the requested data prior to the Bloom Filter. While disabled by default, the row cache can improve the performance of read-heavy workloads.

If the Bloom Filter was unable to determine which SSTables to check, the **Partition Key Cache** is queried next. The key cache is enabled by default, and uses a small, configurable amount of RAM.[6] If a partition key is located, the request is immediately routed to the **Compression Offset**.

 The Partition Key Cache can be tuned in the cassandra.yaml file, by adjusting the key_cache_size_in_mb and key_cache_save_period properties.

If a partition key is not located in the Partition Key Cache, the **Partition Summary** is checked next. The Partition Summary contains a sampling of the partition index data, which helps determine a range of partitions for the desired key. This is then verified against the **Partition Index**, which is an on-disk structure containing all of the partition keys.

Once a seek is performed against the Partition Index, its results are then passed to the **Compression Offset**. The Compression Offset is a map structure which[6] stores the on-disk locations for all partitions. From here, the SSTable containing the requested data is queried, the data is then merged with the Memtable results, and the result set is built and returned.

One important takeaway, from analyzing the Cassandra read path, is that queries that return nothing do consume resources. Consider the possible points where data stored in Cassandra may be found and returned. Use of several of the structures in the read path only happens if the requested data is not found in the prior structure. Therefore, using Cassandra to check for the mere existence of data is not an efficient use case.

# Data modeling in Cassandra

The single most important aspect of ensuring that your cluster will be successful and high-performing is in getting the data model right. The main aspect of data modeling is in designing a proper primary key. Primary keys in Cassandra are split into two parts: the **partition key**, and the **clustering key**.

## Partition keys

Partition keys are the first part(s) of the primary key. Their main job is to determine which node(s) a piece of data must be written to and read from. When we talk about ensuring that a query can be served by a single node, we mean ensuring that query operates on a single partition key. When a query is processed by Cassandra, the partition key is hashed to produce a token number. This token number is then checked against the token ranges that each node is responsible for.

## Clustering keys

All keys in a Cassandra primary key that are not partition keys are clustering keys. Clustering keys serve two functions. First of all, they enforce the on-disk sort order in which the data is written. Secondly, they allow you to control the uniqueness of your data model.

# Putting it all together

Now that we know what partition and clustering keys are, we can put them to use. Assume that I have to design a table to track user logins to an application. I could solve that with a table like this:

```
CREATE TABLE packt.logins_by_user (
  user_id text,
  login_datetime timestamp,
  origin_ip text,
  PRIMARY KEY ((user_id), login_datetime)
) WITH CLUSTERING ORDER BY (login_datetime DESC);
```

 Keyspace and table creation will be covered in the *Using Cassandra* section that comes later in the chapter.

Next, I'll write some data to test with:

```
INSERT INTO logins_by_user (user_id, login_datetime, origin_ip) VALUES
    ('aploetz','2017-06-01 12:36:01','192.168.0.101');
INSERT INTO logins_by_user (user_id, login_datetime, origin_ip) VALUES
    ('aploetz','2017-06-01 12:53:28','192.168.0.101');
INSERT INTO logins_by_user (user_id, login_datetime, origin_ip) VALUES
    ('aploetz','2017-06-02 13:23:11','192.168.0.105');
INSERT INTO logins_by_user (user_id, login_datetime, origin_ip) VALUES
    ('aploetz','2017-06-03 09:04:55','192.168.0.101');
```

Take notice of the primary key definition in the preceding code. I am specifying a partition key of user_id. This means that data for each user_id will be stored together. By specifying a clustering key of login_datetime, data returned from this table will be sorted by login_datetime, in descending order. You can see this when I query for a particular user_id:

```
aploetz@cqlsh:packt> SELECT * FROM logins_by_user WHERE user_id='aploetz';
 user_id | login_datetime | origin_ip
---------+---------------------------------+---------------
 aploetz | 2017-06-03 14:04:55.000000+0000 | 192.168.0.101
 aploetz | 2017-06-02 18:23:11.000000+0000 | 192.168.0.105
 aploetz | 2017-06-01 17:53:28.000000+0000 | 192.168.0.101
 aploetz | 2017-06-01 17:36:01.000000+0000 | 192.168.0.101
(4 rows)
```

As you can see, there are four entries for the `aploetz user_id`. When I query this table, I can also use the `token()` function to see the hashed token for each partition key:

```
aploetz@cqlsh:packt> SELECT token(user_id),
  user_id, login_datetime
  FROM logins_by_user
  WHERE user_id='aploetz';
 system.token(user_id) | user_id | login_datetime
-----------------------+---------+----------------------------------
 -1472930629430174260  | aploetz | 2017-06-03 14:04:55.000000+0000
 -1472930629430174260  | aploetz | 2017-06-02 18:23:11.000000+0000
 -1472930629430174260  | aploetz | 2017-06-01 17:53:28.000000+0000
 -1472930629430174260  | aploetz | 2017-06-01 17:36:01.000000+0000
(4 rows)
```

Looking at the first column of the result set, you can see that the `user_id` all match to the same token. This means that they will be stored in the same partition, and thus, together on any node responsible for the token range that encompasses `-1472930629430174260`. Within this partition, the results are ordered by `login_datetime`, descending.

`WHERE` clauses in a query can only contain components of the primary key. Furthermore, they must respect the order of the keys. You can omit clustering keys, but you cannot skip them. For instance, I can omit `login_datetime` because I am specifying the keys that precede it. I cannot omit `user_id` and only query by `login_datetime`, because Cassandra needs to know which partition to look at, and cannot figure that out from a clustering key. If there was a clustering key defined between `user_id` and `login_datetime`, I would have to specify that key too if I wanted to specify `login_datetime` in my `WHERE` clause.

# Optimal use cases

A use case requiring time series or log-based, event-driven data is a very good fit for Cassandra. In this case, rows are written once, never updated, and are seldom subject to random deletes. Business logic for time series data typically results in queries for data that occurred around a similar period of time, usually resulting in reads that can be served by a single node.

Datasets that are large and will grow over time are another good use case for Cassandra. This is where horizontal scalability comes into play. Additional nodes can be added over time to support an expanding data footprint. However, it is important in this scenario to ensure that your data model is designed to distribute well, while simultaneously supporting single-partition queries.

Another good use case for Cassandra is where the query pattern is well defined and not subject to change (either by adding support for new or altering existing queries). Remember that one key to building a successful cluster is to ensure that tables are designed to meet query requirements. Therefore, if those query patterns are not subject to change, the chances for the long-term success of the cluster are greatly improved.

# Cassandra anti-patterns

Cassandra is a great tool for solving specific problems, but it is not a general-purpose data store. Considering the prior section where we discussed the read and write paths, there are some obvious scenarios in which Cassandra is not the correct choice of the data store. These are important to remember, and we will discuss them in this section:

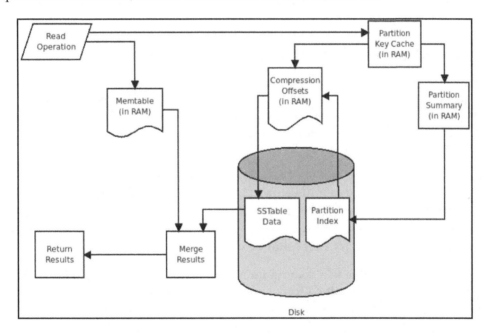

Cassandra reconciles data returned from both memory, disk, and read-time.

# Frequently updated data

Primary keys in Cassandra are unique. Therefore there is no difference between an insert and an update in Cassandra; they are both treated as a write operation. Given that its underlying data files are immutable, it is possible that multiple writes for the same key will store different data in multiple files. The overwritten data doesn't automatically go away. It becomes obsolete (due to its timestamp).

When Cassandra processes a read request, it checks for the requested data from both memory and disk. If the requested data was written recently enough, it may still be in memory. Additionally, if data was written multiple times for a key that has been persisted to disk, it could be spread across multiple SSTable files. This can dramatically increase read latency. This is especially true when multiple pieces of obsoleted data for a specific key need to be reconciled to determine its most recent value.

# Frequently deleted data

As previously mentioned, a delete in Cassandra writes a tombstone. Therefore, it is fair to say that deletes are also treated as write operations. Tombstones can be written at both the row and the column level for a key. As the tombstones also need to be reconciled at read-time, queries for data that contain tombstones become cumbersome, and get slower over time.

It should be noted that one of the most common ways tombstones are created in Cassandra is through the explicit setting of null values. Cassandra's concept of null is slightly different from its relational counterpart. Each row is not required to contain a value for each column. Querying these columns may return `null`, but that is simply Cassandra's way of stating that it just doesn't have data for that column.

Writing an explicit null value to a column for a key tells Cassandra that that row doesn't need to concern itself with a value for that column. The only way it can do that is to write a tombstone. Application code that uses prepared statements containing empty values is an unfortunate yet common way that tombstones get propagated in a table.

# Queues or queue-like data

As you may have surmised, implementing Cassandra as a backend for an application that uses its data store like a queue will not function well. Using a database as a queue in general probably isn't a good idea, but with Cassandra that is a sure path to failure. The constant writing and deleting of the same keys will eventually generate problems associated with overwhelming tombstone exceptions, too much obsoleted data, or both.

# Solutions requiring query flexibility

Tables in Cassandra should be designed according to the required query patterns. This is important to do, in order to ensure the queries can be served by a single node. However, this requires a balancing act to ensure that the required amount of query flexibility can be met. In Cassandra, typically one table is designed to serve one query. If you require the data to be consumed by additional queries, it is usually advisable to store it redundantly with a primary key designed to match the new query.

Of course, managing multiple tables essentially containing the same data can be cumbersome and subject to inconsistency. Thus it is recommended to keep the number of query tables relatively small (low single digits). Cassandra does allow the creation of secondary indexes, but these are horribly inefficient in clusters with a large number of nodes.

Therefore, applications requiring multiple, dynamic, or ad hoc queries should avoid using Cassandra. This includes applications requiring search-engine capability, reporting, or business analysis. Some similar edge cases may be made to work in Cassandra, but, by and large, there are other tools that are better suited to provide that functionality.

# Solutions requiring full table scans

Support of reporting functionality, as mentioned, is not an optimal use case for Cassandra. This is because many reports are rooted in requests for things such as *query all sales for 2017* or *list all transactions for the last 5 years*. Even a **Cassandra Query Language (CQL)** query as simple as `SELECT COUNT(*) FROM my_table;` is considered to be a Cassandra anti-pattern.

This violates a key design principle of Cassandra data modeling, in that queries should be served from a single node. Unbound queries (SELECT without a WHERE clause) or queries with liberal filters violate this principle, in that several or even every node will have to be checked for data that can satisfy the query. When this happens, a single node in the cluster is chosen as a coordinator, which does the work of reaching out to the other nodes and compiling the result set. It is not unheard of to have a Cassandra node crash due to a coordinator being required to do too much.

# Incorrect use of BATCH statements

Cassandra provides the capability to group writes together to be handled in a single transaction, similar to other databases. However, unlike other databases, BATCH statements in Cassandra really just ensure atomicity. The Cassandra BATCH mechanism was designed to write similar data to keep four or five query tables consistent. It was not designed to apply 60,000 writes to the *same* table. Relational databases may work that way, but Cassandra does not. Large batches can also cause nodes to crash, so use with care!

## Using Byte Ordered Partitioner

Cassandra currently ships with three partitioners: ByteOrderedPartitioner, RandomPartitioner, and the (default) Murmur3Partitioner . It should be noted that the **Byte Ordered Partitioner (BOP)** was deprecated long ago (due to issues with hot-spotting and performance), and only exists to provide an upgrade path to users of very old Cassandra implementations. Do not try to build a new cluster using the BOP. When building a new cluster, you should stick with Murmur3Partitioner.

## Using a load balancer in front of Cassandra nodes

Do not put a load balancer between an application and a Cassandra cluster. Cassandra has its own load balancing policies that this can interfere with.

## Using a framework driver

Framework drivers are those written for popular data access patterns, capable of accessing several different types of databases. Their main purpose is to abstract the database from the developer and provide consistent methods for data access from within application code. While this is generally a good idea, these types of drivers are typically first written for relational databases, and then *augmented* to work with NoSQL databases such as Cassandra.

There are drivers available for many languages to work with Cassandra. Your best chances for success are in using the open source drivers written by DataStax. Avoid using framework drivers, such as Spring Data Cassandra, which typically take longer to implement new features and bug fixes. This happens because these types of drivers are usually dependent on a specific version of the DataStax drivers, and have to issue a new release to keep up with the features and fixes offered in the base driver. The best option here is to cut out the middleman and use the recommended DataStax driver for your language.

Spring Data Cassandra specifically uses known anti-patterns in its code base behind the scenes (improper use of BATCH and unbound queries for obtaining row counts). This can cause unnecessary resource consumption and potential node instability.

# Cassandra hardware selection, installation, and configuration

Cassandra is designed to be run in the cloud or on commodity hardware, so (relative to relational databases) you usually don't need to worry about breaking the bank on expensive, heavy-duty hardware. Most documentation on hardware recommendations for Cassandra is somewhat cryptic and reluctant to put forth any solid numbers on hardware requirements. The Apache Cassandra project documentation[1] has a section titled *Hardware Choices*, which states:

> *While Cassandra can be made to run on small servers for testing or development environments (including Raspberry Pis), a minimal production server should have at least 2 cores and 8 GB of RAM. Typical production servers have 8 or more cores and 32 GB of RAM.*

# RAM

One aspect to consider is that Cassandra runs on a JVM. This means that you need to have at least enough random access memory (RAM) to hold the JVM heap, plus another 30-50% or so for additional OS processes and off-heap storage. Note that this recommendation is dependent on the heap size specified. Apache's recommendation of 32 GB of RAM is a good guideline for on-the-metal deployments. For cloud (production) deployments, do not go below 16 GB.

# CPU

It is recommended to ensure that your nodes have a sufficient amount of CPU cores at their disposal. The project documentation[1] states:

> *The Cassandra write path tends to be heavily optimized (writing to the commit log and then inserting the data into the* memtable*), so writes, in particular, tend to be CPU bound. Consequently, adding additional CPU cores often increases throughput of both reads and writes.*

Between 8 and 12 CPU (24 hyper-threaded) cores should be sufficient for a production deployment.

# Disk

Because Cassandra's storage engine is very write-heavy, solid state drives (SSDs) should be considered for production. Cassandra should still run fine on a spinning disk. But in that case, be sure to configure the commit log[1] to be on a separate physical disk from the data directory. It is not necessary to employ a **redundant array of independent disks (RAID)** on your data or commit log drives (RAID 0 should be fine). Cassandra's replication to other nodes protects against data loss. To ensure the proper handling of larger files, be sure to format the drive using either the XFS (preferable) or ext4 filesystems.

Be absolutely sure not to provision Cassandra disks on **network attached storage (NAS)**. Essentially, this turns disk operations into network traffic and generally exhibits poor performance.

Additionally, be sure to disable swap space. Cassandra uses RAM the way it does because it is fast. Swapping RAM to disk slows this down tremendously. If your node is using swap space, you can use the swapoff command, and then edit your /etc/fstab and remove or comment out the swap entry.

# Operating system

Cassandra runs just fine on almost any recent version of Linux. Ubuntu and CentOS are among the most popular chosen flavors of Linux. Make sure to use the latest, full-patched version of your desired Linux flavor to ensure that Cassandra will run optimally.

The newer versions of Cassandra use the 4.4 version of the JNA library, which requires glibc 2.14 or higher. For example, CentOS 6.5 uses glibc 2.12, which could cause Cassandra to throw a JNA-related exception on a startup attempt.

On Linux, you should adjust the following lines in your `/etc/security/limits.conf` configuration file:

```
*  -  memlock unlimited
*  -  nofile 100000
*  -  nproc 32768
*  -  as unlimited
```

Cassandra is officially supported (by several third-party companies) in production as of version 3 on Windows. Be aware that there were several bugs that had to be fixed before Cassandra could work properly on Windows. Running Cassandra on Windows is still a very new thing, and is not recommended. Your best chance for building a successful, high-performing Cassandra cluster is to run it on Linux.

# Network/firewall

Cassandra requires the following (TCP) ports to be accessible:

- `7199`: JMX
- `7000`: Internode communication
- `7001`: Internode communication via SSL
- `9042`: Native Binary Protocol for applications and CQLSH

Older versions of Cassandra may require port `9160` to be open for Thrift communication. However, the Thrift protocol was deprecated as of Cassandra 2.2, and it should not be opened unless deemed necessary.

# Installation using apt-get

If you are using a Debian flavor of Linux, such as Ubuntu, you can install via the **advanced packaging tool** (**APT**).[2] Start by adding the Apache repository to APT's list of sources. This command will add the repository for Cassandra 3.10:

```
echo "deb http://www.apache.org/dist/cassandra/debian 310x main" | sudo tee
-a
   /etc/apt/sources.list.d/cassandra.sources.list
```

Next, pull down the repository keys and add them to APT's list of keys:

```
curl https://www.apache.org/dist/cassandra/KEYS | sudo apt-key add -
```

Once that is done, update via `apt-get` and `install`:

```
sudo apt-get update
sudo apt-get install cassandra
```

Be aware that this method will install Cassandra as a service, and start it. By default, Cassandra will start with the cluster named `test_cluster`, and will be configured only to listen and broadcast on `localhost`. This may be fine for local development, but you may want to stop it in order to customize your configuration:

```
sudo service cassandra stop
```

If you intend to change the cluster name, you will need to wipe any files that were written to the data directory (`$CASSANDRA_HOME/data` by default).

# Tarball installation

Cassandra can also be installed from a downloaded Tarball. Navigate to the Apache Cassandra project download page[2] at http://cassandra.apache.org/download/, and look for the most recent release. If you require a specific, older version of Cassandra, you can find a link to the archived releases there as well.

Once you have downloaded the Tarball, put it in the directory where you intend to install it. For this example, we will download Apache Cassandra 3.10, create a `local` directory on the system, and move it there:

```
sudo mkdir /local
sudo chown $USER:$USER /local
cd /local
mv ~/Downloads/apache-cassandra-3.10-bin.tar.gz
```

 In this example we change ownership to the current user with the $USER environment variable, and this is fine for your own development instance. However, production systems should have a `cassandra` user, and that user should have ownership of the underlying Cassandra directories.

The browser interaction can be skipped entirely, by hitting Apache's Cassandra archive site from the command line with `wget` or `curl`:

```
curl -O
https://archive.apache.org/dist/cassandra/3.10/apache-cassandra-3.10-bin.ta
r.gz
```

Now we can untar it, and it should create a directory and expand the files into it:

```
tar -zxvf apache-cassandra-3.10-bin.tar.gz
```

Many people find it more convenient to rename this directory:

```
mv apache-cassandra-3.10/ cassandra
```

# JVM installation

For best results, use the most recent version of Java 8, from Oracle. Other JVMs (such as OpenJDK) can also be used with Cassandra. If you decide to use a non-Oracle JVM, be sure to thoroughly test your cluster to ensure acceptable levels of performance and stability.

# Node configuration

To configure your node properly, you will need your machine's IP address (assume 192.168.0.100, for this exercise). Once you have that, look inside your configuration directory (`$CASSANDRA_HOME/conf` for Tarball installs, `/etc/cassandra` for `apt-get` installs) and you will notice several files: `cassandra.yaml`, `cassandra-env.sh`, and `cassandra-rackdc.properties` among them.

In the `cassandra.yaml` file, make the following adjustments:

I'll name the cluster `PermanentWaves`:

```
cluster_name: "PermanentWaves"
```

Next, I'll designate this node as a seed node. Basically, this means other nodes will look for this node when joining the cluster. Do not make all of your nodes seed nodes:

```
seeds: "192.168.0.100"
```

Usually, `listen_address` and `rpc_address` will be set to the same IP address. In some cloud implementations, it may be necessary to also set `broadcast_address` and/or `broadcast_rpc_address` to your instances' external IP address, instead. But for a basic, on-the-metal setup, this will work fine:

```
listen_address: 192.168.0.100
rpc_address: 192.168.0.100
```

By default, Cassandra sets your `endpoint_snitch` to the SimpleSnitch. The snitch is a component that makes Cassandra aware of your network topology. This way, the snitch can efficiently route requests, and ensure that an appropriate amount of replicas are being written in each data center. Change the `endpoint_snitch` to the following:

```
endpoint_snitch: GossipingPropertyFileSnitch
```

The `GossipingPropertyFileSnitch` will require additional configuration to the `cassandra-rackdc.properties` file, which will be detailed shortly.

Like many NoSQL databases, Cassandra comes with all security features completely disabled. While it is recommended to run Cassandra on a network secured by an enterprise-grade firewall, that alone is not enough. High profile hackings of unsecured MongoDB databases have made their way into the news.[3] Shortly thereafter, an unknown hacker attacked unsecured Cassandra databases around the world,[5] giving everyone a warning by simply creating a new keyspace on their clusters named `your_db_is_not_secure`. Long story short, enabling user authentication and authorization should be one of the first things that you configure on a new cluster:

```
authenticator: PasswordAuthenticator
authorizer: CassandraAuthorizer
```

Configuring the authenticator and the authorizer, as mentioned, will create the `system_auth` keyspace, with a default username and password of `cassandra`/`cassandra`. Obviously, you should change those once you start your cluster.

> To increase the level of security around a cluster, Cassandra also provides options for a client-to-node SSL and a node-to-node SSL. A Client-to-node SSL requires each connecting client/application to have a valid SSL (secure socket layer) certificate, which needs to be present in the target node's truststore to connect. A Node-to-node SSL works on the same principle, where the truststores on all nodes must contain an SSL certificate used by each node in the cluster (preventing unauthorized nodes from being bootstrapped).

In the `cassandra-rackdc.properties` file, you can define the data center and rack for this particular node. For cloud deployments, you should define the data center as your cloud provider's region, and logical rack as the **availability zone** (or an equivalent thereof). The idea is that Cassandra will use the snitch to figure out which nodes are on which racks, and store replicas in each as appropriate. In this way, you could lose an entire rack (or availability zone), and your cluster could continue to function:

```
dc=LakesidePark
rack=r40
```

Next, you will want to configure settings specific to your JVM and desired method of garbage collection. If you are running on a release of Cassandra prior to version 3, these changes are made in the `cassandra-env.sh` file. For version 3 and up, these settings can be altered in the `jvm.options` file.

By default, Cassandra will use concurrent mark and sweep (CMS) as its method of garbage collection. It will also specify the minimum/maximum JVM heap sizes and new generation size, based on the node's maximum RAM and CPU cores. Heap size is determined by this formula:

$$Heap\ Size\ \rightarrow\ max(min(1/2\ RAM,\ cap\ at\ 1024MB),\ min(1/4\ RAM,\ cap\ at\ 8192MB))$$

Essentially, if left to the defaults, your heap size will be between 1 GB and 8 GB. This may be fine for a local development configuration, but for a cluster, in production (and even a commonly used development or staging cluster), you will want to override these settings.

It is my opinion that an entire chapter (or even a book) could be written about efficient tuning and configuration of your JVM's garbage collector. Given the limited overview that is being provided here, some quick guidelines will be given. If your cluster will be provisioned with smaller nodes, and your JVM heap will be small (8 GB or less), CMS garbage collection should be used. It is not recommended to exceed an 8 GB heap size while using CMS garbage collection, unless you know what you are doing.

However, if you have the available RAM, there are some gains to be realized with Cassandra while using the newer **Garbage-First Garbage Collector (G1GC)**. Good (JVM option) starting points for G1GC are:

```
+UseG1GC
-Xms=20GB
-Xmx=20GB
G1RSetUpdatingPauseTimePercent=5
InitiatingHeapOccupancyPercent=25
G1HeapRegionSize=32m
MaxGCPauseMillis=500
```

It is not advisable to use G1GC with JDK versions 1.7 or older. If you are stuck running on an old JDK, you should opt for the CMS garbage collector instead.

The heap size will be dependent on how much RAM you have available. A good starting point is 20 GB, assuming that your node has at least 32 GB of RAM. It is important to note, that you should not set a young generation size (mn) for G1GC. The main property to watch here is `MaxGCPauseMillis`. If you find that GC pauses inhibit your workload, reduce the target pause time down to 300 ms or so.

`MaxGCPauseMillis` is simply the target pause time. G1GC will attempt to keep collection times under this limit, but it is not a hard stop, and it is possible that GC times may exceed this limit.

# Running Cassandra

With the configuration complete, start up your node.

If you used the Tarball install:

```
bin/cassandra -p cassandra.pid
```

It is not recommended to run Cassandra as the `root` user or as a user with access to `sudo`. You should create a Cassandra user, and ensure that Cassandra runs as that user instead.

If you used `apt-get` for the install:

```
sudo service cassandra start
```

Cassandra comes with the nodetool utility, which is very useful for performing operational duties, as well as for assessing the health of your node and/or cluster. To verify that your node has started, running a `nodetool status` should return information on your cluster, based on the gossip information held by the node that you are logged into:

```
nodetool status

Datacenter: LakesidePark
================
Status=Up/Down
```

```
|/ State=Normal/Leaving/Joining/Moving
-- Address Load Tokens Owns (effective) Host ID Rack
UN 192.168.0.100 1.33 MiB 256 100.0% 954d394b-f96f-473f-ad23-cbe4fd0672c8
R40
```

See the *Using Cassandra* section for more information on `nodetool status`.

Of course, you can always verify that it is running by checking the process scheduler and `grep` for Cassandra:

```
ps -ef | grep cassandra
```

If your node fails to start, check your `system.log` file (location defined in `conf/logback.xml`).

To bring your node down cleanly, it is a good idea to disable gossip and drain the node (includes flushing data in RAM to disk) first:

```
nodetool disablegossip
nodetool drain
```

Once those commands are complete, then the Cassandra process can be stopped.

For the Tarball install:

```
kill cat cassandra.pid
```

For the `apt-get` install:

```
sudo service cassandra stop
```

# Adding a new node to the cluster

Once `.100` is up and running, I can add a second node to the cluster quite easily. We will assume that I now want to add `192.168.0.100` as a new node in my cluster.

All of the configuration properties mentioned prior to all of the files (`cassandra.yaml`, `cassandra-env.sh`, `cassandra-rackdc.properties`, `jvm.options`) should be specified exactly the same as the first node. The exceptions are these two lines in the `cassandra.yaml` file:

```
listen_address: 192.168.0.101
rpc_address: 192.168.0.101
```

Start the new node up, and tail the log to make sure it joins the cluster.

```
tail -f /var/log/cassandra/system.log
```

The seed node will stay the same for `101`'s configuration:

```
seeds: "192.168.0.100"
```

The `seed node` designation in Cassandra doesn't make a node any different. The seed list simply specifies nodes that should be contacted to gain information about the cluster when joining it. It is usually a good idea to have one or two seed nodes per logical data center.

The `cluster_name` of a new node must match the `cluster_name` of the target cluster that it aims to join.

While the node is joining, running a `nodetool` status should yield similar output to this:

```
$ nodetool status
Datacenter: LakesidePark
=========================
Status=Up/Down
|/ State=Normal/Leaving/Joining/Moving
-- Address          Load        Tokens  Owns      Host ID
Rack
UJ 192.168.0.101   83.99 MiB  16        100.0%
fd352577-6be5-4d93-8251-15a74... r40
```

The `status` column for `192.168.0.101` shows as `UJ`, indicating that it is both `Up` and `Joining`.

# Using Cassandra

Now that we have a running cluster, we will cover some simple examples to explore some of Cassandra's basic functionality. This section will introduce command-line tools, such as **nodetool** and **CQLSH**, as well as examples for interacting with Cassandra via Python and Java.

# Nodetool

Nodetool is Cassandra's collection of delivered tools that help with a variety of different operational and diagnostic functions. As previously mentioned, probably the most common nodetool command that you will run is `nodetool status`, which should produce output similar to this:

```
$ nodetool status
Datacenter: LakesidePark
========================
Status=Up/Down
|/ State=Normal/Leaving/Joining/Moving
-- Address          Load        Tokens  Owns     Host ID
Rack
UN 192.168.0.100  84.15 MiB  16      100.0%   71700e62-2e28-4974-93e1-
a2ad3f... r40
UN 192.168.0.102  83.27 MiB  16      100.0%   c3e61934-5fc1-4795-
a05a-28443e... r40
UN 192.168.0.101  83.99 MiB  16      100.0%
fd352577-6be5-4d93-8251-15a74f... r40
```

Additional information about your node(s) and cluster can be obtained by running commands such as `nodetool info` or `nodetool describecluster`:

```
$ nodetool info

ID                     :71700e62-2e28-4974-93e1-a2ad3f8a38c1
Gossip active          : true
Thrift active          : false
Native Transport active: true
Load                   :84.15MiB
Generation No          : 1505483850
Uptime (seconds)       : 40776
Heap Memory (MB)       : 422.87 / 4016.00
Off Heap Memory (MB)   : 0.00
Data Center            :LakesidePark
Rack                   :r40
Exceptions             : 0
Key Cache              : entries 24, size 2.02 KiB, capacity 100 MiB, 210
hits, 239 requests, 0.879 recent hit rate, 14400 save period in seconds
Row Cache              : entries 0, size 0 bytes, capacity 0 bytes, 0 hits,
0 requests, NaN recent hit rate, 0 save period in seconds
Counter Cache          : entries 0, size 0 bytes, capacity 50 MiB, 0
```

```
hits, 0 requests, NaN recent hit rate, 7200 save period in seconds
Chunk Cache           : entries 19, size 1.19 MiB, capacity 480 MiB, 85
misses, 343 requests, 0.752 recent hit rate, 583.139 microseconds miss
latency
Percent Repaired      : 100.0%
Token                 : (invoke with -T/--tokens to see all 16 tokens)
```

`nodetool info` is useful for ascertaining things such as heap usage and uptime. `nodetool describecluster` is helpful when diagnosing issues such as schema disagreement.

```
Name: PermanentWaves
Snitch: org.apache.cassandra.locator.DynamicEndpointSnitch
Partitioner: org.apache.cassandra.dht.Murmur3Partitioner
Schema versions: 22a8db59-e998-3848-bfee-a07feedae0d8:
[192.168.0.100,192.168.0.101,192.168.0.102]
```

If there is a node in the cluster that needs to be removed, there are three methods to accomplish this. The determining factor is whether or not the node is still running.

If the node is still functioning and the Cassandra process is still running, you can execute a `nodetool decommission` from any node in the cluster. For example, decommission `192.168.0.102`:

```
nodetool -h 192.168.0.102 decommission
```

At this point, the data on `192.168.0.102` will be streamed to the other nodes in the cluster, and control will be returned to the command line when the process is complete. If you were to run a `nodetool status` during this time, the cluster would look like this:

```
Datacenter: LakesidePark
=========================
Status=Up/Down
|/ State=Normal/Leaving/Joining/Moving
-- Address         Load       Tokens Owns     Host ID
Rack
UN 192.168.0.100  84.15 MiB  16     100.0%   71700e62-2e28-4974-93e1-
a2ad3f... r40
UL 192.168.0.102  83.27 MiB  16     100.0%   c3e61934-5fc1-4795-
a05a-28443e... r40
UN 192.168.0.101  83.99 MiB  16     100.0%
fd352577-6be5-4d93-8251-15a74f... r40
```

The `status` column for 192.168.102 has changed to `UL`, indicating that it is both `Up` and `Leaving`.

This method is useful for scaling back a cluster that may have too many computing resources available.

If a node happens to crash, and it is unable to be restarted, the decommissioning process will not work. In this case, the node will have to be forcibly removed. First of all, log into another node in the cluster, and run `nodetool status`:

```
Datacenter: LakesidePark
========================
Status=Up/Down
|/ State=Normal/Leaving/Joining/Moving
-- Address          Load       Tokens  Owns     Host ID
Rack
UN 192.168.0.100  84.15 MiB  16      100.0%   71700e62-2e28-4974-93e1-
a2ad3f... r40
DN 192.168.0.102  83.27 MiB  16      100.0%   c3e61934-5fc1-4795-
a05a-28443e... r40
UN 192.168.0.101  83.99 MiB  16      100.0%
fd352577-6be5-4d93-8251-15a74f... r40
```

 The `status` column for `192.168.102` has changed to `DN`, indicating that it is both `Down` and `Normal`.

In this case, the only recourse is to remove the `down` node by its host ID:

```
nodetool removenode c3e61934-5fc1-4795-a05a-28443e2d51da
```

Once this process has begun, the node processing the removal can be queried with `nodetool removenode status`. And if the removal is taking a long time, it can be forced with `nodetool removenode force`.

If for some reason the node will not disappear from the cluster with either `decommission` or `removenode`, then `nodetool assassinate` should do the trick:

```
nodetool assassinate 192.168.0.102
```

Always try to use decommission first (or removenode if the Cassandra process cannot be started on the node) and assassinate as a last resort.

# CQLSH

Cassandra installs with the **Cassandra Query Language Shell (CQLSH)** tool. This command-line interface allows you to perform schema changes, user maintenance, and run queries.

 CQLSH requires Python 2.7.

To run cqlsh , you can invoke it from the command line. If you have authorization and authentication enabled (and you should), you can start it like this:

```
cqlsh 192.168.0.100 -u cassandra -p cassandra
```

You should see output similar to the following, and beat a cqlsh prompt:

```
Connected to PermanentWaves at 192.168.0.100:9042.
[cqlsh 5.0.1 | Cassandra 3.10 | CQL spec 3.4.4 | Native protocol v4]
Use HELP for help.
cassandra@cqlsh>
```

The first administrative task that should be completed is to tighten up security. You'll want to create a new administrative user (so that you don't need the default Cassandra user), and change the password on the default cassandra/cassandra user. The recommendation is to change it to something long and indecipherable because you shouldn't need to use it again:

```
cassandra@cqlsh> CREATE ROLE cassdba
  WITH PASSWORD='flynnLives' AND SUPERUSER=true AND LOGIN=true;
cassandra@cqlsh> ALTER ROLE cassandra
  WITH PASSWORD='2f394084e98a4bec92405f73e2e634ea';
```

Now, log in with your newly created user. You should see that the `cqlsh` prompt changes:

```
cqlsh 192.168.0.100 -u cassdba -p flynnLives
Connected to PermanentWaves at 192.168.0.100:9042.
[cqlsh 5.0.1 | Cassandra 3.10 | CQL spec 3.4.4 | Native protocol v4]
Use HELP for help.
cassdba@cqlsh>
```

Now that we are logged in as a non-default user, let's go ahead and create a keyspace (database) to work in. As we want our cluster to be data center aware, and we are already using `GossipingPropertyFileSnitch`, we will create our new keyspace using the `NetworkTopologyStrategy` replication strategy. Creating a keyspace using the default `SimpleStrategy` does not work properly with a plural data center configuration, and it offers no benefits over `NetworkTopologyStrategy`. Therefore, it is best not to get into the habit of using it at all. For the purposes of this exercise, I will suggest the keyspace name of `packt`:

```
CREATE KEYSPACE packt WITH replication = {
   'class':'NetworkTopologyStrategy', 'LakesidePark':'1'}
   AND durable_writes = true;
```

As previously discussed, this command creates a new keyspace named `packt` using `NetworkTopologyStrategy`. Our data center is named `LakesidePark`, and we are specifying a **replication factor** (**RF**) of one to store only a single replica of all data in that data center. The `durable_writes` property is set to `true`. This is the default setting for durable writes (so our setting is superfluous). Note that disabling durable writes (setting it to `false`) prevents write operations for this keyspace from being written to the commit log. Disabling it is not advised unless you have a specific use case for it, so use with caution!

The RF of one specified is only recommended for single-node clusters. If you joined additional nodes, as detailed in the preceding instructions, you will want to increase that. The accepted practice is to set the RF equal to (not greater than) the number of nodes with a maximum RF of three. I have seen RFs set higher than three in two cases, as mentioned here:

- A specific use case for a higher level of consistency
- The keyspace was created by someone who didn't really understand (or care about) the extra overhead involved in maintaining additional replicas

Now, let's go ahead and create a table to demonstrate a few examples. We will create a table called `astronauts_by_group`, and design it to work with a query to select NASA astronauts by selection group (`group`):

```
CREATE TABLE packt.astronauts_by_group (
  name text, year int, group int, status text, dob text,
  birthplace text, gender text, alma_mater text, spaceflights int,
  spaceflight_hours int, spacewalks int, spacewalk_hours int,
  missions text,
  PRIMARY KEY (group,name))
WITH CLUSTERING ORDER BY (name asc);
```

Next, we will use the CQLSH `copy` command to import a **comma-separated values (CSV)** file containing data on more than 350 NASA astronauts:

```
COPY packt.astronauts_by_group (name, year, group, status, dob, birthplace,
  gender, alma_mater, spaceflights, spaceflight_hours, spacewalks,
  spacewalk_hours, missions)
  FROM '~/Documents/Packt/astronauts.csv' WITH HEADER=true;
```

The CSV file can be found in the GitHub repo at `https://github.com/aploetz/packt`.

 It is also important to remember that the copy command is not a part of CQL. It is specific to CQLSH, and only works from within CQLSH.

Now, running a query for the astronaut's group where group is equal to 1 yields this result set:

```
cassdba@cqlsh:packt> SELECT name, alma_mater, birthplace FROM
astronauts_by_group WHERE group=1;
     name                 | alma_mater                        |
birthplace
    ----------------------+-----------------------------------+----------
-------
      Alan B. Shepard Jr. |                 US Naval Academy | East
Derry, NH
      Donald K. Slayton |           University of Minnesota |
Sparta, WI
      John H. Glenn Jr. |                 Muskingum College |
Cambridge, OH
      L. Gordon Cooper Jr. | Air Force Institute of Technology |
Shawnee, OK
      M. Scott Carpenter |             University of Colorado |
Boulder, CO
```

```
        Virgil I. Grissom |                 Purdue University |
Mitchell, IN
        Walter M. Schirra Jr. |            US Naval Academy |
Hackensack, NJ
    (7 rows)
```

This particular query shows data for the famous Mercury Seven astronauts. To exit `cqlsh` and return to your Linux prompt, simply type `exit`:

```
cassdba@cqlsh:packt> exit
```

# Python

Now, let's try working with Cassandra from Python. First, make sure to install the DataStax Cassandra Python driver:

```
pip install cassandra-driver
```

Let's write a simple script to query the `system.local` table, and call it `cassHelloWorld.py`.

First, we will add our imports. We will need the cluster and (since we have enabled `auth`) `PlainTextAuthProvider` items. Additionally, we will need the `sys` module to pull in command-line arguments:

```
from cassandra.cluster import Cluster
from cassandra.auth import PlainTextAuthProvider
import sys
```

Now we will pull in our hostname, username, and password from the command-line arguments. Cassandra uses an array of endpoints to connect to, so we 'll also create a new array and add our `hostname` to it:

```
hostname=sys.argv[1]
username=sys.argv[2]
password=sys.argv[3]
nodes = []
nodes.append(hostname)
```

Now we will use `PlainTextAuthProvider` to pass along our username and password to authenticate with the cluster. Then we will set a local session object to keep our connection and pass it the system keyspace to connect to:

```
auth = PlainTextAuthProvider(username=username, password=password)
cluster = Cluster(nodes,auth_provider=auth)
session = cluster.connect("system")
```

Our CQL query will pull down a few columns from the `system.local` table. This particular data will reveal some information about the cluster that we are connecting to:

```
strCQL = """ SELECT cluster_name,data_center,listen_address,release_version
FROM local WHERE key='local'
"""
```

Next, we'll execute our query and process the result set. The `system.local` table will only ever contain a single row, but it is still a good idea to get into the habit of processing a complete result set. Once the result set has been printed, we will close our connection to Cassandra:

```
rows = session.execute(strCQL)
print("Hello world from:")
for row in rows:
  print(row[0] + " " + row[1] + " " + row[2] + " " + row[3])

#closing Cassandra connection
session.shutdown()
```

Running this from the command line yields the following output:

```
python cassHelloWorld.py 192.168.0.100 cassdba flynnLives
Hello world from:
PermanentWaves 'LakesidePark' 192.168.0.100 3.10
```

We can also use Python to interact with the existing tables in our `packt` keyspace (that we created in the preceding sections). We will name this script `queryUser.py`. It will require the `logins_by_user` table which was introduced earlier in the chapter. If you have not created it, go ahead and do that now:

```
CREATE TABLE packt.logins_by_user (
  user_id text,
  login_datetime timestamp,
  origin_ip text,
  PRIMARY KEY ((user_id), login_datetime)
) WITH CLUSTERING ORDER BY (login_datetime DESC);
```

The imports and command-line arguments will be similar to the previous ones, except that we will add a variable to process as `user_id` from the command line. We will also define our keyspace as a variable:

```
from cassandra.cluster import Cluster
from cassandra.auth import PlainTextAuthProvider
import sys
hostname = sys.argv[1]
username = sys.argv[2]
password = sys.argv[3]
userid = sys.argv[4]
nodes = []
nodes.append(hostname)
```

The code to define the connection to Cassandra will remain the same as shown here:

```
auth = PlainTextAuthProvider(username=username, password=password)
cluster = Cluster(nodes,auth_provider=auth)
session = cluster.connect(keyspace)
```

We will prepare and execute an `INSERT` to our `logins_by_user` table to record a new entry. For the `login_datetime`, we will pass the `dateof(now())` nested function, which will add the current time as a timestamp from the server-side Cassandra:

```
strINSERT = """
INSERT INTO logins_by_user (user_id,login_datetime,origin_ip)
VALUES (?,dateof(now()),?)
"""
pINSERTStatement = session.prepare(strINSERT);
session.execute(pINSERTStatement,['aploetz','192.168.0.114'])
```

Then we will prepare a query for the last three entries for that user:

```
strSELECT = """
SELECT * FROM logins_by_user WHERE user_id=? LIMIT 3;
"""
pSELECTStatement = session.prepare(strSELECT);
```

Finally, we'll process the result set and close our connection:

```
rows = session.execute(pSELECTStatement,[userid])
print("Data for user %s:" % userid)
for row in rows:
    #only one row in system.local
    print(row[0] + " " +
            str(row[1]) + " " +
            row[2])
```

```
#closing Cassandra connection
session.shutdown()
```

Running this from the command line yields the following output:

```
python queryUser.py 192.168.0.100 cassdba flynnLives aploetz
aploetz 2017-06-10 15:26:23.329000 192.168.0.114
aploetz 2017-06-03 14:04:55 192.168.0.101
aploetz 2017-06-02 18:23:11 192.168.0.105
```

Notice the difference between inserting a timestamp without milliseconds, and `dateof(now())`.

Complete code for both scripts can be found at https://github.com/aploetz/packt/.

# Java

Of course, applications using Java (and many other languages) can connect to, and work with, data in Cassandra. The easiest way to do so is with the DataStax Cassandra Java driver, via Apache Maven. To accomplish this, I'll create a new Maven project (naming it `CassHelloWorld`) with the following entries in the `pom.xml`:

```
<dependencies>
  <dependency>
    <groupId>com.datastax.cassandra</groupId>
    <artifactId>cassandra-driver-core</artifactId>
    <version>3.3.0</version>
  </dependency>
</dependencies>
```

Look for the most recent version at https://github.com/datastax/java-driver.

Once that is done, we will create a class, named `CassandraConnection`, to handle our Cassandra connections:

```
import com.datastax.driver.core.Cluster;
import com.datastax.driver.core.Session;
import com.datastax.driver.core.ResultSet;

public class CassandraConnection {
  private Cluster cluster;
  private Session session;
```

We will create two constructors: one without arguments, and one that accepts a node, username, and password:

```
public CassandraConnection() {
}
public CassandraConnection(String node, String user, String pwd) {
  connect(node,user,pwd);
}
```

Then we'll create a public `connect` method that takes an endpoint and our credentials and then connects to our `cluster`:

```
public void connect(String node, String user, String pwd) {
  cluster = Cluster.builder()
    .addContactPoint(node)
    .withCredentials(user,pwd)
    .build();
  session = cluster.connect();
}
```

We will also create methods to handle queries and close the connection:

```
public ResultSet query(String strQuery) {
  return session.execute(strQuery);
}
public void close() {
  cluster.close();
}
}
```

Finally, we will create a short main class to connect to our cluster, query the `system.local` table, and print the result set:

```
import com.datastax.driver.core.ResultSet;
import com.datastax.driver.core.Row;

public class CassHelloWorld {
    public static void main(String[] args) {
        CassandraConnection conn = new CassandraConnection();
        conn.connect("192.168.0.100", "cassdba", "flynnLives");
        String strSELECT ="SELECT cluster_name,data_center,"
                + "listen_address,release_version "
                + "FROM system.local WHERE key='local'";
        ResultSet rows = conn.query(strSELECT);
        for (Row row : rows) {
            System.out.print(
                row.getString("cluster_name") + " " +
                row.getString("data_center") + " " +
                row.getString("release_version"));
        }
        conn.close();
    }
}
```

The `cassdba` account is used here for brevity in this example. You typically would not want to use a superuser account to query data for an application. The best practice is to create a new user account with privileges assigned only to the specific required keyspace or tables.

When running this code in my integrated developer environment (IDE), I get the following results:

```
PermanentWaves LakesidePark 3.10
```

Next, we will write code to use prepared/bound statements to read and write from Cassandra (much like the second Python example). We will use the same `CassandraConnection` class, with three new methods:

```
public ResultSet query(BoundStatement bStatement) {
  return session.execute(bStatement);
}
public void insert(BoundStatement bStatement) {
  session.execute(bStatement);
}
public Session getSession() {
  return session;
}
```

The `query` method will be an overload of the existing one, with the new method allowing a bound statement object to be passed in. The `insert` method will take a bound statement, and execute it. And the `getSession` method will return the local, private session so that queries can be prepared and variables can be bound.

Next, we will create a new main class called `QueryUser`. It will need the following imports:

```
import com.datastax.driver.core.BoundStatement;
import com.datastax.driver.core.PreparedStatement;
import com.datastax.driver.core.ResultSet;
import com.datastax.driver.core.Row;
import com.datastax.driver.core.Session;
```

The main class will connect in much the same way as the last Java example, except that we will create a local variable to hold the state of the session object:

```
public static void main(String[] args) {
  CassandraConnection conn = new CassandraConnection();
  conn.connect("192.168.0.100", "cassdba", "flynnLives");
  Session session = conn.getSession();
```

Create a local variable for the current `userID`:

```
String userID = System.getProperty("user.name");
```

Here we will create our insert query, prepare it, and bind our user-ID variable and IP address to it. Once that is done, we will pass the bound statement for the insert to the `CassandraConnection` class `insert` method:

```
String strINSERT = "INSERT INTO packt.logins_by_user "
    + "(user_id,login_datetime,origin_ip) "
    + "VALUES (?,dateof(now()),?)";
PreparedStatement pIStatement = session.prepare(strINSERT);
BoundStatement bIStatement = new BoundStatement(pIStatement);
bIStatement.bind(userID, "192.168.0.119");
conn.insert(bIStatement);
```

Similarly, with the select query, we will prepare the statement and bind our user-ID variable to it. We will then pass our bound statement to the `query` method on the `CassandraConnection` class, and process the returned result set:

```
String strSELECT = "SELECT * "
    + "FROM packt.logins_by_user WHERE user_id=? "
    + "LIMIT 3";
PreparedStatement pSStatement = session.prepare(strSELECT);
BoundStatement bSStatement = new BoundStatement(pSStatement);
```

```
bSStatement.bind(userID);
ResultSet rows = conn.query(bSStatement);
  for (Row row : rows) {
    System.out.println(row.getString("user_id") + " " +
      row.getTimestamp("login_datetime") + " " +
      row.getString("origin_ip"));
  }
  conn.close();
}
```

When I run this code in my IDE, I see the following results:

```
aploetz Sun Jun 11 08:49:58 CDT 2017 192.168.0.119
aploetz Sat Jun 10 15:26:23 CDT 2017 192.168.0.114
aploetz Sat Jun 03 14:04:55 CDT 2017 192.168.0.101
```

The complete code for both classes can be found at
https://github.com/aploetz/packt/.

# Taking a backup with Cassandra

In a multi-data center, high-availability deployment, it may seem like taking backups of your Cassandra nodes is unnecessary. After all, if a node crashes and doesn't come back, there are usually other nodes in the data center containing replicas of the data lost. If an entire data center is lost, a new data center can be deployed into the existing Cassandra cluster, with data streamed from another data center.

Even if a copy of the data directory of a node was to be taken and copied off site, those files are of limited use in a large-scale deployment. This is because a node will only store data for specific token ranges. With Vnodes, token ranges are numerous and non-contiguous, making the backed-up data only valid for that specific node. Additionally, if you should happen to add or remove nodes from your cluster, the token ranges will be recalculated, essentially invalidating any off-site copies of node-specific data.

Despite these challenges, having a solid backup and restore strategy for your cluster(s) is essential. And while deploying multiple nodes across multiple data centers might help for disaster recovery, it does not help in situations where data has been corrupted, tampered with, or accidentally deleted.

Cassandra does allow its operators to take snapshots. Snapshots are periodic, point-in-time bookmarks for your data. They can be taken on a table, keyspace, or system-wide basis. Additionally, you can also enable incremental backups, which essentially backs up data changed since the last snapshot. To enable incremental backups, edit the `incremental_backups` property in your `cassandra.yaml` configuration file, and set it to `true`:

```
incremental_backups: true
```

It is very easy to take a snapshot in Cassandra. Simply invoke it through `nodetool` and provide as much focus as you require, such as `nodetool snapshot [keyspace_name].[table_name]`:

```
nodetool snapshot packt.logins_by_user
Requested creating snapshot(s) for [packt.logins_by_user] with snapshot
name [1504986577085] and options {skipFlush=false}
Snapshot directory: 1504986577085
```

# Restoring from a snapshot

Let's say that after taking a snapshot, one of our tables ends up with corrupted data for a particular user. The application team fixes the problem on their end, and simply asks for us to restore the `logins_by_user` table to the last snapshot.

First of all, let's take a look at the data in question:

```
cassdba@cqlsh> use packt ;
cassdba@cqlsh:packt> SELECT * FROM logins_by_user WHERE user_id='avery'
LIMIT 1;

 user_id | login_datetime                 | origin_ip
---------+--------------------------------+-----------
   avery | 1970-01-01 19:48:33.945000+0000 | 10.0.15.2

(1 rows)
```

Obviously, the new user did not recently log in on January 1, 1970, so our corrupted data has been presented to us. To ensure that we are starting from a clean slate, truncate the table:

```
cassdba@cqlsh:packt> truncate table packt.logins_by_user;
```

Assuming the data for our keyspace is in `/var/lib/cassandra/data/packt`, let's take a look at it:

```
cd /var/lib/cassandra/data/packt
ls -al
total 20
drwxrwxr-x  5 aploetz aploetz 4096 Jul 18 09:23 .
drwxr-xr-x 18 aploetz aploetz 4096 Jun 10 09:06 ..
drwxrwxr-x  3 aploetz aploetz 4096 Jul 18 14:05 astronauts-
b27b5a406bc411e7b609c123c0f29bf4
drwxrwxr-x  3 aploetz aploetz 4096 Jul 18 14:05 astronauts_by_group-
b2c163f06bc411e7b609c123c0f29bf4
drwxrwxr-x  4 aploetz aploetz 4096 Sep  9 14:51 logins_by_user-
fdd9fa204de511e7a2e6f3d179351473
```

We see a directory for the `logins_by_user` table. Once a snapshot has been taken, each table directory should also have a "snapshots" directory, so let's `cd` into that and list it out:

```
cd logins_by_user-fdd9fa204de511e7a2e6f3d179351473/snapshots
ls -al
total 16
drwxrwxr-x 4 aploetz aploetz 4096 Sep  9 14:58 .
drwxrwxr-x 4 aploetz aploetz 4096 Sep  9 14:58 ..
drwxrwxr-x 2 aploetz aploetz 4096 Sep  9 14:55 1504986577085
drwxrwxr-x 2 aploetz aploetz 4096 Sep  9 14:58 truncated-1504987099599-
logins_by_user
```

Recalling the output from our earlier `nodetool snapshot` command, the `1504986577085` directory was the name of the snapshot taken. Enter that directory, and list it out:

```
ls -al
total 52
drwxrwxr-x 2 aploetz aploetz 4096 Sep  9 14:49 .
drwxrwxr-x 3 aploetz aploetz 4096 Sep  9 14:49 ..
-rw-rw-r-- 1 aploetz aploetz   31 Sep  9 14:49 manifest.json
-rw-rw-r-- 2 aploetz aploetz   43 Jun 10 10:53 mc-1-big-
CompressionInfo.db
-rw-rw-r-- 2 aploetz aploetz  264 Jun 10 10:53 mc-1-big-Data.db
-rw-rw-r-- 2 aploetz aploetz    9 Jun 10 10:53 mc-1-big-Digest.crc32
-rw-rw-r-- 2 aploetz aploetz   16 Jun 10 10:53 mc-1-big-Filter.db
-rw-rw-r-- 2 aploetz aploetz   11 Jun 10 10:53 mc-1-big-Index.db
-rw-rw-r-- 2 aploetz aploetz 4722 Jun 10 10:53 mc-1-big-Statistics.db
-rw-rw-r-- 2 aploetz aploetz   65 Jun 10 10:53 mc-1-big-Summary.db
-rw-rw-r-- 2 aploetz aploetz   92 Jun 10 10:53 mc-1-big-TOC.txt
-rw-rw-r-- 1 aploetz aploetz  947 Sep  9 14:49 schema.cql
```

All of these files need to be copied into the `logins_by_user-fdd9fa204de511e7a2e6f3d179351473` directory. As we have navigated our way down to the directory containing the snapshot files, we can do this with a simple command:

```
cp * ../../
```

This copies all files from the current directory into the directory two levels up, which is `/var/lib/cassandra/data/packt/logins_by_user-fdd9fa204de511e7a2e6f3d179351473`. Now, we will bounce (stop/restart) our node. Go back into `cqlsh`, and rerun the prior query:

```
cassdba@cqlsh> use packt ;
cassdba@cqlsh:packt> SELECT * FROM logins_by_user WHERE user_id='avery'
LIMIT 1;

 user_id | login_datetime                   | origin_ip
---------+----------------------------------+-----------
   avery | 2017-09-09 19:48:33.945000+0000  | 10.0.15.2

(1 rows)
```

It is important to note that snapshots and incremental backups are essentially hard links created to `sstable` files on disk. These hard links prevent `sstable` files from being removed once compacted. Therefore, it is recommended to build a process to remove old snapshots and backups that are no longer needed.

# Tips for success

Following are some tips you may need while using Cassandra:

# Run Cassandra on Linux

Cassandra *may* work on Windows, but remember that this is a fairly new development in the Cassandra world. If you want the best chance of building a successful cluster, build it on Linux.

# Open ports 7199, 7000, 7001, and 9042

Cassandra needs 7199 for JMX (nodetool), 7000 for gossip, 7001 for gossip over SSL, and 9042 for native binary (client connections). You shouldn't need Thrift (port 9160), so don't open the port or enable the protocol unless you have a reason to.

# Enable security

At the very least, you should enable authorization and authentication.

# Use solid state drives (SSDs) if possible

The primary bottleneck on Cassandra is disk I/O, and SSDs will help you to mitigate that. The cassandra.yaml file also contains some specific settings for optimizing an instance backed by SSDs, so be sure to look those up and activate them where appropriate. Never use a NAS or SAN for Cassandra.

# Configure only one or two seed nodes per data center

Do not make every node a seed node, as the new nodes will not bootstrap data. Remember those seed nodes do not have any kind of special designation; all Cassandra nodes in a cluster are considered equal to each other.

# Schedule weekly repairs

Even if you never delete any data, this is a good idea, just to make sure all of your data is properly replicated.

# Do not force a major compaction

Let Cassandra decide when compaction should be run. Once you run compaction manually, you'll have to run it manually from that point on.

# Remember that every mutation is a write

Updates, inserts, and deletes are all treated the same... as writes! Any previous data will be obsoleted, and not immediately removed. Deletes and TTLs will create tombstones. Consider these points when building your data models. Avoid deleting data or writing data in place as much as possible, and build your tables to match specific query patterns.

# The data model is key

Probably the most important, determining factor of building a good cluster is getting your data model right. Bad data models can bring an otherwise well-performing cluster to a grinding halt. From the perspective of a DBA, there is usually little that can be done to improve performance if the data model is rife with anti-patterns.

# Consider a support contract

If you are new to Cassandra, enterprise support is available through third-party providers (DataStax, Instaclustr, The Last Pickle, and so on). If your organization is new to Cassandra and has only a few individuals who are experienced with it, having a company you can go to for help is good insurance to have.

# Cassandra is not a general purpose database

Cassandra is a great, high-performance, highly available data store. It will run well if deployed for a proper use case, with a query-based data model, while following best practices on the application side for data access. However, implementing it with the wrong use case is a recipe for failure. Remember to avoid deleting data or writing data in place as much as possible, and to build your tables to match specific query patterns.

# Summary

In this chapter, we introduced the Cassandra database, and discussed its features and acceptable use cases, as well as providing some example code for working with it. Cassandra has some intrinsic features that certainly make it a desirable backend data store. It can serve data in an environment with no single point of failure, as well as provide tunable consistency, linear scalability, and best-in-class data center awareness.

Common use cases for Cassandra include time series or event-driven data. It has also shown its ability to support large datasets, which continue to grow over time. Applications backed by Cassandra are successful when they use tables designed to fit well-defined, static query patterns.

It is important to remember that Cassandra also has its share of anti-patterns. Cassandra typically does not perform well with use cases architected around frequently updating or deleting data, queue-like functionality, or access patterns requiring query flexibility. Improper setup can also lead to issues, so it is important to refrain from using a load balancer or a NAS with Cassandra. And of course, never use the `ByteOrderedPartitioner`.

# References

1. Apache Software Foundation (2016). *Cassandra Documentation - Operations - Hardware Choices.* Apache Software Foundation - Cassandra project site. Retrieved on 20170603 from: `http://cassandra.apache.org/doc/latest/operating/hardware.html`

2. Apache Software Foundation (2016). *Cassandra Documentation - Downloads.* Apache Software Foundation - Cassandra project site. Retrieved on 20170603 from: `http://cassandra.apache.org/download/`

3. Brenner B. (2017). *Thousands of MongoDB databases compromised and held to ransom.* Naked Security by Sophos. Retrieved on 20170604 from: `https://nakedsecurity.sophos.com/2017/01/11/thousands-of-mongodb-databases-compromised-and-held-to-ransom/`

4. Brewer E., Fox, A. (1999). *Harvest, Yield, and Scalable Tolerant Systems.* University of California at Berkeley. Berkeley, CA Doi: 10.1.1.24.3690. Retrieved on 20170530 from: `http://citeseerx.ist.psu.edu/viewdoc/download?doi=10.1.1.24.3690rep=rep1type=pdf`

5. Cimpanu C. (2017). *A Benevolent Hacker Is Warning Owners of Unsecured Cassandra Databases*. Bleeping Computer. Retrieved on 20170604 from: `https://www.bleepingcomputer.com/news/security/a-benevolent-hacker-is-warning-owners-of-unsecured-cassandra-databases/`

6. DataStax. (2017). *How is data read?* DataStax 3.0 documentation. Retrieved on 20170916 from: `http://docs.datastax.com/en/archived/cassandra/3.x/cassandra/dml/dmlAboutReads.html`

7. Decandia G., Hastorun D., Jampani M., Kakulapati G., Lakshman A., Pilchin A., et-al. (2007). *Dynamo: Amazon's Highly Available Key-value Store*. Proceedings of the Twenty-First ACM SIGOPS Symposium on Operating Systems Principles (pp. 205-220). Doi: 10.1145/1294261.1294281

# 6
# HBase

Systems aren't designed in a vacuum. Each system reflects a long line of prior work. HBase is no exception. So where did HBase's developers draw their inspiration from?

In 2006, engineers at Google published a paper on a system they called Bigtable. It described the data model, semantics, and inner workings of a distributed database, which itself drew inspiration from a line of prior work, such as Chord, Tapestry, and C-Store.

Bigtable followed **Google File System** (**GFS**), the inspiration behind HDFS at Google, and was meant to offer record-level random read/write capabilities that were missing in GFS. Bigtable was initially used to serve workloads such as Google Analytics (for storing site metrics), and continues to be a popular storage choice at Google, despite newer systems, such as Spanner, that have been developed since then.

In 2007, engineers at a search startup called Powerset decided to draw from the material in Google's publication and build an open source rendition of Bigtable. HBase was initially structured as a contrib module within the Hadoop project, which at that time included the MapReduce framework and HDFS, the file system that HBase was and still is built on top of. In 2008, HBase became a full subproject of Hadoop and became a top-level Apache project in 2010.

Today, HBase is among the top five most popular and widely-deployed NoSQL databases. It is used to support critical production workloads across hundreds of organizations. It is supported by multiple vendors (in fact, it is one of the few databases that is multi vendor), and more importantly has an active and diverse developer and user community.

# Architecture

First, let's take a look at some of the terminology that is specific to HBase:

- **Table:** A table in HBase roughly means the same thing as a table in an RDBMS. Data in an HBase cluster is organized into tables, which are distributed across a set of nodes:

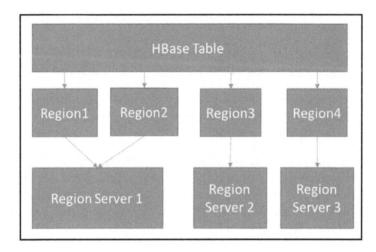

HBase tables are divided into Regions, which are assigned to RegionServers.

- **Namespace:** A collection of tables is stored in a namespace. Typically, an application gets its own namespace on the cluster. The application consists of a bunch of tables stored within that namespace.
- **Region:** An HBase table is broken up into individual shards, or partitions, called regions, which are distributed across nodes in the cluster. Each region corresponds to a unique slice of the key space. A key and the value stored against that key uniquely maps to a region, based on the key range that it falls within. A region is the basic unit of assignment of data within the cluster.
- **RegionServer:** The HBase RegionServer is the JVM instance that hosts a given region. A single RegionServer instance typically hosts tens to hundreds of regions. Typically, there is just a single RegionServer instance per physical node, though it is possible to run more than one instance per node.

# Components in the HBase stack

The Unix philosophy has promoted the use of tools that do one thing and do it well. The tools are designed in a modular fashion so that they can be put together to achieve complex functionality. HBase follows this philosophy to the hilt. HBase leverages two well-known distributed technologies, HDFS and Zookeeper:

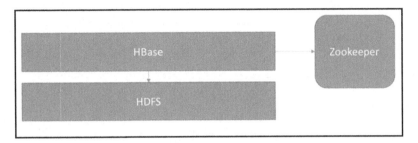

HBase depends on two external components, HDFS and Zookeeper.

# Zookeeper

Apache Zookeeper is a well-known framework for providing primitives for distributed consensus. It provides features such as the following:

- Recipes that allow a set of nodes in a distributed system to conduct elections for leadership, to partition work in an equitable manner, and so on.
- It can be used as a highly-available state store for persisting small amounts of metadata. Zookeeper, like HBase, is strongly consistent and accepts a write only once it's been safely persisted to the majority of nodes in the Zookeeper cluster.
- Zookeeper implements a heartbeat mechanism between the Zookeeper client and the server nodes. So, if a Zookeeper client instance stops sending a heartbeat, the server will consider that client instance to be dead.
- Zookeeper allows clients to set watches on specific events of interest. When those specific events of interest come to pass, interested clients can be notified.
- If a given Zookeeper client instance's heartbeat stopped, depending on how things are set up, it's possible for other client instances to be notified so that corrective action can be taken.
- Zookeeper represents state variables as nodes in a logical file system. These nodes are called znodes. Watches can be kept on any znode. When there is any change to the znode, all client instances that are maintaining watches on it will be notified.

HBase uses Zookeeper for a number of things:

- The state of all regions, the key range they represent, and the RegionServers they are assigned to are kept in Zookeeper
- All RegionServers in the cluster, both the ones that are active and the ones that appear dead, are tracked in Zookeeper
- Various other pieces of metadata related to replication, region splits, merges, and transitions are also kept track of in Zookeeper, and are leveraged heavily for various operations in HBase

# HDFS

HDFS is the Hadoop Distributed File System. Modeled on GFS, Google File System, it allows the storage and processing of large amounts of data. HDFS is modeled as a file system, with support for files larger than what could fit on a single machine. Files are stored as collections of blocks, spread out across a collection of machines.

The data blocks are stored at DataNodes, which handles all of the I/O for the blocks they are responsible for. The block assignment metadata is stored at the **NameNode**. The **NameNode** is responsible for admin and meta operations, such as creating directories, listing directories, file moves, and so on. The **HDFS** client implements the file system interface and provides client applications the logical abstraction of dealing with single, large files, hiding the complexity of dealing with a distributed file system behind the scenes. To read or write a file, the HDFS client interacts with the **NameNode**, which identifies the **DataNode** to read or write the block to. After that, the client directly interacts with the **DataNode** for the block I/O.

**HDFS** provides the persistent storage for **HBase**. It's a similar sort of relationship to GFS and Bigtable. **HBase** uses the **HDFS** client to store collections of records as data blocks in HDFS. The commit logs are also stored in **HDFS**. We'll cover these file structures in more detail in a later section.

Through its inherent replication capabilities, **HDFS** provides high availability to **HBase**. Since block writes to **HDFS** can be replicated across multiple DataNodes, even if a **RegionServer** process goes down, it can come back quickly without losing data. If the **DataNode** process went down, the **RegionServer** can still fetch data from a replica **DataNode**.

There are two questions that always come up in the context of **HBase** and HDFS. When do we use **HBase**, and when should we pick **HDFS** for a given use case?

**HDFS** exposes a file system interface, while **HBase** exposes a key-value API. **HDFS** optimizes for throughput. **HBase** optimizes for low-latency reads or updates to a small set of keys. The fact that **HBase** achieves random reads/writes on top of an append-only file system is remarkable.

So, if you have a batch processing use case that needs to scan a dataset in its entirety and compute some aggregates, **HDFS** is what you need. If you also need random reads and writes to that dataset, **HBase** is what you should go with:

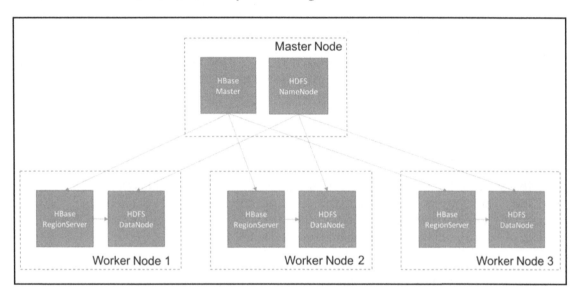

HBase RegionServers and HDFS DataNodes are co-located on each Worker node. HBase Master and HDFS NameNodes are typically co-located on the Master node

# HBase master

The HBase master is responsible for orchestrating various admin operations in an HBase cluster. Operations such as creating a table, adding a column family, or taking a snapshot, require coordination across multiple nodes in the cluster. The HBase master handles this coordination.

Before we describe the HBase master, we need to understand the role of the META region:

- META is a special region in an HBase cluster. It is the region that keeps the state of all the other regions in the cluster. Specifically, it tracks what the regions are, what the associated key ranges are, the RegionServers they've been assigned to, and other information. The META region is hosted on one of the RegionServers in the cluster. It's the master that is responsible for keeping the META region up to date to reflect the current state of the cluster. As regions get split, merged, and moved around, the master updates its internal state as well as the META region.
- The master is responsible for ensuring that the cluster is balanced, and that each node in the cluster is pulling its weight equally. The master periodically looks at the current distribution of regions, and if it is unbalanced, generates a plan of how to move regions around to get to an optimal distribution.

The **assignment manager**, which is a component within the master, is responsible for taking that plan and executing it. It handles coordination with RegionServers to close and open regions and to update META once the ownership transfer is complete.

When an HBase node dies, Zookeeper detects the lack of a heartbeat and lets the master know. The master coordinates the ownership transfer of regions hosted on the dead node to another live node in the cluster (the exact mechanics of this are covered later).

The HBase master is on the critical path for admin operations. For data operations, such as read and write requests, the HBase master is on the critical path only for new client connections. Once an HBase client has an already established connection with the cluster, the loss of the HBase master doesn't interrupt the client traffic flow.

HBase allows for multiple instances of the master to be brought up in an active-standby configuration. Once the active instance stops sending its heartbeat to Zookeeper, one of the backup instances takes over and becomes the active master.

# HBase RegionServers

The HBase RegionServers are the processes that run on every node in the cluster. Typically, there is one RegionServer (or RS) and one HDFS DataNode per physical node in the cluster. It is possible to run more than one RegionServer per physical node, but that's not common.

Each RegionServer is responsible for a set of regions in the cluster and serves all read and write requests to them from HBase clients. A region is end-of-day persisted in one or more files on HDFS. So, to service reads and writes to a region, the RegionServer communicates with the DataNode process on the same or a different machine. The RegionServer also maintains an LRU cache of the blocks that were retrieved to speed up subsequent accesses to those same blocks.

Next, we will explore the inner workings of the RegionServer.

# Reads and writes

Let's look at the internal mechanics of how reads and writes are executed within a RegionServer instance.

# The HBase write path

HDFS is an append-only file system, so how could a database that supports random record updates be built on top of it?

HBase is what's called a log-structured merge tree, or an LSM, database. In an LSM database, data is stored within a multilevel storage hierarchy, with movement of data between levels happening in batches. Cassandra is another example of an LSM database.

When a write for a key is issued from the HBase client, the client looks up Zookeeper to get the location of the RegionServer that hosts the META region. It then queries the META region to find out a table's regions, their key ranges, and the RegionServers they are hosted on.

The client then makes an RPC call to the RegionServer that contains the key in the write request. The RegionServer receives the data for the key, immediately persists this in an in-memory structure called the Memstore, and then returns success back to the client. The Memstore can fill up once a large enough amount of data accumulates within it. At that point, the contents of the Memstore get emptied out onto the disk in a format called HFile.

What happens if the RegionServer crashes before the Memstore contents can be flushed to disk? There would have been irrevocable data loss. To avoid this data loss, each update to the Memstore is first persisted in a write-ahead log. The write-ahead log is maintained on HDFS to take advantage of the replication that is offered by HDFS, thereby ensuring high availability. If the RegionServer goes down, the contents of the WAL are replayed from the same or a replicant DataNode in order to recover the edits that were in the Memstore at the time of the RegionServer crash.

The Memstore is divided into memory segments that are maintained in each region. The flush of the memory segment associated with a region can be done independently of other regions. When the contents of the memory segment are ready to be flushed, data is sorted by key before it is written out to disk. These sorted, disk-based structures allow for performant access to individual records.

On the other hand, the WAL contains edits in the time order in which they were processed by the RegionServer. While data files in HBase are partitioned by region, each RegionServer today maintains a single active WAL for all of the regions hosted on the RegionServer:

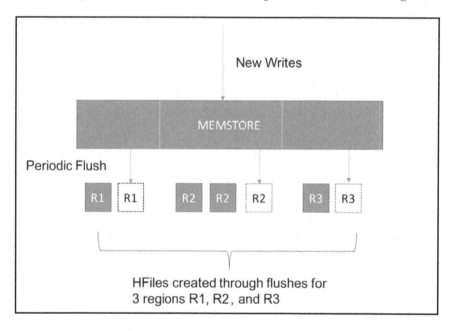

Writes go into the Memstore. Once the Memstore is full, the data gets flushed into HFiles on disk. Each Region has one or more corresponding HFiles.

# HBase writes – design motivation

Why does it work this way? Why is there a single WAL per RS? What is the point of recording the edits in a WAL rather than applying the updates in place?

The original motivation from a decade ago was that spinning disks were slow and SSDs were too expensive to be practical. In mechanical spinning disks, the seek costs were high, but if the disk head was already in the right position, writes could be performed with relatively low latency. In other words, the latency of an append operation is less than a random write. The lower latencies translate to higher throughput.

The LSM structure allows a sequence of random writes to be handled as append-only operations, as random writes are buffered in memory and then written out as a single batch.

The disk writes are only for persisting edits in the commit log itself. By having a single commit log for all regions in the RegionServer, writes for different keys are converted into a stream of append-only edits to a singular commit log.

Since HBase and other such LSM databases only needs a file system that supports append-only operations, it can be layered on top of HDFS, which provides only append-only operations. Hence, HBase and HDFS are a unique fit in terms of capabilities exposed (by HDFS) and capabilities required (by HBase).

Over the past decade, there's been a dramatic lowering in the cost and increase in the capacity of SSD devices. They are now cost-effective enough that these days they are the preferred storage medium in many enterprises, even for big data workloads.

SSDs don't have a mechanical disk head. In SSDs, the latency of sequential and random writes is the same. So, given this change in technology, is there any benefit in a database that converts random writes into append-only operations?

In SSDs, the reading and writing of data happens at page level, typically 512 bytes or more. So, if you need to write a 100-byte value into a page on disk, SSDs need to read 512 bytes of data, merge the 100 bytes into this 512-byte page, and then write the 512 bytes back to disk. So, a 100-byte write has become amplified into a write for 512 bytes. This is called write amplification. The lifetime of an SSD device is measured in terms of how many times a page can be rewritten, after which the error rates tend to go up.

An append-only database, such as HBase, has a write amplification of one (which means, each logical write from the database translates to exactly one physical write within the SSD). Hence, append-only databases put less stress on SSD devices, leading to longer device lifetimes.

# The HBase read path

When a read for a key is issued from the HBase client, as with writes, the client needs to query the META table to identify the RegionServer that contains the data for the given key.

Once the RegionServer receives the read request, it looks it up in the Memstore. However, this by itself is insufficient. The contents of the Memstore might have been flushed to disk by the time the read request arrives, so the RegionServer has to look for the key in the HFile that the Memstore contents were previously flushed into. However, it's not sufficient to look at the most recent HFile for the region since writes for that key could have arrived at any time in the past, so the RegionServer has to look for the key in every HFile that exists for that region.

In other words, fragments of the record exist in the Memstore and various HFiles. On a read request, these record fragments have to be retrieved to reconstruct the latest snapshot of the record to be served out.

This displays one of the fundamental trade-offs that exists in HBase. By converting random writes to append-only operations, disk seeks are minimized on the write path, but this comes at the cost of multiple seeks on the read path.

There are a couple of additional structures that exist to optimize reading data from the Files:

- **Ordering**: At the time of flushing the Memstore segment for a given region, the data is sorted by key at the time it is flushed to disk. Within a given row, data is sorted by column. To retrieve data for a given row and column, it is possible to do something akin to a binary search to quickly triangulate to a given value.

- **Indexes**: Since data is sorted, it is possible to create an index. The index is made up of multiple index blocks, with each index block recording the start key for a given set of data blocks. A quick scan of the index blocks makes it easy to triangulate more quickly to a given value. It's possible to index these index blocks to create a multilevel index to further minimize the number of seeks required to triangulate to a value within an HFile.

- **Bloom filters**: HBase uses a probabilistic data structure called a bloom filter to avoid reading an HFile altogether if it doesn't contain data for a given key. A bloom filter can be thought of as a collection of bit vectors and hash functions. Each key is hashed using each of the hash functions, and the bit in the corresponding hash index is toggled. The same logic is used to check whether a key is present in the bloom filter. Only if the bits in the corresponding hash index in all of the bit vectors are one will we conclude that the key is present in the bloom filter. A bloom filter can produce false positives since multiple keys might hash to the same hash indices in different bit vectors. A bloom filter might claim to have a key that it doesn't have, but it never fails to claim a key that it does have.

  Each HFile comes with a bloom filter that describes all the keys that are present in that HFile. If the bloom filter doesn't have that key, the HFile is never queried. If the bloom filter has the key, the HFile is queried to retrieve data for the key.

# HBase compactions

As we've discussed previously, over time, a large number of HFiles gets created for each region. Each additional HFile that is created increases the read latency, as it's one more disk seek to query whether there is data for a given key in that HFile. To avoid an unbounded increase in read latencies, HBase performs a background operation called a compaction.

The idea behind compactions is simple. A set of HFiles for a given region are consolidated into a single HFile. This has the effect of merging record fragments for a given key into a single record fragment. During this merge operation, multiple updates are squashed and delete markers/tombstones are purged, often resulting in a more compact record footprint. Since the individual HFiles are sorted, the compaction process itself is similar to a disk-based merge sort.

The only remaining question is what HFiles should be merged and when to do so. This is governed by the compaction policy, which can be configured by the operator. There are different compaction policies that one could set depending on query patterns and data characteristics for a given table. An in-depth discussion of these compaction policies is beyond the scope of this chapter.

# System trade-offs

In the introduction to this book, we discussed some of the principles in the design of distributed systems and talked about inherent system trade-offs that we need to choose between while setting out to build a distributed system.

How does HBase make those trade-offs? What aspects of its architecture are affected by these design choices, and what effect does it have on the set of use cases that it might be a fit for?

At this point, we already know HBase range partitions the key space, dividing it into key ranges assigned to different regions. The purpose of the META table is to record the range assignments. This is different from Cassandra, which uses consistent hashing and has no central state store that captures the data placement state.

We already know that HBase is an LSM database, converting random writes into a stream of append operations. This allows it to achieve higher write throughputs than conventional databases, and also makes the layering on top of HDFS possible.

How does it handle other trade-offs, such as consistency versus availability?

HBase, like Bigtable, chooses consistency over availability. In HBase, a given key has to be in a single region, and a region hosted on a single RegionServer. As a result, all operations on a key are processed by a single RegionServer. This ensures strong consistency, since there is only a single arbiter responsible for handling updates to a given record. This makes operations such as increment and checkAndPut possible, since there is one and only one RegionServer responsible for handling both the read and write phases in a read-modify-write operation, and hence it can ensure that no updates to the data can happen outside its realm.

However, this stronger notion of consistency comes at the cost of availability. If the RegionServer goes down, there is a period of downtime before a new RegionServer can take over ownership of the regions. On the face of it, it might seem like this makes HBase unsuitable for mission-critical applications. However, there is some difference between theoretical and practical notions of availability, and we'll discuss techniques to improve the availability of HBase clusters in a later section.

Our second consideration was about the transaction model and the isolation levels that the database seeks to provide.

HBase provides ACID only at the row level, so updates to multiple columns in the same row can be done atomically, but no atomic updates are possible for updates spanning multiple rows. This means dirty writes from a transaction are invisible to other concurrent transactions operating on the same row, but once our transaction modifies an R1 row and moves on to the next row, R2, the updated R1 is immediately visible to other transactions operating on R1.

Finally, HBase is a type of row store. To be specific, it is what we'd call a column-family oriented store. We'll discuss what this means in our next section on the HBase data model.

# Logical and physical data models

An HBase cluster is divided into namespaces. A namespace is a logical collection of tables, representing an application or organizational unit.

A table in HBase is made up of rows and columns, like a table in any other database. The table is divided up into regions such that each region is a collection of rows. A row cannot be split across regions:

| Row Key | Version | Metrics: Humidity | Metrics: Temperature |
|---------|---------|-------------------|----------------------|
| Key 1 | T1 | V1 | V11 |
| Key 1 | T2 | V2 | V12 |
| Key 2 | T1 | V3 | V13 |
| Key 3 | T1 | V4 | V14 |
| Key 3 | T3 | V5 | V15 |
| Key 3 | T4 | V6 | V16 |

Values are identified by the combination of the Row Key, a Version Timestamp, the Column Family (Metrics) and the Column Qualifier (Temperature)

However, in addition to rows and columns, HBase has another construct called a ColumnFamily. A ColumnFamily, as the name suggests, represents a set of columns. For a given set of rows, all data for columns in a column family is stored physically together on a disk. So, if a table has a single region with 100 rows and two column families with 10 columns each, then there are two underlying HFiles, corresponding to each column family.

What should the criteria be for grouping columns within a column family? Columns that are frequently queried together can be grouped together to achieve locality of reference and minimize disk seeks. Within a column family are a collection of columns that HBase calls column qualifiers. The intersection of every row plus column family plus column qualifier is called an HBase cell and represents a unit of storage.

Within an HBase cell, rather than storing a single value, HBase stores a time series of edits to the cell. Each update is associated with the timestamp of when the update was made. HBase allows you to provide a timestamp filter in the read requests, thus enabling you to not just read the latest value in a cell, but the value of the cell as of a point in time. Each row in HBase is identified by a row key. The row key, like the value in the cells, is stored as an array of bytes:

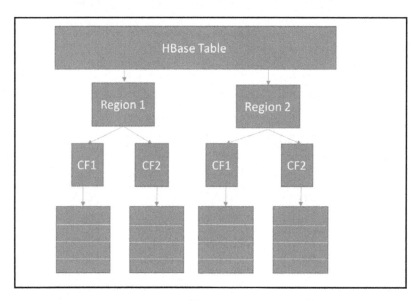

If a Table has two column-families (CF), each Region will contain at least two HFiles which store the individual rows of that Region for that CF.

How do all these logical entities map to a physical representation on a disk? A detailed description of the HFile structure is outside the scope of the book, but we'll discuss it at a high level here.

HBase sorts data on the row key (lexicographic byte ordering). Within the row, data is sorted by the column name. Within each cell, data is sorted in reverse order of the timestamp. This ordering allows HBase to quickly triangulate a specific cell version.

HBase stores the row key along with each cell, instead of once per row. This means that if you have a large number of columns and a long row key, there might be some storage overhead. HBase allows for data in tables to be compressed via multiple codecs, snappy, gzip, and lzo. Typically, snappy compression helps achieve a happy medium between the size of the compressed object and the compression/decompression speeds.

HBase also supports a variety of data block encoding formats, such as prefix, diff, and fast diff. Often, column names have repeating elements, such as timestamps. The data block encoders help reduce the key storage overhead by exploiting commonalities in the column names and storing just the diffs.

As discussed before, HFiles also contain a multilevel index. Top-level index blocks are loaded from the HFiles and pinned in the RegionServer memory. And as discussed, HFiles also contain probabilistic data structures ("bloom filters"), allowing for entire HFiles to be skipped if the bloom filter probe turned up empty.

Data is stored as a byte array within an HBase cell. There are no data types in HBase, so the bytes within an HBase cell might represent a string, an int, or a date. HBase doesn't care. It's left to the application developer to remember how a value was encoded and decode it appropriately.

HBase itself is schemaless. This not only means that there is no native type system, it means that there is no well-defined structure for each row. This means that when you create a table in HBase, you only need to specify what the column family is. The column qualifiers aren't captured in the table schema. This makes it a great fit for sparse, semi-structured data since each row only needs to allocate storage for the columns that will be contained within it.

So how does someone store data in HBase if there are so many degrees of freedom in terms of how the data is modeled? Often, novice HBase users make assumptions about expected performance based on a theoretical understanding of its internal workings. However, they are often surprised when the actual footprint is different from their back-of-an-envelope calculations, or when latencies are worse than they expected. The only scientific approach here is to do a quantitative evaluation of schemas and understand the storage footprint and the latencies for reading and writing data at scale.

# Interacting with HBase – the HBase shell

The best way to get started with understanding HBase is through the HBase shell.

 Before we do that, we need to first install HBase. An easy way to get started is to use the Hortonworks sandbox. You can download the sandbox for free from `https://hortonworks.com/products/sandbox/`. The sandbox can be installed on Linux, Mac and Windows. Follow the instructions to get this set up.

On any cluster where the HBase client or server is installed, type `hbase shell` to get a prompt into HBase:

```
hbase(main):004:0> version
1.1.2.2.3.6.2-3, r2873b074585fce900c3f9592ae16fdd2d4d3a446, Thu Aug  4
18:41:44 UTC 2016
```

This tells you the version of HBase that is running on the cluster. In this instance, the HBase version is 1.1.2, provided by a particular Hadoop distribution, in this case HDP 2.3.6:

```
hbase(main):001:0> help
HBase Shell, version 1.1.2.2.3.6.2-3,
r2873b074585fce900c3f9592ae16fdd2d4d3a446, Thu Aug  4 18:41:44 UTC 2016
Type 'help "COMMAND"', (e.g. 'help "get"' -- the quotes are necessary) for
help on a specific command.
Commands are grouped. Type 'help "COMMAND_GROUP"', (e.g. 'help "general"')
for help on a command group.
```

This provides the set of operations that are possible through the HBase shell, which includes DDL, DML, and admin operations.

```
hbase(main):001:0> create 'sensor_telemetry', 'metrics'
0 row(s) in 1.7250 seconds
=> Hbase::Table - sensor_telemetry
```

This creates a table called `sensor_telemetry`, with a single column family called `metrics`. As we discussed before, HBase doesn't require column names to be defined in the table schema (and in fact, has no provision for you to be able to do so):

```
hbase(main):001:0> describe 'sensor_telemetry'
Table sensor_telemetry is ENABLED
sensor_telemetry
COLUMN FAMILIES DESCRIPTION
{NAME => 'metrics', BLOOMFILTER => 'ROW', VERSIONS => '1', IN_MEMORY =>
'false',
KEEP_DELETED_CELLS => 'FALSE', DATA_BLOCK_ENCODING
```

```
=> 'NONE', TTL => 'FOREVER', COMPRESSION => 'NONE', MIN_VERSIONS => '0',
BLOCKCACHE => 'true', BLOCKSIZE => '65536', REPLICATION_SCOPE =>'0'}
1 row(s) in 0.5030 seconds
```

This describes the structure of the `sensor_telemetry` table. The command output indicates that there's a single column family present called `metrics`, with various attributes defined on it.

`BLOOMFILTER` indicates the type of bloom filter defined for the table, which can either be a bloom filter of the `ROW` type, which probes for the presence/absence of a given row key, or of the `ROWCOL` type, which probes for the presence/absence of a given row key, col-qualifier combination. You can also choose to have `BLOOMFILTER` set to `None`.

The `BLOCKSIZE` configures the minimum granularity of an HBase read. By default, the block size is 64 KB, so if the average cells are less than 64 KB, and there's not much locality of reference, you can lower your block size to ensure there's not more I/O than necessary, and more importantly, that your block cache isn't wasted on data that is not needed.

`VERSIONS` refers to the maximum number of cell versions that are to be kept around:

```
hbase(main):004:0> alter 'sensor_telemetry', {NAME => 'metrics', BLOCKSIZE
=> '16384', COMPRESSION => 'SNAPPY'}
Updating all regions with the new schema...
1/1 regions updated.
Done.
0 row(s) in 1.9660 seconds
```

Here, we are altering the table and column family definition to change the `BLOCKSIZE` to be 16 K and the `COMPRESSION` codec to be `SNAPPY`:

```
hbase(main):004:0> version
1.1.2.2.3.6.2-3, r2873b074585fce900c3f9592ae16fdd2d4d3a446, Thu Aug 4
18:41:44 UTC 2016 hbase(main):005:0> describe 'sensor_telemetry'
Table sensor_telemetry is
ENABLED
sensor_telemetry
COLUMN FAMILIES DESCRIPTION
{NAME => 'metrics', BLOOMFILTER => 'ROW', VERSIONS => '1', IN_MEMORY =>
'false',
KEEP_DELETED_CELLS => 'FALSE', DATA_BLOCK_ENCODING
=> 'NONE', TTL => 'FOREVER', COMPRESSION => 'SNAPPY', MIN_VERSIONS => '0',
BLOCKCACHE => 'true', BLOCKSIZE => '16384', REPLICATION_SCOPE => '0'}
1 row(s) in 0.0410 seconds
```

This is what the table definition now looks like after our ALTER table statement. Next, let's scan the table to see what it contains:

```
hbase(main):007:0> scan 'sensor_telemetry'
ROW COLUMN+CELL
0 row(s) in 0.0750 seconds
```

No surprises, the table is empty. So, let's populate some data into the table:

```
hbase(main):007:0> put 'sensor_telemetry', '/94555/20170308/18:30',
'temperature', '65'
ERROR: Unknown column family! Valid column names: metrics:*
```

Here, we are attempting to insert data into the sensor_telemetry table. We are attempting to store the value '65' for the column qualifier 'temperature' for a row key '/94555/20170308/18:30'. This is unsuccessful because the column 'temperature' is not associated with any column family.

In HBase, you always need the row key, the column family and the column qualifier to uniquely specify a value. So, let's try this again:

```
hbase(main):008:0> put 'sensor_telemetry', '/94555/20170308/18:30',
 'metrics:temperature', '65'
 0 row(s) in 0.0120 seconds
```

Ok, that seemed to be successful. Let's confirm that we now have some data in the table:

```
hbase(main):009:0> count 'sensor_telemetry'
 1 row(s) in 0.0620 seconds
 => 1
```

Ok, it looks like we are on the right track. Let's scan the table to see what it contains:

```
hbase(main):010:0> scan 'sensor_telemetry'
 ROW COLUMN+CELL
/94555/20170308/18:30 column=metrics:temperature,
timestamp=1501810397402,value=65
1 row(s) in 0.0190 seconds
```

This tells us we've got data for a single row and a single column. The insert time epoch in milliseconds was 1501810397402.

In addition to a `scan` operation, which scans through all of the rows in the table, HBase also provides a `get` operation, where you can retrieve data for one or more rows, if you know the keys:

```
hbase(main):011:0> get 'sensor_telemetry', '/94555/20170308/18:30'
COLUMN CELL
metrics:temperature timestamp=1501810397402, value=65
```

OK, that returns the row as expected. Next, let's look at the effect of cell versions. As we've discussed before, a value in HBase is defined by a combination of Row-key, Col-family, Col-qualifier, Timestamp.

To understand this, let's insert the value `'66'`, for the same row key and column qualifier as before:

```
hbase(main):012:0> put 'sensor_telemetry', '/94555/20170308/18:30',
'metrics:temperature', '66'
0 row(s) in 0.0080 seconds
```

Now let's read the value for the row key back:

```
hbase(main):013:0> get 'sensor_telemetry', '/94555/20170308/18:30'
COLUMN CELL
metrics:temperature timestamp=1501810496459,
value=66
1 row(s) in 0.0130 seconds
```

This is in line with what we expect, and this is the standard behavior we'd expect from any database. A `put` in HBase is the equivalent to an `upsert` in an RDBMS. Like an `upsert`, `put` inserts a value if it doesn't already exist and updates it if a prior value exists.

Now, this is where things get interesting. The `get` operation in HBase allows us to retrieve data associated with a particular timestamp:

```
hbase(main):015:0> get 'sensor_telemetry', '/94555/20170308/18:30', {COLUMN
=>
'metrics:temperature', TIMESTAMP => 1501810397402}
COLUMN CELL
metrics:temperature timestamp=1501810397402,value=65
1 row(s) in 0.0120 seconds
```

We are able to retrieve the old value of 65 by providing the right timestamp. So, puts in HBase don't overwrite the old value, they merely hide it; we can always retrieve the old values by providing the timestamps.

Now, let's insert more data into the table:

```
hbase(main):028:0> put 'sensor_telemetry', '/94555/20170307/18:30',
'metrics:temperature', '43'
0 row(s) in 0.0080 seconds

hbase(main):029:0> put 'sensor_telemetry', '/94555/20170306/18:30',
'metrics:temperature', '33'
0 row(s) in 0.0070 seconds
```

Now, let's scan the table back:

```
hbase(main):030:0> scan 'sensor_telemetry'
ROW COLUMN+CELL
/94555/20170306/18:30 column=metrics:temperature, timestamp=1501810843956,
value=33
/94555/20170307/18:30 column=metrics:temperature, timestamp=1501810835262,
value=43
/94555/20170308/18:30 column=metrics:temperature,
timestamp=1501810615941,value=67
3 row(s) in 0.0310 seconds
```

We can also scan the table in reverse key order:

```
hbase(main):031:0> scan 'sensor_telemetry', {REVERSED => true}
ROW COLUMN+CELL
/94555/20170308/18:30 column=metrics:temperature, timestamp=1501810615941,
value=67
/94555/20170307/18:30 column=metrics:temperature, timestamp=1501810835262,
value=43
/94555/20170306/18:30 column=metrics:temperature,
timestamp=1501810843956,value=33
3 row(s) in 0.0520 seconds
```

What if we wanted all the rows, but in addition, wanted all the cell versions from each row? We can easily retrieve that:

```
hbase(main):032:0> scan 'sensor_telemetry', {RAW => true, VERSIONS => 10}
ROW COLUMN+CELL
/94555/20170306/18:30 column=metrics:temperature, timestamp=1501810843956,
value=33
/94555/20170307/18:30 column=metrics:temperature, timestamp=1501810835262,
value=43
/94555/20170308/18:30 column=metrics:temperature, timestamp=1501810615941,
```

```
value=67
/94555/20170308/18:30 column=metrics:temperature, timestamp=1501810496459,
value=66
/94555/20170308/18:30 column=metrics:temperature, timestamp=1501810397402,
value=65
```

Here, we are retrieving all three values of the row key `/94555/20170308/18:30` in the scan result set.

HBase scan operations don't need to go from the beginning to the end of the table; you can optionally specify the row to start scanning from and the row to stop the scan operation at:

```
hbase(main):034:0> scan 'sensor_telemetry', {STARTROW => '/94555/20170307'}
ROW COLUMN+CELL
/94555/20170307/18:30 column=metrics:temperature, timestamp=1501810835262,
value=43
/94555/20170308/18:30 column=metrics:temperature, timestamp=1501810615941,
value=67
2 row(s) in 0.0550 seconds
```

HBase also provides the ability to supply filters to the `scan` operation to restrict what rows are returned by the scan operation. It's possible to implement your own filters, but there's rarely a need to. There's a large collection of filters that are already implemented:

```
hbase(main):033:0> scan 'sensor_telemetry', {ROWPREFIXFILTER =>
'/94555/20170307'}
ROW COLUMN+CELL
/94555/20170307/18:30 column=metrics:temperature, timestamp=1501810835262,
value=43
1 row(s) in 0.0300 seconds
```

This returns all the rows whose keys have the prefix `/94555/20170307`:

```
hbase(main):033:0> scan 'sensor_telemetry', { FILTER =>
    SingleColumnValueFilter.new(
        Bytes.toBytes('metrics'),
        Bytes.toBytes('temperature'),
        CompareFilter::CompareOp.valueOf('EQUAL'),
        BinaryComparator.new(Bytes.toBytes('66')))}
```

The `SingleColumnValueFilter` can be used to scan a table and look for all rows with a given column value:

# Interacting with HBase – the HBase Client API

Now that we have an understanding of how to execute basic HBase operations via the shell, let's try and attempt them through the Java API:

```
Configuration conf = HBaseConfiguration.create();
Connection conn = ConnectionFactory.createConnection(conf);
```

The recommended way in which the configuration should be provided to an HBase client application is to copy over the `hbase-site.xml` from the cluster and make it available on the classpath of the client application (typically included in `src/main/resources`).

The `HBaseConfiguration` class reads the `hbase-site.xml` and populates properties such as the Zookeeper quorum hosts and ports, within a `Configuration` object.

The `ConnectionFactory` class handles the lifecycle management of `Connections` to an HBase cluster. The `Connection` class encapsulates TCP connections to the RegionServers, as well as a local cache of the META region, which contains the region assignments.

Connections are heavyweight objects. Thankfully, they are also thread safe, so `Connection` objects only need to be created once per service lifetime, and are reused on every request, whether it's a DDL or a DML action.

Failing to ensure that connections are only created once at service startup, doing so on every request, and creating a ton of the `Connection` objects is a common mistake, and puts quite a bit of stress on the cluster:

```
Admin admin = conn.getAdmin();
 HTableDescriptor descriptor = new
               HTableDescriptor(TableName.valueOf("sensor_telemetry"));
 descriptor.addFamily(new HColumnDescriptor("metrics"));
 admin.createTable(descriptor);
```

Once you have the `Connection` object, an `Admin` object is what you need to execute DDL operations, such as creating a table or altering the attributes of an existing table. `Admin` objects are not thread safe, but are thankfully lightweight to create for each DDL operation. The `HTableDescriptor` is simply a holding object for all of the attributes an HBase table can be created with:

```
Table table = conn.getTable(TableName.valueOf("sensor_telemetry"));

String key = "/94555/20170308/18:30";
```

```
Double temperature = 65;

Put sensorReading = new Put(Bytes.toBytes(key));
sensorReading.addColumn("metrics",
                        "temperature", Bytes.toBytes(temperature));
table.put(sensorReading);
```

This code snippet gets a `Table` object, which, like the `Admin` object, is not thread safe, but is lightweight to create. Just as one common developer mistake is creating connections on each request, putting pressure on the RegionServers, another mistake comes from going to great lengths to reuse `Table` objects across requests. Since these are not thread safe, they create thread local variables to stash these `Table` objects. This is overkill. It's quite okay to create `Table` objects for each read/write request and discard them after the request has been serviced:

```
String key = "/94555/20170308/18:30";
 Result sensorReading = table.get(new Get(Bytes.toBytes(key));
 Double temperature = Bytes.toDouble(
result.getValue("metrics","temperature"));
```

This code snippet should be fairly self explanatory. We are providing a row key and getting back the temperature value:

```
Scan scan = new Scan();
 ResultScanner scanner = table.getScanner(scan);
 for (Result sensorReading : scanner) {
     Double temperature =
Bytes.toDouble(sensorReading.getValue("metrics", "temperature"));
 }
```

This code snippet initiates a scan on an HBase table. Once we get a `scanner` object, we use it to step through the results of the scan. Iterating using the `scanner` object gives you a `Result` row. The `Result` row object can be used to extract individual column values.

Before executing the scan, it's often important to disable scanner caching via the following:

```
ResultScanner scanner = table.getScanner(scan);
scanner.setCaching(false);
```

When executing a large scan, data blocks are being read off the disk and brought to memory. By default, these blocks are cached. However, a large sequential scan is unlikely to access the same blocks again, so not only is caching the blocks not useful, we may have evicted other potentially useful blocks from the cache. Hence, we should turn off server-side caching for the blocks that are being read from a `scan` operation.

Now that we understand how scans can be executed through the API, let's try to understand how to define a filter and execute a scan with the filter:

```
FilterList filters = new FilterList();
  SingleColumnValueFilter filter =
          new SingleColumnValueFilter(
                                    Bytes.toBytes("metrics"),
                                    Bytes.toBytes("temperature"),
                                    CompareOp.EQUAL,
                                    Bytes.toBytes(65));

  filter.setFilterIfMissing(true);
  filters.addFilter(filter);

  Scan scan = new Scan();
  scan.setFilter(filters);

  ResultScanner scanner = table.getScanner(scan);
  scanner.setCaching(false);

  for (Result sensorReading : scanner) {
        Double temperature =
  Bytes.toDouble(sensorReading.getValue("metrics", "temperature"));
  }
```

In this code snippet, we define a `SingleColumnValueFilter` to check whether there are any rows where the `metrics:temperature` column has the value 65. We store this filter in a `FilterList` object. As you might expect, we can chain together multiple filters and store them within the same `FilterList` object (we can control whether the filters are applied conjunctively or disjunctively). We then associate the `FilterList` with the `scan` object and then execute a scan like we did before.

# Interacting with secure HBase clusters

HBase supports strong notions of security through integration with Kerberos. Kerberos is a widely deployed network authentication protocol. A detailed explanation of Kerberos is beyond the scope of this chapter.

An HBase cluster that supports Kerberos requires some additional setup steps. Kerberos works with the notion of principals and keytabs. A Kerberos principal is what identifies a client attempting to talk to HBase. A Kerberos keytab is a file that contains authentication keys (similar to a password). A client can authenticate itself by providing both its principal and keytab.

On a Kerberized cluster, the `hbase-site.xml` has the following additional entries:

```
<property>
    <name>hbase.security.authentication</name>
    <value>kerberos</value>
</property>
<property>
    <name>hbase.security.authorization</name>
    <value>true</value>
</property>
```

To interact with a secure HBase, the client application will need to ensure that the `hbase-site.xml` is included on its classpath.

In addition, the following API calls need to be invoked before creating a `Connection` object:

```
Configuration conf = HBaseConfiguration.create();

UserGroupInformation.setConfiguration(conf);
UserGroupInformation.loginUserFromKeytab(principal, keytabLocation);

Connection conn = ConnectionFactory.createConnection(conf);
```

The `UserGroupInformation` or UGI is the class that handles all of the Kerberos authentication in an HBase client application. In the `loginUserFromKeytab()` method, the client needs to provide the Kerberos principal name and the file location of the Kerberos keytab. Once the client is authenticated, it will create a `Connection` object to the cluster like it did before.

# Advanced topics

For readers who feel they have a good grasp of HBase fundamentals at this point, we will now cover advanced topics such as high availability, coprocessors, and SQL over HBase.

# HBase high availability

In any enterprise looking to build mission-critical applications on top of HBase, the main questions on everybody's minds are *Is the database reliable? What if it goes down? Under what conditions does it fail? How long will it take for the system to be functional again? Will there be lingering effects?*

Let's try and understand each piece of this puzzle. As we've discussed, HBase favors strong consistency, and consequently makes a single RegionServer responsible for all reads and writes for a given key. When that RegionServer goes down, we lose access to the data stored within it and are unable to perform reads and writes with that data. However, since the underlying data is stored on HDFS, the loss of access is only temporary. Once the regions are reassigned to a different RegionServer, reads and writes can resume.

What exactly are the recovery steps involved when a RegionServer goes down? The first step in addressing a failure is to detect that a failure has occurred. Each RegionServer sends a heartbeat to Zookeeper periodically. When Zookeeper doesn't get a heartbeat over a certain period of time, it concludes that the RegionServer has gone offline and notifies the master to initiate corrective steps.

Region reassignment would be easy if all we had to do was recover the HFiles on HDFS. Since the HFiles are on HDFS, new RegionServers can access existing HFiles right away. The issue, however, is that the contents of the Memstore are lost upon RS failure. This has to be recovered before the regions can be brought online. The contents of the Memstore can be reconstructed by replaying edits in the commit log. Since the commit log is also stored in HDFS, it can be accessed remotely from any one of the three DataNodes that maintain a copy of it. The primary challenge is that the commit log has the edits interspersed for all of the regions that are hosted on the RegionServer. However, these regions might be reassigned to different RegionServers upon recovery to prevent undue load on any one RegionServer.

To achieve this, the commit log has to be split by region. Once split, per-region HFiles are generated from the commit log and placed back into HDFS. At this point, all the regions on the RegionServer have up-to-date HFiles. The regions can now be reassigned to new RegionServers (essentially a metadata operation), where they are opened and made available for reads and writes.

# Replicated reads

For a number of applications, availability isn't something that can be sacrificed. However, in some cases, availability requirements for read operations might be different from availability requirements for write operations. There's a category of applications for which the database always needs to be available for reads. However, often these systems have a robust ingestion pipeline that can buffer writes. So, if certain regions are unavailable, the writes will simply backlog and resume once the regions come back online.

So, if the application can't tolerate read unavailability, can we reduce the duration of the downtime? HBase provides a feature called region replication. If this feature is turned on, each region in the table will have a set of replicas. One of the replicas is considered active, while the rest are standby replicas. Each RegionServer hosts some active region replicas and some standby replicas. Naturally, the active and standby of the same region will not be hosted in the same RegionServer. The client issues a read against the active replica and if that times out, it reissues the query against all of the standby replicas. This way, there's a higher probability that a query can be serviced. A detailed explanation of how replicated reads work is outside the scope of this chapter.

So, what do we lose out by gaining this high availability? This comes at the cost of consistency. The active and standby replicas are kept in sync via asynchronous replication, so it's possible that the active replica might reflect writes that might not have been processed by the standby replica yet. So, if the application wants higher availability and can accept a weaker consistency level, using replicated reads is a good option to explore.

# HBase in multiple regions

What if we wanted to run HBase in multiple datacenters? Typically, it is not recommended to run a single HBase cluster stretched across datacenters. What we want to do instead is to set up independent HBase clusters in each datacenter. If this is what we want, how do we ensure that the same data is available from both clusters? We've a couple of options.

We can have the application do a dual ingest. In other words, the application is aware that multiple HBase clusters exist. It explicitly connects to each of the HBase clusters and stores the data. In this setup, if one or more clusters are unavailable, it is the responsibility of the application to keep track of what data has been written to what clusters and ensure all of the writes have landed on all clusters.

The other option is to leverage HBase's native replication to achieve synchronization between clusters. HBase's replication is asynchronous, which means that once a write has been persisted in the source cluster, the client immediately receives the write acknowledgement. At some point in the future, the source cluster attempts to forward the write to the target cluster. The target cluster receives the write, applies it locally, and acknowledges this to the source cluster. The source cluster now knows that the target cluster is caught up till that point in the stream. The replication is weaker than strong consistency and is timeline consistent, in the sense that the updates are applied in the same order in both the source and target cluster, but might be arbitrarily delayed at the target cluster. Hence, there's a potential for stale reads at the target cluster.

Let's next examine how HBase replication performs under different types of workloads and the kind of inconsistency that can arise during failover. Firstly, let's define what failover means. Let's assume we are running clusters in an active-standby configuration. By this, we mean that readers and writers are both connected to a single HBase cluster at any point in time. The edits on the HBase cluster are asynchronously replicated to a peer cluster. When the cluster becomes unavailable, both readers and writers switch over to another cluster.

HBase asynchronous replication isn't just about traditional master-slave replication. HBase also supports multimaster replication. In multimaster replication, both clusters are asynchronously replicating to their peer. Wouldn't this cause race conditions? Wouldn't updates clobber each other? As we've discussed previously, in HBase, the cells are versioned with a timestamp. The timestamp is, by default, the timestamp of the insert in the source cluster. When the update is replicated over to the target cluster, it is inserted with the timestamp from the source cluster. Hence, the update is recorded with the same timestamp in the source and target clusters.

This means that if the two clusters were partitioned off from each other and some writers were writing to cluster A and others were writing to cluster B, when the partition is resolved, updates will flow again between A and B. Both sets of updates will be recorded in the same way in the two clusters and, eventually, the clusters will be in sync.

However, if failover is implemented from the perspective of writers switching over to a peer cluster when the local cluster is unavailable, there is a potential for inconsistency, depending on the type of write workload.

If the writers are issuing blind writes (that is, writes that aren't preceded by a read), there is no potential for inconsistency. Let's say that the writers were sending their updates to cluster A and then cluster A went down and the writers switched to cluster B. When cluster A eventually comes back up, cluster B will send over all the delta updates to cluster A. Cluster A will eventually be caught up.

What if the workload was a read-modify-write? Say that the client read the value 2 for a given cell, incremented it by 2, and wrote the value 4 back into the database. At this point, the cluster became unavailable, before the new value 4 could be replicated to the peer database. When the client fails over to the new database and needs to increment the value in the cell again, it applies the increment on the 2, not the new value 4. Hence, this results in inconsistent data within the database. Such inconsistency is unavoidable in any database that supports only asynchronous replication between peer clusters.

# HBase coprocessors

HBase has a powerful feature called coprocessors, which we will briefly explain to raise awareness with the reader, but a deeper coverage is outside the scope of this book.

One of the tenets of large-scale data processing is to ensure that the analytics are executed as close to the data layer as possible in order to avoid moving large amounts of data to where the processing is being done. HBase filters are an example of server-side processing that reduces the amount of data flowing back into the client.

HBase offers a set of constructs called coprocessors that allow for arbitrary server-side processing. Since this is arbitrary code running without any sandboxing within the RegionServers, they can also be a source of instability if proper deployment and testing procedures are not followed. Coprocessors are of two types: **observers** and **endpoints**.

Observers are similar to triggers in traditional RDBMs. They allow for some business logic to be executed before or after operations such as reads and writes are performed on a table. The following are some examples of observers and their use:

- If we wanted to do some permission checking on whether a given user is allowed to access data for a given key, the permission checking could be implemented in a preGet().
- If we wanted to do post-processing on the value for a given key, it could be done in a postGet().
- If we wanted to update a secondary index after the base data table has been updated, it could be done in a postPut().

The other kind of coprocessor is endpoints, which are similar to stored procedures in RDBMSs. Endpoints can be invoked via distributed RPC calls and will run concurrently on all of the RegionServers. For example, if you wanted to average the values in a given column in a table, the average operation can be implemented as an endpoint coprocessor. In general, any distributive operation (such as map-reduce) can be expressed within an endpoint coprocessor.

# SQL over HBase

Given that SQL is the lingua franca in the database world, a low-level get/put/scan API puts a bit of adoption friction on HBase since developers now need to learn a new API to interact with the database. Similarly, the lack of a type system puts the burden on the application developer to ensure that the encoding and decoding of the bytes stored in HBase remains in-sync. To mitigate this developer friction, there are now various projects that provide an SQL interface over HBase. Of these projects, the most popular and, arguably, most well developed is Apache Phoenix.

Apache Phoenix allows developers to use a subset of standard ANSI SQL to interact with their HBase tables.

The features supported include the following:

- Creating a table with well-defined types
- Performing standard `Insert/Update/Delete/Select` operations on the table
- Building and maintaining secondary indices
- Building and maintaining materialized views
- Performing inner/outer joins between tables
- Invoking grouping, ordering, and standard SQL aggregate functions

Phoenix works by efficiently translating standard SQL queries into HBase API calls and executing them against the cluster. Phoenix heavily uses HBase coprocessors to push down as much of an operation into the RegionServers as possible, instead of executing them at the client side.

We recommend that a user new to HBase looks into Phoenix since it represents standard recipes and best practices on how to efficiently store and query data from HBase.

# Summary

In this chapter, we dived deep into HBase, one of the most widely deployed NoSQL databases. We looked at the system architecture and design motivations of HBase in great detail. We then reviewed the logical and physical data model within HBase. We looked at how to interact with the database and execute common operations. We looked at interactions via the HBase shell as well as the programmatic Java API. We finished the chapter by looking at advanced topics, such as high availability, coprocessors, and SQL interfaces to HBase.

# 7
# DynamoDB

DynamoDB is a managed NoSQL database service provided by Amazon. To use DynamoDB, you have to pay for throughput only—that is, read/write operations per second; you don't have to worry about storage, server, or other infrastructure-related issues. All infrastructure is managed by Amazon.

The following are some key features provided by DynamoDB:

- DynamoDB spreads data and request traffic to multiple servers to provide better throughput and storage.
- Data is stored on a **solid state drive** (**SSD**) and is replicated over multiple availability zones to provide high availability and fault tolerance.
- It provides data backup using S3 storage.
- It allows you to decide the expiry time of items by allowing you to set a time-to-live parameter. The item will be deleted after this time expires, which makes storage management more efficient.
- We only have to pay for throughput, which makes DynamoDB cost effective.
- It allows you to integrate with other Amazon services, such as the **Identity and Access Management** (**IAM**) service, which secures our DynamoDB database.

DynamoDB supports a wide range of data types, including string, number, binary, and set, and document types, such as list and map. It also provides data types to deal with the date and calendar.

The core components of DynamoDB are the tables, items, and attributes. The table is the same as the table in a relational database. The item represents each record in a table, which contains multiple attributes. Each attribute is a key-value pair.

Each table must have a primary key attribute that identifies each item in the table uniquely. DynamoDB tables are schemaless. Attributes can vary from item to item.

# The difference between SQL and DynamoDB

DynamoDB uses the NoSQL model, which means that it is a non-relational database system. The difference between a relational database and DynamoDB is outlined in the following table:

| SQL | DynamoDB |
|---|---|
| The SQL database system uses the persistent connection and SQL commands. | DynamoDB uses HTTP/HTTPS requests and API operations. |
| RDBMS's fundamental structure is a table, and its schema must be defined in advance before any operation happens on a table. | DynamoDB uses the primary key, and a schema is not required to be defined in advance. It also uses various data sources. |
| All table information is accessible and we can query almost all data. SQL is rich in query processing. | Only the primary key is available for querying. To get more flexibility in querying data, one must use secondary indexes. |
| In RDBMS, information is stored in rows of tables. | In DynamoDB, information is stored as items in a table and the item structure can vary as it is schemaless. |
| SQL databases use a select statement and filtering statements to load the data. | DynamoDB uses `GetItem`, `Query`, and `Scan` APIs to load the data. |
| RDBMS uses standard indexes created using a SQL statement. Changes that happen in the table are automatically managed in the indexes. | DynamoDB uses secondary indexes for faster retrieval of data. Secondary indexes uses partition keys and sort keys. |
| To modify table data, RDBMS uses the `update` statement with the `set` operator. | DynamoDB uses `UpdateItem` to handle the `update` operation on table data. |
| To delete the data from a table, RDBMS uses the `delete` statement. | DynamoDB uses `DeleteItem` to handle the `delete` operation. |
| To delete a table from the database, RDBMS uses the `drop table` command. | DynamoDB uses the `DeleteTable` operation to handle the deletion of a table. |
| The foreign key concept is used extensively to query data from multiple tables. | DynamoDB has no foreign key concept. |

We shall now see the advantages of DynamoDB:

- In DynamoDB, we only have to pay for throughput and read/write operations per second, so cost-effectiveness is a key benefit of DynamoDB.
- It has the best programming support using languages such as Java, .NET and Ruby, which allow easy interaction with DynamoDB. It also provides RESTful API calls.
- It is distributed—DynamoDB scales up horizontally, and so we can distribute a single table across multiple servers.
- It is scalable—we can store any amount of data with DynamoDB. It will automatically increase storage whenever needed.
- It is flexible—DynamoDB supports a large range of data types. Its table structure is also schemaless, so new changes can be easily adopted.
- Amazon also provides a free tier account for DynamoDB, which allows 40 million operations per month.
- Amazon provides a data replication option for DynamoDB, which makes the recovery of data easier.
- DynamoDB provides a method to authenticate users through access keys and API calls. We can also use the Amazon IAM service to secure our data.

The following are some of the disadvantages of DynamoDB:

- For production use, we have to go with AWS deployment. It does not provide any software that can be installed and used in our own environment.
- When we query data, we can only access 1 MB of data at a time. To access the entirety of the data, we have to do a subsequent query operation with pagination.
- We cannot store more than 64 KB of data in a single row.
- DynamoDB does not provide support for ACID properties. We have to manually perform transaction management to achieve consistency and integrity.
- The query operation only works on a primary key. To access data more efficiently, we need to work with scan and secondary indexes.
- As DynamoDB does not support foreign keys, joins are not possible.
- Triggers are not available; instead, we have to use DynamoDB streams.

# Setting up DynamoDB

To work with DynamoDB, we have to set up an AWS account. Amazon provides local JAR support where we can test our application. Now we will look into both setups in detail.

# Setting up locally

AWS provide a version of DynamoDB for local installation. It supports the creation of an application without the web services or connection. It reduces provisioned throughput, data storage, and transfers by allowing local databases. When we are ready for deployment, we can make some changes for it to be used with AWS.

To use DynamoDB locally, we have to use the `.jar` executable file. We can download `.tar` or `.zip`, based on the operating system we are using. For the Unix OS, we have to use `.tar`, and for Windows, we have to download a `.zip` file.

Use the following links to download the respective files:

- `.tar` file:
  http://dynamodb-local.s3-website-us-west-2.amazonaws.com/dynamodb_local_latest.tar.gz
- `.zip` file:
  http://dynamodb-local.s3-website-us-west-2.amazonaws.com/dynamodb_local_latest.zip

Once the file is downloaded, we have to extract the content. We have to go to the directory where we have `DynamoDBLocal.jar` and run the following command:

```
devram@devram-Inspiron-3542:~/Desktop/packtpub/d-jar$ java -jar DynamoDBLocal.jar -sharedDb
Initializing DynamoDB Local with the following configuration:
Port:   8000
InMemory:        false
DbPath: null
SharedDb:        true
shouldDelayTransientStatuses:    false
CorsParams:      *
```

Now DynamoDB is set up locally, and you can use it to connect your application. In the preceding command, we used the `-sharedDb` option. This instructs DynamoDB to use a single database file instead of separate files for each credential and region. If you specify the `-sharedDb` option, all clients will interact with the same set of tables, regardless of the credential files and region.

By default, DynamoDB SDK uses an endpoint for AWS; to use locally, we have to specify the local endpoint `http://localhost:8000`.

To access DynamoDB, use the following command locally:

```
devram@devram-Inspiron-3542:~$ aws dynamodb list-tables --endpoint-url http://localhost:8000
{
    "TableNames": []
}
```

We can also access the user interface for local installation through `http://localhost:8000/shell`. It has a console to execute the request, as shown in the following screenshot:

The preceding command uses a local endpoint and lists all the tables currently available.

Except for the endpoint, an application that runs with the downloadable version of DynamoDB should also work with DynamoDB web services. However, while using DynamoDB locally, we should consider the following points:

- If we use the `-shareDb` option, DynamoDB creates a single database file name `shared-local-instance.db`. Every program that connects to DynamoDB accesses this file. If you delete this file, you will lose all the data.

- If you skip the `-shareDb` option, the database file will be named `myaccesskeyid_region.db`, with the AWS access key ID and region that you configured in the application.
- If you use the `-inMemory` option, DynamoDB does not write any database file. All data is written in memory, and once you exit DynamoDB, all data is lost.
- If you use the `-optimizeDbBeforeStartup` option, you must specify the `dbPath` parameter so that DynamoDB can find the database file.
- The AWS SDK for DynamoDB requires that your application configuration must define the access key value and the AWS region value. If you do not use the `-sharedDb` and `-inMemory` options, DynamoDB will use this value to create local database files.

# Setting up using AWS

To work with AWS DynamoDB services, we have to set up an AWS account. The following are the steps to sign up with an AWS account:

1. Go to `https://aws.amazon.com/` and then choose **Create an AWS account**:

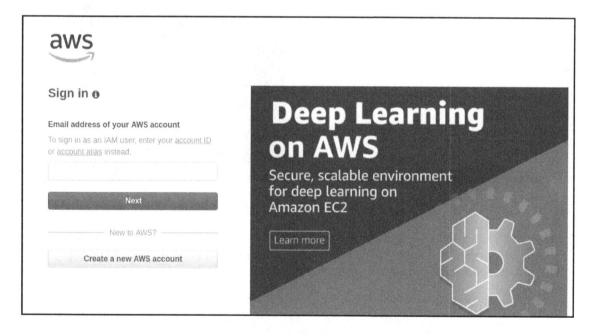

Follow the online instructions to create the account. This involves adding personal information, creating a password, and adding a payment method:

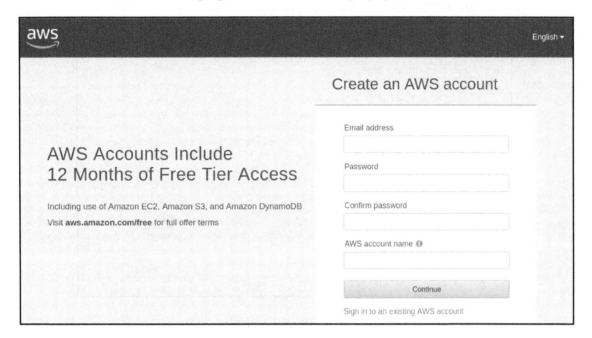

2. Before you can start accessing DynamoDB programmatically or through the AWS command-line interface, you must have the AWS access key. You don't need an access key if you plan to only use the DynamoDB console.

2. To get the access key, go through the following steps:
   1. Open the IAM console:

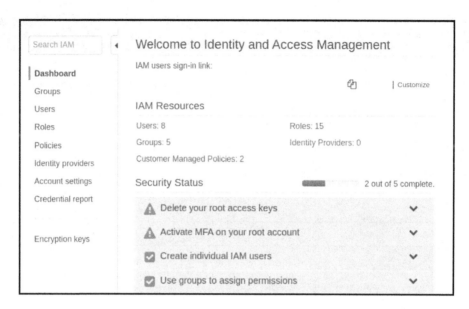

2. In the navigation panel of the console, choose **Users**.
3. Choose your IAM username:

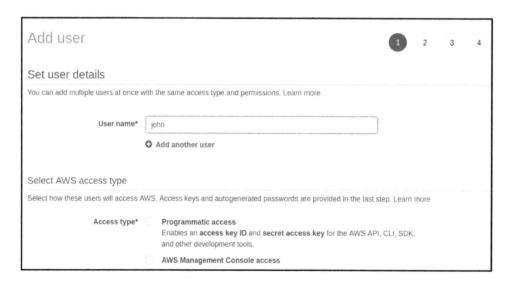

4. Click the **Security credentials** tab and then choose to **Create access key**:

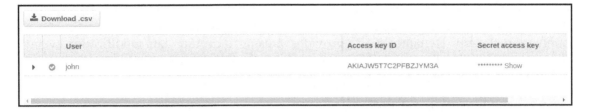

5. To see the new access key, click **Show**. It will show the credentials as follows:
   - **Access key ID:** `AKIBHBDBKHKDHDLJD`
   - **Secret access key:** `ajgjhsjhjahjgs/HGFSHGFhjJHGJHGJH`
6. To download the key pair, choose **Download .csv file**.

3. To access DynamoDB programmatically or through the AWS CLI, you must configure your credentials to enable authorization for your application.
For this, you can manually create a credentials file or you can use the `configure` command of the AWS CLI to automatically create the file.

# The difference between downloadable DynamoDB and DynamoDB web services

We have seen how to set up DynamoDB locally and how to create a DynamoDB AWS account. Now we will see what the advantages and disadvantages of both are:

- Regions and distinct AWS accounts are not supported at the client level
- Provisioned throughput settings are ignored in downloadable DynamoDB
- Scan operations are performed sequentially and parallel scans are not supported in downloadable DynamoDB
- The speed of read/write operations is based on the configuration of your computer
- Read operations are eventually consistent, but as they are running on your computer, most reads appear to be more consistent
- Both web and downloadable services have a data retrieval limit of 1 MB

# DynamoDB data types and terminology

In DynamoDB tables, items and attributes are the core component that you work with. A table is a collection of items, and each item is a collection of attributes. DynamoDB uses the primary key to uniquely identify each item in the table and secondary indexes to fire the query more flexibly. DynamoDB also provides streams to capture data modification events in DynamoDB tables. DynamoDB has size limits on the following components—this may vary from region to region:

- Tables, items, and attributes
- Primary key
- Secondary indexes
- DynamoDB streams

In the next section, we will look at these components in detail.

# Tables, items, and attributes

Similar to other database systems, DynamoDB stores data in tables. A table is a collection of data. For example, if we have a table called `Person`, you could use this to store personal information, contact information, information about friends and family, and other such information. You could also have a table called `Cars` to store the information about the vehicles that people drive.

Each table contains multiple items. An item is a group of attributes that are uniquely identified among all of the other items. In the `People` table, each item represents a person. In the `Cars` table, each item represents a vehicle. Items in DynamoDB are similar in many ways to rows, records, or tuples in other database systems. In DynamoDB, there is no limit to the number of items you can store in the table.

Each item is composed of one or more attributes. An attribute is the fundamental data element that cannot be broken down further. For example, an item in the `People` table contains attributes called `PersonId`, `LastName`, `FirstName`, and so on. For the `Department` table, we could have attributes such as `DepartmentId`, `Name`, `Manager`, and so on.

Attributes in DynamoDB are similar in many ways to fields or columns in other database systems:

```
{
        PersonID : 101,
        FirstName:"John",
        LastName:"smith",
        Age:26,
        Email:"john.smith@co.in"
},
{
        PersonID : 102,
        FirstName:"Ryan",
        LastName:"Henry",
        Age:27,
        Email:"john.smith@co.in"
},
{
        PersonID : 201,
        FirstName:"Kedar",
        LastName:"Sam",
        Age:23,
        Email:"kedar.sam@co.in"
}
```

The following are the key points about the `People` table:

- Each item in the table has a unique identifier, or primary key, that differentiates items from all other items in the table. In the `People` table, the primary key consists of one attribute—`PersonId`.
- The `People` table is schemaless, which means that we don't have to define attributes or their data types in advance. Each item can have its own distinct attributes.
- Most of the attributes are scalar, which means they have only one value. Strings and numbers are the common examples of a scalar data type.
- Some of the items have nested attributes—for example, `Address`. DynamoDB supports nested attributes up to 32 levels.

# Primary key

The primary key uniquely identifies each item in the table. Two items in a table cannot have the same primary key value. Even if DynamoDB tables are schemaless, we have to define a primary key attribute while creating the table. A null value is not applicable for the primary key attribute value. The following figure represents items in the `Person` table. Here, `PersonID` is a primary key that uniquely identifies each `Person` item in the table:

```
{
        PersonID : 101,
        FirstName:"John",
        LastName:"smith",
        Age:26,
        Email:"john.smith@co.in"
},
{
        PersonID : 102,
        FirstName:"Ryan",
        LastName:"Henry",
        Age:27,
        Email:"john.smith@co.in"
},
{
        PersonID : 201,
        FirstName:"Kedar",
        LastName:"Sam",
        Age:23,
        Email:"kedar.sam@co.in"
}
```

DynamoDB supports two kinds of primary key: the partition key and the composite primary key, which is a combination of the partition key and the sort key. Let us discuss both keys in detail:

- **Partition key:** With the partition key, we only have to use one attribute as the primary key, which is known as a partition key. DynamoDB uses the partition key to determine the partition (physical location) in which to store the item. For example, if our internal hash function is the mod function, then the item with `PersonID 101` will be stored in partition 1, as 101 % 100 = 1, in the same way, the item with `PersonID 102` will be stored in partition 2:

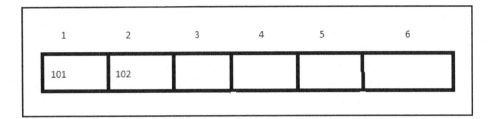

This will make the retrieval of data very much faster. We can immediately access the item by giving the partition key. We can create a partition key while creating a table by choosing the key attribute, as shown in the following screenshot:

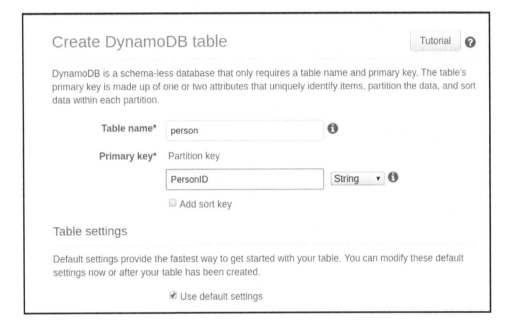

- **Composite primary key:** The composite primary key has two attributes. The first attribute is used as a partition key and the second attribute is used as a sort key. The partition key is used to determine the partition of the item. If two items have the same hash output, they are stored in the single partition. The sort key is used to determine the order of the item in a partition if two or more items receive the same partition. For example, say that we have `PersonID 101, 102` already stored in the partition, and if we now insert an item with `PersonID 201`, we will get partition 1. As we defined age as the sort key item, `201` will be inserted before `101` as its age is less than `23`. In a composite primary key, we can have two items with the same partition key, but the sort key must be different. The partition key in DynamoDB is also called a hash attribute as it is used by the hash function. Partition key values must be scalar values. String, number, and binary are the only data types allowed for a primary key. To create a composite key, we can add a sort key while creating the table:

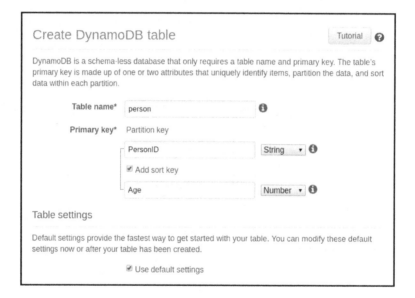

## Secondary indexes

DynamoDB allows you to create an index on an attribute other than the primary key attribute, known as a secondary index. We can use these indexes in `scan` and `query` operations to retrieve data more efficiently.

If an item is inserted, deleted, or updated in the table, DynamoDB will automatically maintain any related secondary index for that table.

DynamoDB supports two types of secondary index:

- **Global secondary index:** The global secondary index is called *global* because any attribute in the base table can be used as a partition key in the index. For the global secondary index, you must define one partition key attribute. Here, the sort key attribute is optional, so this can have a simple key as well as a composite key. A user can create a maximum of five global secondary indexes per table. Global secondary indexes can be created while creating the table, and you can also add them at a later point. The global secondary index allows us to query across multiple partitions. We can create an index by clicking the index tab and providing the partition key. You can also define the sort key:

- **Local secondary index:** The local secondary index is called *local* because it has the same partition key as the base table. We can use other attributes of the base table to define the sort key, and thus the local secondary index is always the composite key. We have to create a local secondary index while creating the table itself. We cannot add or delete a local secondary index at a later point in time. The local secondary index allows you to query only one partition, the same as the base table. In the local secondary index we have to use the partition key, which we created for the base key. For example, if we created the partition key on field `id`, we have to use same the partition key, we cannot create a partition key on another attribute like `Email`, which is allowed in global secondary indexes.

# Streams

The DynamoDB stream feature is a feature local to DynamoDB that allows you to see the changes to your DynamoDB table items.

When you turn on the DynamoDB stream feature, it will present all changes to the items as a stream in real time, as changes happen to the items. When you turn on the stream feature, you have to choose what it is going to write to the stream. The options are as follows:

- **Keys only**: Only the key attribute of a modified item will be written to the stream
- **New image**: This will write the item to the stream as the item appears once it has been modified
- **Old image**: This will write the item to the stream as the item appeared before it was modified
- **New and old image**: When you choose this option, both the new and the old image of an item is written to the stream upon the modification of the item

Whenever we create, update, or delete an item in a DynamoDB table, the DynamoDB stream will write a stream record. The order of the stream record is maintained by the DynamoDB stream, and will change in the same sequence as the actual modification of the item:

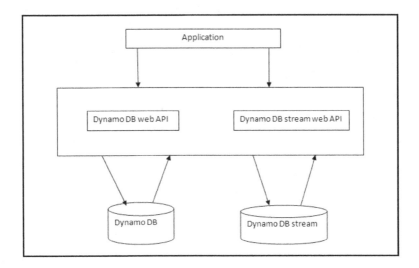

When modification happens in a DynamoDB table, the DynamoDB stream API records the changes. Both work independently. The stream API works asynchronously, so there is no performance impact on the application.

The following are the steps to enable DynamoDB streams:

1. Open the DynamoDB console:

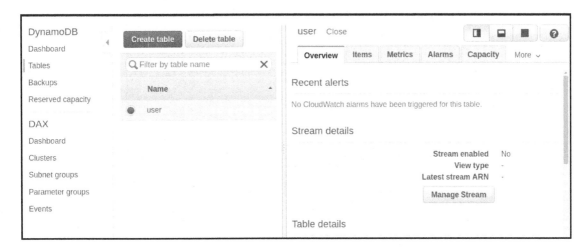

2. In the console dashboard, choose **Manage Stream**:

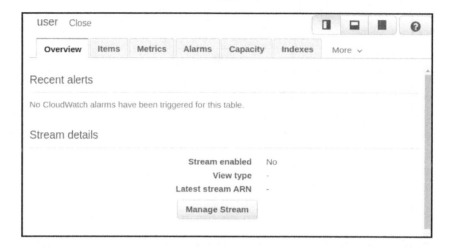

3. In the `Manage Stream` dialog box, choose which information will be written to the stream whenever data is inserted, deleted, or modified in the table:

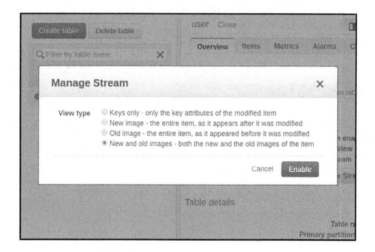

4. To disable the stream, click **Disable**, as follows:

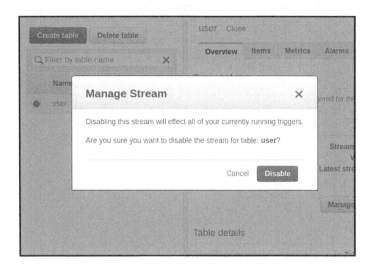

DynamoDB streams are used for the replication of data, table audits, and to trigger another event, such as sending an email when data is modified.

# Queries

The `query` operation searches for, or filters, data based on primary key values. We can apply the `query` operation on the table, as well as on secondary indexes that have the composite primary key.

When we apply the `query` operation on a secondary index, we have to provide a specific value for the partition key using the `KeyConditionExpression` parameter. Then, the `query` operation will return all items with the given partition key from the table. If we have defined a sort key, then we have to provide the `comparison` operator, along with the sort key value in the `KeyConditionExpression` parameter.

To filter the query result, we can also provide the `FilterExpression`. If the matching items are not found in the table, the `query` operation will return the empty result set.

If the composite primary key is the sort key, then the result is always sorted by the sort key values. By default, the sort order is in ascending order; to get the descending order, we have to set the `ScanIndexForward` parameter to false.

The following code shows the request syntax:

```
{
    "FilterExpression" : "String",
    "KeyConditionExpression" : "String",
    "ScanIndexForward" :  boolean,
    "Select" : "String",
    "TableName" : "String",
    .
    .
    .
}
```

# Scan

The `scan` operation in DynamoDB is used to retrieve and filter the data from the table. The `scan` operation scans all the items from the table and returns only those items that meet the filtering criteria. To filter items, we have to provide the conditions in which the filtering should take place, in the `FilterExpression` parameter in the request header.

If the `scan` operation does not match any items in the table, it will return the empty result set.

Also, if the `scan` operation result exceeds 1 MB, the scan will stop and the result returned will be `LastEvaluatedKey`. With this key, we can continue with the `scan` operation again and get the subsequent data.

We can paginate data if it exceeds the 1 MB limit, using `LastEvaluatedKey` to paginate other pages of data. We can read all of the data using pagination even if we are limited to 1 MB data at a time. However, we can also perform a parallel scan on the large table to achieve fast performance.

To perform a parallel scan, we have to provide the `Segment` and `TotalSegment` parameters.

The following code shows the syntax:

```
{
    "TableName":"String",
    "FilterExpression":"String",
```

```
    "Select":"String",
    "Segment":number,
    "TotalSegment":number,
        .
        .
        .
}.
```

# Data types

DynamoDB supports `boolean`, `byte`, `int`, `long`, `float` and `double` primitive data types. It also supports wrapper classes for these primitive data types, such as `Boolean`, `Byte`, `Integer`, `Long`, `Float`, and `Double`. In addition to this, it also supports the String data type, which can represent alphanumeric values, as well as special characters. To manipulate date and calendar related functionality, DynamoDB provides the `Date` and `Calendar` data type also. It also supports `BigDecimal` and `BigInteger` data types to support a very large number of numeric values.

These data types are categorized into three types:

- **Scalar type**: The scalar type represents a single value. The data types such as `string`, `number`, `boolean`, and `null` come under the scalar type definition.
- **Document types**: Document types give you key–value pairs of scalar types. It includes list and map types and supports up to 32 levels of nesting. Document types are generally shown in JSON format.
- **Set types**: Set types can be described as a group of multiple scalar values represented using an array. We have the string set, number set, and binary set.

Now we will discuss each category in detail:

- **Scalar types**: Scalar types include `string`, `number`, `boolean`, `binary`, and `null` values
    - **String**: String types are widely used in programming to represent alphanumeric values, as well as special characters. DynamoDB strings are Unicode with UTF-8 encoding, and should not exceed the size limit of 400 KB. We can also represent the date using a string value.
    - **Number**: Number types represent numerical values, including both positive and negative numbers. We can also use the number data type to represent a floating point number. DynamoDB also supports BigDecimal and BigInteger in the number data type.

- **Boolean**: Boolean types represent true and false values. Boolean data is very useful in condition-checking and logical operations.
- **Binary**: Binary types represent any type of binary data, such as images, audio files, videos, encrypted data, or compressed files. DynamoDB treats each byte of binary data as unsigned and has a size limit of 400 KB.
- **Null**: DynamoDB provides special support for null values. They represent an unknown or undefined state of the attribute.

- **Document types**: DynamoDB supports two document types: list and map
    - **List**: List types store multiple values in order. Each value is accessible using `index`, and `index` starts at zero. We can access the first element using `index` `0` as `list[0]`; `index` `1` represents the second element, and so on. The list is enclosed within square brackets. A list of cities can be written as `cities = ["NY", "London", "Paris"]`.
    - **Map**: Map types are represented as key–value pairs. Each value is accessible using the key. Here, the key must be unique in the keyset of a map. Duplicate keys are not allowed. Maps are enclosed within curly braces. A map of users' age could be written as `users = {"john":27, "ryan":34, "smith":28 }`.
- **Set types**: DynamoDB supports sets of number, string, and binary values. Sets are always homogeneous, which means that all elements within the set must be of the same type. Each value within a set must be unique. Also, DynamoDB does not support empty sets. The following are some examples of sets:
    - `stringSet = ["Black", "Green","Red"]`
    - `numberSet = [42.2, -19, 7.5, 3.14]`
    - `binarySet = ["xy3?=", "UzCPhk=","zj788shbd="]`

# Data models and CRUD operations in DynamoDB

To perform CRUD operations in DynamoDB, select **DynamoDB** from the database services in the AWS Account Service section, as shown in the following screenshot:

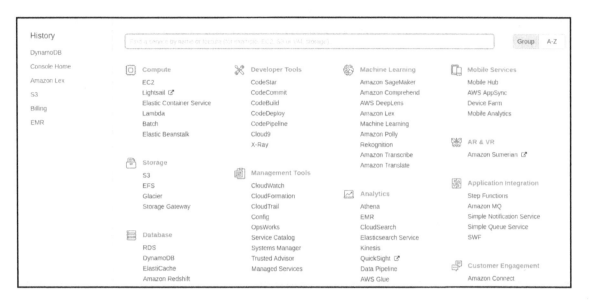

Once you select DynamoDB from the section, it will redirect you to the DynamoDB console, where it will show an option for creating the table:

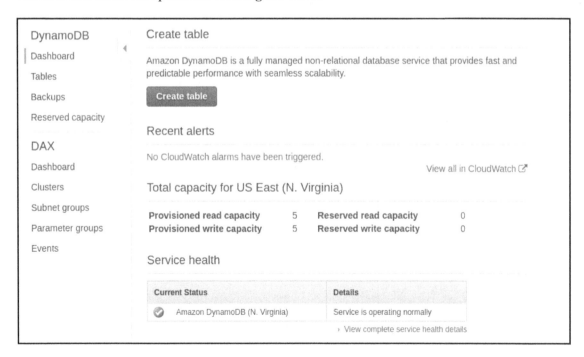

To create a table, click on the **Create table** button. This will take you to the **Create table** screen. During the creation of the table, you have to provide the primary key, along with the table name.

Here, we are creating a table called `customer`, and each customer is identified by `customer_id`:

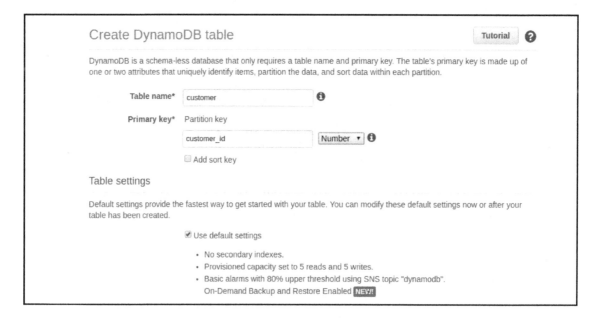

Once the table is created, it is listed in the console, and other operations that can be performed on the table, such as delete table, insert item, and so on, are also shown:

Here, we can select the table from the list of created tables and click on the **Delete table** button to delete the table.

If you want to list events on the table, you can click the **Manage Stream** button. The records are inserted if insert, update, and delete operations are performed on the table.

If we click on the **Items** tab on the left side of the pan console, it will list all the items that exist in that table using the scan operation, as shown in the following screenshot:

We can insert an item in the table using the **Create item** option and provide an item value, as shown in the following screenshot:

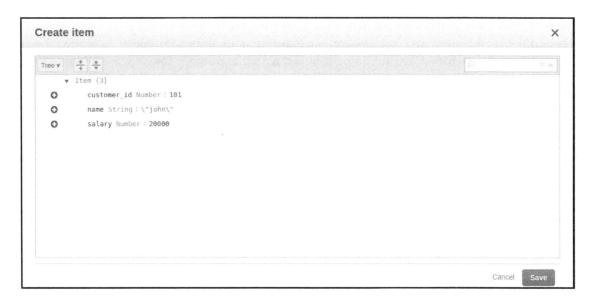

Click on **Save** to create an item:

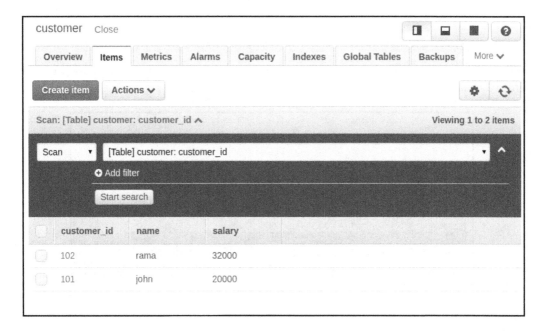

Now we have two items inserted in our table, the first with `customer_id 101` and the second with `customer_id 102`. We can have different attributes for items. As a new customer has been added, we are going to insert a mobile number for him, as shown in the following screenshot:

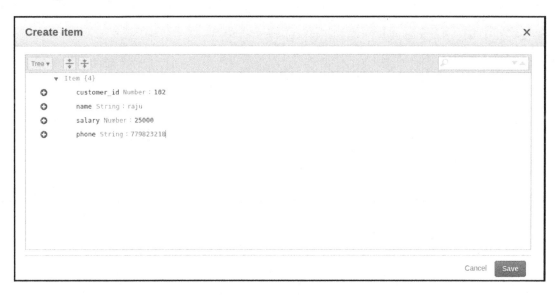

If we list the items now, we can see that the items can vary in the number of attributes for different items:

You can delete the item by selecting the **Delete** option from the drop-down list, as shown in the following screenshot:

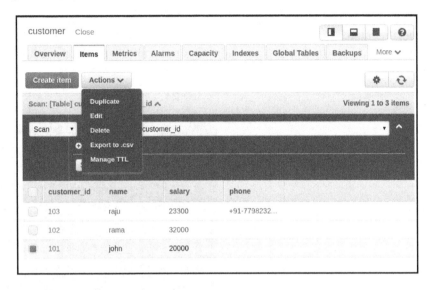

To update the items, we have to choose the **Edit** option from the drop-down list shown in the previous screenshot, which opens a popup to edit the information, as shown in the following screenshot:

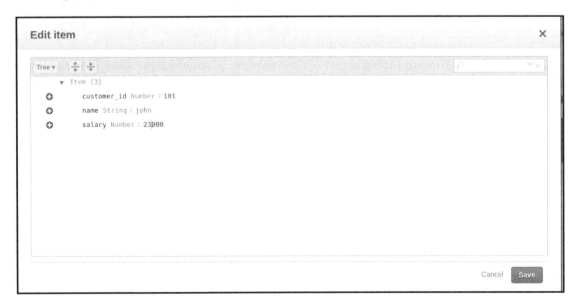

Here, we can update the information and click **Save** to save it. We can see the updated information in the console by listing all the items. Here we can see that John's salary is updated to 23,000 from 20,000.

We can also perform **CRUD** operations using local installation. Here, we need to use request and API calls to perform the operation. Open the shell and start working with CRUD operations:

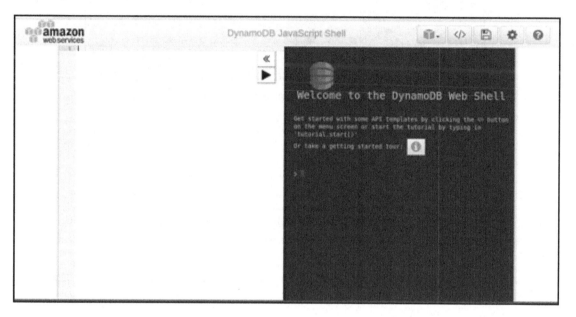

The local shell also provides the template of the request. If you click the **Template** option, you can see the various sample requests:

Let us start by checking the list of all the tables that exist in the database. This request requires you to specify the limit of entries it should return at a time:

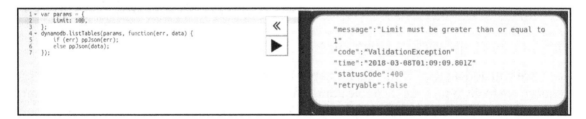

We have to write our request in the left-hand side panel and the result will be displayed in the right-hand side panel. Here we can see the tables that are listed with `TableNames`.

Let us create the table **Person**. To create the table, we have to provide the primary key attribute. In this example, we are defining `PersonID` as a primary key; the other schemas will vary:

```
1 ▾ var params = {
2       TableName: 'person',
3 ▾     KeySchema: [
4 ▾         {
5               AttributeName: 'PersonID',
6               KeyType: 'HASH'
7         },
8       ],
9 ▾     AttributeDefinitions: [
10 ▾        {
11              AttributeName: 'PersonID',
12              AttributeType: 'N',
13        }
14      ],
15 ▾    ProvisionedThroughput: {
16          ReadCapacityUnits: 10,
17          WriteCapacityUnits: 10,
18      },
19  };
20
21 ▾ dynamodb.createTable(params, function(err, data) {
22      if (err) ppJson(err); // an error occurred
23      else ppJson(data); // successful response
24
25  });
```

```
☐ "TableDescription" {
    ☐ "AttributeDefinitions" [
        ☐ 0: {
            "AttributeName":"PersonID"
            "AttributeType":"N"
        "TableName":"person"
    ☐ "KeySchema" [
        ☐ 0: {
            "AttributeName":"PersonID"
            "KeyType":"HASH"
        "TableStatus":"ACTIVE"
        "CreationDateTime":"2018-03-08T01:14:17.341Z"
    ☐ "ProvisionedThroughput" {
        "LastIncreaseDateTime":"1970-01-
        01T00:00:00.000Z"
        "LastDecreaseDateTime":"1970-01-
        01T00:00:00.000Z"
        "NumberOfDecreasesToday":0
        "ReadCapacityUnits":10
        "WriteCapacityUnits":10
        "TableSizeBytes":0
    "ItemCount":0
    "TableArn":"arn:aws:dynamodb:ddblocal:0000000000
    00:table/person"
```

Here, we need to provision throughput when we create the table.

Now we will add an item to the **Person** table, using the `PutItem` API call. For the `PutItem` request, we have to provide the table name and the item to be inserted. We are inserting an item with `PersonID 101`, as shown in the following screenshot:

```
1 ▾ var params = {
2       TableName: 'person',
3 ▾     Item: {
4           PersonID: 101,
5           FirstName : "John",
6           LastName : "Smith",
7           Age : 27,
8           Email : "john.smith@co.in"
9       }
10  };
11 ▾ docClient.put(params, function(err, data) {
12      if (err) ppJson(err);
13      else ppJson(data);
14  });
```

```
1 ▾ var params = {☐};
11 ▸ docClient.put(params, function(err, data) {☐});
```

To retrieve an item from the table, we have to use a `GetItem` call, which needs the table name and the primary key attribute value to retrieve the item:

```
1  var params = {
2      TableName: 'person',
3      Key: {
4          PersonID: 101
5      },
6  };
7  docClient.get(params, function(err, data) {
8      if (err) ppJson(err);
9      else ppJson(data);
10 });
```

```
"Item" {
    "LastName":"Smith"
    "Email":"john.smith@co.in"
    "PersonID":101
    "FirstName":"John"
    "Age":27
}
```

Here, the item with `PersonID 101` is retrieved. To retrieve all the items, we can use the `scan` operation, as shown in the following screenshot:

```
1  var params = {
2      TableName: 'person',
3      Select: 'ALL_ATTRIBUTES'
4  };
5  dynamodb.scan(params, function(err, data) {
6      if (err) ppJson(err); // an error occurred
7      else ppJson(data); // successful response
8  });
```

```
"Items" [
    0: {
        "LastName" {
            "S":"Smith"
        "Email" {
            "S":"john.smith@co.in"
        "PersonID" {
            "N":"101"
        "FirstName" {
            "S":"John"
        "Age" {
            "N":"27"
    "Count":1
    "ScannedCount":1
```

Now we will update the age of the person to 32. To update the item's attribute value, we are using the `UpdateItem` API. Here, we have to pass the primary key attribute to search the item in the table and pass the `UpdateExression` parameter to set the attribute value:

```
1
2  var params = {
3      TableName: 'person',
4      Key: {
5          PersonID: 101,
6      },
7      UpdateExpression: 'SET Age= :age',
8      ExpressionAttributeValues:{
9          ':age':32,
10     },
11 };
12 docClient.update(params, function(err, data) {
13     if (err) ppJson(err); // an error occurred
14     else ppJson(data); // successful response
15 });
```

For deletion, we have to use the `DeleteItem` call. We have to provide the primary key value of the item to be deleted. We are deleting a person with `PersonID 101` in the following operation:

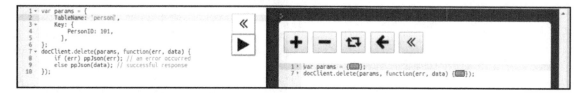

# Limitations of DynamoDB

DynamoDB has size limits on its components, described in the following list. This may vary from region to region:

- **Capacity unit**:
  - One read capacity unit = one strongly consistent read per second or two eventually consistent reads per second, for items up to 4 KB in size
  - One write capacity unit = one write per second for items up to 1 KB in size

- **Table size**:
  There is no practical limit on table size. Tables are unconstrained for the number of items and number of bytes. But for any AWS account, there is an initial limit of 256 tables per region. To increase the limit, you have to raise the request.

- **Secondary indexes**:
  You can define a maximum of five local secondary indexes per table. You can project up to 20 attributes into all of the table's local and global secondary indexes. These should be used to define the attributes. While creating the table operation, if you specify the `ProjectionType` of `INCLUDE`, then the number of `NonKeyAttribute` for all of the secondary indexes should not exceed 20. If you project the same attribute name in two different indexes, it will assume that these are two different attributes while counting.

- **Partition key**:
  The minimum length of the partition key value is 1 byte and the maximum length is 2,048 bytes. There is no limit to the number of distinct partition key values for tables or secondary indexes.

- **Sort key**:
  The minimum length of the sort key value is 1 byte and the maximum length is 1,024 bytes. There is no limit to the number of distinct sort key values per partition key value.
- **Naming rules**:
  Names for tables and secondary indexes must be at least three characters long, but no more than 255 characters are allowed.
- **Accepted characters are as follows**:
  - A-Z
  - Z-z
  - 0-9
  - _(Underscore)
  - -(Hyphen)
  - .(Dot)

- **Attribute names**:
  In general, the attribute name must be at least one character long and should not exceed 64 KB in length. If an attribute name is used in a secondary index partition key name, secondary index sort key name, or any user-specified projected attribute, then it should not be greater than 255 characters long.
  Attribute names must be encoded using UTF-8. The total size of the name of each name cannot exceed 255 bytes.
- **Data types**:
  - **String**: The maximum length for the string of any item should be less than 400 KB. Strings are written in Unicode with UTF-8 binary encoding. DynamoDB determines the length of the string using UTF-8 bytes.
  - **Numbers**: A number can have up to 38 digits of precision, and can be positive, negative, or zero. DynamoDB uses a JSON string to represent numerical data in both the request and the response.
  - **Binary**: The length of the binary is constrained by the maximum item size of 400 KB. An application must encode the data in Base64 format before sending it to DynamoDB. After receiving the data, DynamoDB decodes it into an unsigned byte array and uses that as the length of the attribute.

- **Items**:
  The maximum size of an item in DynamoDB is 400 KB, which includes both the attribute name's binary length and the attribute's value length. Say we have an item with two attributes, one named `shirt-color` with the value R and the other `shirt-size` with the value M. The total size of this item would be 23 bytes.

- **Attributes**:
  The cumulative size of the attributes per item must fit within the maximum DynamoDB item size, namely 400 KB.

# Best practices

To work with DynamoDB more efficiently, we should follow some best practices while designing tables and items:

- **Table best practices**: DynamoDB tables are distributed across multiple partitions. For the best results, design your tables and applications so that read and write activities are spread evenly across all the items on your table, and avoid I/O hotspots that can degrade the performance of your application:
  - Design for uniform data access across items in your table
  - Distribute the write activity during data upload operations
  - Understand the access platform for the time series data

- **Item best practices**: DynamoDB items are limited in size. However, there is no limit to the number of items in the table. Instead of storing large attribute data values in an item, consider the following alternative for your design:
  - Use one-to-many tables instead of a large set of attributes
  - Use multiple tables to support a varied access pattern
  - Compress large attribute values
  - Store large attribute values on Amazon S3
  - Break large attributes across multiple items

- **Query and scan best practices**: Sudden and unexpected read activity can quickly consume the provisioned read capacity of the table. Such activity can be inefficient if it is not evenly spread across the table partitions:
  - Avoid sudden read activities
  - Take advantage of parallel scans

- **Local secondary indexes best practices**: Local secondary indexes let you define alternate keys on the table. You can then issue queries against these keys. This enables the efficient retrieval of data based on your requirement. Before using local secondary indexes, you should know their effects in terms of provisioned throughput cost, storage cost, and query efficiency:
    - Use indexes sparingly
    - Choose your projection carefully
    - Optimize frequent queries
    - Take advantage of sparse indexes
    - Check for expanding item collections

# Summary

DynamoDB, a NoSQL database provided by Amazon, is an alternative to many other NoSQL databases, such as MongoDB. It provides an easy interface, using the console to create the table and perform related operations through the console. Amazon provides a large set of language-specific SDKs and APIs to interface with various programming languages. Thus, DynamoDB is becoming more popular day by day.

# 8
# InfluxDB

The term *big data* is everywhere these days, has now entered the mainstream, and is also merging with traditional analytics. More electronic devices than ever before are connected to the internet, phones, watches, sensors, cars, TVs, and so on. These devices generate enormous amounts of new, unstructured real-time data every minute. Analyzing time-structured data has become the most important problem across many industries. Many companies are looking for a new way to solve their time-series data problems and have utilized their available influx data. As a result, the popularity of the time-series database has rapidly increased over the past few years. InfluxDB is one of the most popular time-series databases in this area.

In this chapter, we will cover the following topics:

- What is InfluxDB?
- Installation and configuration
- Query language and API
- InfluxDB ecosystem
- InfluxDB operations

## Introduction to InfluxDB

InfluxDB is developed by InfluxData. It is an open source, big data, NoSQL database that allows for massive scalability, high availability, fast write, and fast read. As a NoSQL, InfluxDB stores time-series data, which has a series of data points over time. These data points can be regular or irregular type based on the type of data resource. Some regular data measurements are based on a fixed interval time, for example, system heartbeat monitoring data. Other data measurements could be based on a discrete event, for example, trading transaction data, sensor data, and so on.

InfluxDB is written on the go; this makes it easy to compile and deploy without external dependencies. It offers an SQL-like query language. The plug-in architecture design makes it very flexible to integrate other third-party products.

Like other NoSQL databases, it supports different clients such as Go, Java, Python, and Node.js to interact with the database. The convenience HTTP native API can easily integrate with web-based products such as DevOps to monitor real-time data.

Since it's specially designed for time-series data, it became more and more popular in this kind of data use case, such as DevOps monitoring, **Internet of Things (IoT)** monitoring, and time-series based analytics application.

The classic use case of time-series data includes the following:

- System and monitoring logs
- Financial/stock tickers over time in financial markets
- Tracking product inventory in the retail system
- Sensors data generation in IoT and **Industrial Internet of Things (IIoT)**
- Geo positioning and tracking in the transportation industry

The data for each of these use cases is different, but they frequently have a similar pattern.

In the system and monitoring logs case, we're taking regular measurements for tracking different production services such as Apache, Tomcat, MySQL, Hadoop, Kafka, Spark, Hive, Web applications etc. Series usually have metadata information such as the server name, the service name, and the metric being measured.

Let's assume a common case to have 200 or more measurements (unique series) per server. Say we have 300 servers, VMs, and containers. Our task is to sample them once every 10 seconds. This will give us a total of $24 * 60 * 60 / 10 = 8,640$ values per series. For each day, a total distinct point is $8,640 * 300 * 200 = 518,400,000$ (around 0.5 billion data points per day).

In a relational database, there are few ways to structure things, but there are some challenges, which are listed as follows:

- Create a single denormalized table to store all of the data with the series name, the value, and a time. In this approach, the table will get 0.5 billion per day. This would quickly cause a problem because of the size of the table.
- Create a separate table per period of time (day, month, and so on). It required the developer to write code archives and versioning historical data from the different tables together.

After comparing with relational databases, let's look at some big data databases such as Cassandra and Hive.

As with the SQL variant, building a time-series solution on top of Cassandra requires quite a bit of application-level code.

First, you need to design a data mode for structuring the data. Cassandra rows are stored as one replication group, you need to design proper row keys to ensure that the cluster is properly utilized for querying a data load. Then, you need to write the ETL code to process the raw data, build row keys, and other application logic to write the time-series data into the table.

This is the same case for Hive, where you need to properly design the partition key based on the time-series use case, then pull or receive data from the source system by running Kafka, Spark, Flink, Storm, or other big data processing frameworks. You will end up writing some ETL aggregation logic to handle lower precision samples that can be used for longer-term visualizations.

Finally, you need to package all of this code and deploy it to production and follow the DevOps process. You also need to ensure that the query performances are optimized for all of these use cases.

The whole process will typically require the developer team to spend several months to completely coordinate with many other teams.

InfluxDB has a number of features that can take care of all of the features mentioned earlier, automatically.

# Key concepts and terms of InfluxDB

InfluxDB uses particular terms to describe the various components of time-series data, and the techniques used to categorize this data to make InfluxDB unique.

InfluxDB organizes data by database, time series, and point of events. The database is quite similar to other traditional databases such as MySQL, Oracle, and PostgreSQL. It is an organized collection of time-series data and retention policies. The point of events are similar to SQL rows.

The following table is a simple example of a table called `tickers` in a SQL database with the unindexed columns (`close`, `high`, `low`, `open`, and `volume`) and the indexed columns (`ticker`, `company`, and `time`):

```
+---------------------+---------+--------------+---------+---------+---------+--------+--------+
| time                | close   | company      | high    | low     | open    | ticker | volume |
+---------------------+---------+--------------+---------+---------+---------+--------+--------+
| 2017-11-22T14:30:00Z | 1051.16 | Alphabet Inc | 1051.16 | 1051.16 | 1051.16 | GOOGL  | 13622  |
| 2017-11-22T14:30:00Z | 173.45  | Apple Inc    | 173.45  | 173.34  | 173.36  | AAPL   | 300218 |
| 2017-11-22T14:31:00Z | 1051.46 | Alphabet Inc | 1051.78 | 1051.11 | 1051.42 | GOOGL  | 1404   |
| 2017-11-22T14:31:00Z | 173.70  | Apple Inc    | 173.71  | 173.35  | 173.39  | AAPL   | 165442 |
| 2017-11-22T14:32:00Z | 1051.07 | Alphabet Inc | 1051.57 | 1050.72 | 1051.53 | GOOGL  | 7014   |
| 2017-11-22T14:32:00Z | 173.56  | Apple Inc    | 173.80  | 173.51  | 173.70  | AAPL   | 175809 |
| 2017-11-22T14:33:00Z | 1051.35 | Alphabet Inc | 1051.53 | 1050.61 | 1051.00 | GOOGL  | 5973   |
| 2017-11-22T14:33:00Z | 173.62  | Apple Inc    | 173.75  | 173.56  | 173.57  | AAPL   | 109326 |
| 2017-11-22T14:34:00Z | 1051.33 | Alphabet Inc | 1051.75 | 1051.27 | 1051.75 | GOOGL  | 1500   |
| 2017-11-22T14:34:00Z | 173.91  | Apple Inc    | 173.93  | 173.61  | 173.62  | AAPL   | 218830 |
+---------------------+---------+--------------+---------+---------+---------+--------+--------+
```

The same data is shown in InfluxDB as follows:

```
name: tickers
tags: company=Alphabet Inc, ticker=GOOGL
time                  close    high     low      open     volume
----                  -----    ----     ---      ----     ------
2017-11-22T14:30:00Z  1051.16  1051.16  1051.16  1051.16  13622
2017-11-22T14:31:00Z  1051.46  1051.78  1051.11  1051.42  1404
2017-11-22T14:32:00Z  1051.07  1051.57  1050.72  1051.53  7014
2017-11-22T14:33:00Z  1051.35  1051.53  1050.61  1051     5973
2017-11-22T14:34:00Z  1051.33  1051.75  1051.27  1051.75  1500

name: tickers
tags: company=Apple Inc, ticker=AAPL
time                  close    high     low      open     volume
----                  -----    ----     ---      ----     ------
2017-11-22T14:30:00Z  173.45   173.45   173.34   173.36   300218
2017-11-22T14:31:00Z  173.7    173.71   173.35   173.39   165442
2017-11-22T14:32:00Z  173.56   173.8    173.51   173.7    175809
2017-11-22T14:33:00Z  173.62   173.75   173.56   173.57   109326
2017-11-22T14:34:00Z  173.91   173.93   173.61   173.62   218830
```

By comparing the preceding examples, we can see that InfluxDB terms are similar to SQL:

- An InfluxDB database is similar to an SQL database
- An InfluxDB measurement (`tickers`) is similar to an SQL database table (`tickers`)
- InfluxDB tags (`ticker`) are similar to SQL table indexed columns (`ticker`)
- InfluxDB fields (`close`, `high`, and `low`) are similar to an SQL table with unindexed columns (`close`, `high`, and `low`)

The following is the list of important terms used in InfluxDB:

- **Measurement**: This is similar to an SQL database table. The measurement contains the timestamps, fields, and tags; it is a string. The measurement can have many retention policies.
- **Field set**: This is a collection of field keys and field values on a point.
- **Field key**: This is a key part for the field set key-value pair. The key is a string type and stores the metadata.
- **Field value**: This is similar to an SQL table's unindexed columns; it stores your data. It is the value part in a field set key-value pair.
- **Tags**: This is similar to indexed columns in an SQL database. Tag keys and tag values are of the type string and record metadata. It is optional.
- **Continuous query**: Continuous queries in InfluxDB are similar to SQL database's stored procedures.
- **Line protocol**: This is the text-based format for writing points to InfluxDB.
- **Point**: This is similar to an SQL database with a single row of record. It consists of a single collection of fields in a series. Each point is uniquely identified by its series and the given timestamp. For example:

```
time                     close   high    low     open    volume
----                     -----   ----    ---     ----    ------
2017-11-22T14:30:00Z     173.45  173.45  173.34  173.36  300218
```

- **Retention Policy (RP)**: This describes the duration of data points that are kept in InfluxDB and how many data copies are stored in the cluster. It can have shard duration (for example, 7d). Each RP is unique in the database. The default RP is `autogen`. For example:

```
name        duration shardGroupDuration replicaN default
----        -------- ------------------ -------- -------
autogen 0s           168h0m0s                  1 true
```

- **Series**: This is the collection of data in InfluxDB data structure that share a RP, measurement, and tag set.
- **Timestamps**: This is the date and time associated with a point. The time in InfluxDB is UTC. The time is stored in the RFC 3339 UTC format, for example, `2017-11-22T14:30:00Z`.
- **Time Structured Merge (TSM) tree** : This is a data storage engine for InfluxDB.
- **Write Ahead Log (WAL)**: This is the temporary cache for recently written points, it allows for efficient batching of the writes into the TSM.

Here is quick overview of some comparison:

| InfluxDB | SQL Database |
|---|---|
| Database | Database |
| Measurement | Table |
| Points | Rows |
| Tags | Indexed columns |
| Fields | Unindexed columns |
| Continuous queries | Stored procedures |

# Data model and storage engine

The data stored in InfluxDB is generally a sequence of data point based on time. The records often have hundreds of millions of rows, including timestamps and other fields and tags. Typically, the data point is immutable and read only, the new point will automatically write and keep appending to measurement. For a large amount of data, we need careful design for the data mode. Define which attribute we can use for the indexed tag so that we can use the others as unindexed fields. It is critical for query performance. Here are a few recommendations when you design an InfluxDB data model:

- If the data is searched by query frequently, consider storing it in a tag
- If query have `group by`, consider storing the data in a tag
- If you want to use the data with an InfluxQL function, consider storing it in fields
- If you need data of non-string type, consider storing it in fields
- If the data has dynamic values, consider storing it in fields

Try avoiding too many series, tags contain large string information such as hashes and **universally unique identifiers** (**UUIDs**), which can cause high memory usage for database workloads. One of the key roles impacting performance is high series cardinality, which often causes high RAM usage. Based on the recent InfluxDB hardware guidelines, for less than 100k unique series, it recommends approximately 2-4 GB of RAM. When one measurement has few highly dynamic value of tags, like more than thousands, it can easily consume more than 32 GB memory usage. It will cause high series cardinality. On the other hand, when tag keys and values are stored only once, it only needs more storage and doesn't impact the memory footprint.

# Storage engine

The earlier InfluxDB release supports different storage engines, LevelDB, RocksDB, HyperLevelDB, and LMDB. Most of them are based on log-structured merge-tree (LSM Tree). Since the 0.9.5 InfluxDB release, it has its own storage engine called the **Time Structured Merge Tree (TSM Tree)**.

**Log-Structured Merge-Tree (LSM Tree)** creates indexing files, which provide efficient indexing for high transactional data such as log data. One of the implementations of LSM Tree is called **Sorted String Table (SSTable)**. When data is saved in SSTable, it will be stored as a key-value pair. The index files contain batch data changes for a certain duration. LSM Tree utilizes batch information from index files to merge-sort for each fragment of data file and cache in the memory. It will provide high performance data retrieval for later search. Since the cache file is immutable, new records will be inserted into new files.

Periodically, the algorithm merges files together to keep a small number of files. However, indexed search requiring immediate response will lose I/O efficiency in some cases, so the LSM Tree is most useful for index inserts than the finds that retrieve the entries. To make reads in LSM Trees faster, the common approach is to hold a page-index in memory. Since the data is sorted, you can look up your target key. LSM is used in LevelDB, RocksDB, HBase, MongoDB, Apache Cassandra, and so on:

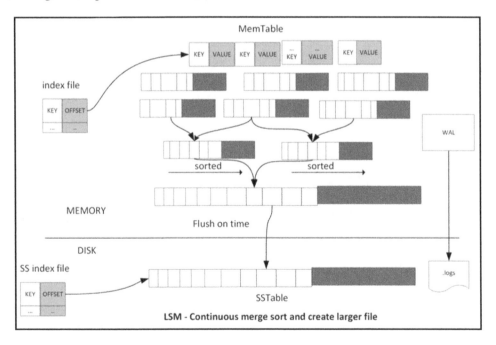

LSM - Continuous merge sort and create larger file

TSM Tree is similar to LSM Tree. TSM Tree has a **write ahead log (WAL)** and a collection of read-only data files or TSM files, which are similar in concept to SSTables in a LSM Tree. The storage engine uses WAL to write an optimized storage format and map the index files to memory.

The .wal file is created and organized by WAL, the file size will monotonically increase. When the size becomes 10 MB, the current .wal file will close and a new .wal file will be created and opened. Each .wal segment file contains a compress block of write and delete. For new data point arrival, it will be compressed using Snappy and written as a .wal file. An entry will be added to a memory index file. When it reaches a certain number of data points, the data point will flush to disk storage. This batch feature achieves high throughput performance. Data point is stored as TSM files; these files have compressed series data in a columnar format.

Each TSM file has four sections: **Header**, **Blocks**, **Index**, and **Footer**.

- In the **Header** section, it is composed of a magic number to identify the file type and a version number
- In the **Blocks** section, it contains CRC and data
- In the **Index** section, it contains key length, key (includes the measurement name, tag set, and one time-related field), block min and max time, and so on
- In the **Footer** section, it stores the index offset:

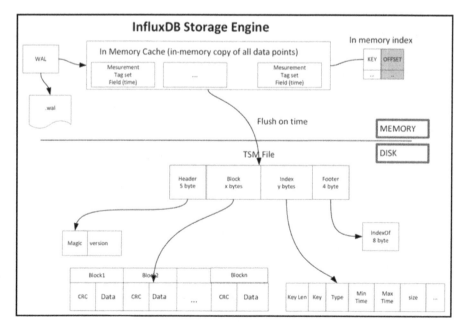

# Installation and configuration

In this section, we will discuss how to install InfluxDB and set up InfluxDB configuration.

## Installing InfluxDB

To install InfluxDB, the official installation guide can be found here: `https://docs.influxdata.com/influxdb/v1.5/introduction/installation/`.

Ubuntu is built from the Debian distribution. In this chapter, we use Ubuntu as the lab environment to run InfluxDB. Here is a link to install Ubuntu in a VirtualBox: `https://askubuntu.com/questions/142549/how-to-install-ubuntu-on-virtualbox`.

Once Ubuntu is installed in your VM, we will install InfluxDB in Ubuntu. We use the `apt-get` package manager to install InfluxDB. Enter the following five commands:

```
curl -sL https://repos.influxdata.com/InfluxDB.key | sudo apt-key add -

source /etc/lsb-release

echo "deb https://repos.influxdata.com/${DISTRIB_ID,,} ${DISTRIB_CODENAME} stable" | sudo tee /etc/apt/sources.list.d/InfluxDB.list

sudo apt-get update && sudo apt-get install influxdb

sudo systemctl start influxdb
```

In this step, a file `/etc/apt/sources.list.d/InfluxDB.list` is created. We can check whether this file exists here:

```
ls /etc/apt/sources.list.d/InfluxDB.list
```

## Configuring InfluxDB

To see the current InfluxDB configuration, just run the InfluxDB `config` command:

```
$influxd config
```

This command will return all of the configuration sections. The options part in each configuration is optional. The default value will be used if the option is not specified. Here is the list of configuration sections:

`reporting`, `meta`, `data`, `cluster`, `retention`, `shard-precreation`, `admin`, `monitor`, `subscriber`, `graphite`, `collectd`, `opentsdb`, `udp`, `continuous_queries`, `hinted-handoff`.

- `[meta]`: This maintains InfluxDB cluster parameters
- `[data]`: This tells **write ahead log (WAL)** how to store and flush data
- `[cluster]`: This controls how the data is shared between shards in a non-raft cluster
- `[retention]`: This handles the InfluxDB retention polices behavior
- `[shard-precreation]`: This makes sure that new shards are created and are available before the data arrives
- `[http]`: It handles the InfluxDB HTTP endpoints configuration when called from CLI or an other client

In the most use cases, the default configuration is sufficient. In case the application needs customized configuration, you can open the configuration file and edit them. The file is located in the directory `/etc/InfluxDB/InfluxDB.conf`:

```
sudo nano /etc/InfluxDB/InfluxDB.conf
```

At long last, you are ready to get your hands dirty. It is time to run and use InfluxDB.

To start InfluxDB instance, use the following command:

```
sudo service InfluxDB start
```

This command doesn't show any output. Now connect to InfluxDB:

```
$ influx
Connected to http://localhost:8086 version 1.5
InfluxDB shell version: 1.5
>
```

Congratulations! Your InfluxDB installation is completed.

# Production deployment considerations

InfluxDB is easy to install and use for development in the production environment. It is typically a user faced, business-critical enterprise environment. This can be very different from a lower environment such as development. Some important factors to consider are high availability, fault tolerance, recovery, security, performance, and so on to make InfluxDB production ready:

- **High Availability**: InfluxDB supports a high availability cluster, which can be reliably utilized with a minimum amount of downtime. Each instance will have a data node and a meta node. The meta node contains system information, while the data node contains actual data. Data can be replicated and distributed across networks to achieve high availability.
- **Backups**: Backup is critical for almost every production database. InfluxDB has the ability to snapshot an instance at a point-in-time and restore it, all backups are full backups. Once a backup is taken, it is important to verify your backups regularly.
- **Security**: Many known attacks are possible only once the physical access to a machine has been acquired.

For this reason, it is best to separate the application server and the database server on different machines. If it has to be in the same machine, you must make sure to execute remote commands via an application server, otherwise, an attacker may be able to harm your database even without permissions. For this reason, always enable authentication password protect for your InfluxDB instance to keep any unauthorized individuals from accessing your data.

Manage users and their permissions and restrict access by creating individual users and assigning them relevant read and/or write permissions. InfluxDB has three levels of user permission, cluster admin, database admin, and database user. Based on user entitlement, some users may only read data, while some users can read and write.

 Database admin can typically add or remove database admin or user, and assign read/write permission to them.

Cluster admin is the highest permission role among all of the roles. In this role admin can add or remove database admin and users, grant or invoke user permissions, and kill a query process in that database. Cluster admin also has the privilege to create, alert, delete and drop database and measurement.

Always enable HTTPS in production to secure the communication between clients and the InfluxDB server. It is highly recommend to close port 8088 for remote backups and restore it in the production environment. Provide the remote machine with a specific permission to perform a remote backup.

# Query language and API

In this section, we will discuss InfluxDB query language and how to use InfluxDB API.

## Query language

InfluxDB provides an SQL-like query language; it is used for querying time-series data. It also supports HTTP APIs for write and performs admin-related work.

Let's use the InfluxDB CLI tool to connect to an InfluxDB instance and run some queries.

Start and connect to the InfluxDB instance by typing the following commands:

```
sudo service InfluxDB start
$ influx -precision rfc3339
```

By default, InfluxDB shows the time as nanosecond UTC value, it is a very long number, like 1511815800000000000. The argument -precision rfc3339 is for the display time field as a human readable format - YYYY-MM-DDTHH:MM:SS.nnnnnnnnnZ:

```
Connected to http://localhost:8086 version 1.5
InfluxDB shell version: 1.5
>
```

We can check available databases by using the show databases function:

```
> show databases;
name: databases
name
----
_internal
```

To use the command to switch to an existing database, you can type the following command:

```
use _internal
```

This command will switch to the existing database and set your default database to
_internal. Doing this means all subsequent commands you write to CLI will
automatically be executed on the _internal database until you switch to another database.

So far, we haven't created any new database. At this stage, it shows the default database
_internal provided by the product itself. If you want to view all of the available
measurements for the current database, you can use the following command:

```
show measurements
```

Let's quickly browse the measurements under the _internal database.

```
> use _internal
Using database _internal
> show measurements
name: measurements
name
----
cq
database
httpd
queryExecutor
runtime
shard
subscriber
tsm1_cache
tsm1_engine
tsm1_filestore
tsm1_wal
write
```

We can see that the _internal database contains lots of system-level statistical data, which
can store very useful system information and help you analyze the system information.

For example, if you want to check heap usage over the time, you can run an SQL-like
SELECT statement command to query and get more information:

```
SELECT HeapAlloc, HeapIdle, HeapInUse, NumGC, Mallocs, TotalAlloc from
runtime limit 3;
```

```
> SELECT HeapAlloc, HeapIdle, HeapInUse, NumGC, Mallocs, TotalAlloc from runtime limit 3;
name: runtime
time                  HeapAlloc HeapIdle HeapInUse NumGC Mallocs TotalAlloc
----                  --------- -------- --------- ----- ------- ----------
2017-11-27T04:39:00Z  2818392   196608   4521984   1     80921   4652552
2017-11-27T04:39:10Z  2835344   1081344  4685824   2     94765   5918456
2017-11-27T04:39:20Z  3265608   679936   5087232   2     96718   6348720
```

It's time to create our first InfluxDB database! In our sample project, we will use real-time intra day stock quotes market data to set up our lab. The sample data contains November 27, 2017 to November 29, 2017 market stock data for three companies: Apple Inc, JPMorgan Chase & Co., and Alphabet Inc. The interval is 60 seconds.

Here is the example data format:

```
tickers,ticker=JPM company="JPMorgan Chase &
Co",close=98.68,high=98.7,low=98.68,open=98.7,volume=4358 151179804
tickers,ticker=JPM company="JPMorgan Chase &
Co",close=98.71,high=98.7,low=98.68,open=98.68,volume=1064 151179810
```

In the data shown here, we separated measurement, tag set and field set use comma, each tag set and field set are separated by space: `measurement, tag set..., field set....`. Define the ticker as tag set and define `company, close, high, low, open, volume` as fields set. The last value is UTC time. The measurement name is `tickers`.

```
> create database market;
> exit
```

Download the sample data to the Unix box:

**/tmp/data/ticker_data.txt**

Then, load the data to the market database:

```
/tmp/data$ influx -import -path=/tmp/data/ticker_data.txt -database=market
-precision=s
2017/11/30 12:13:17 Processed 1 commands
2017/11/30 12:13:17 Processed 3507 inserts
2017/11/30 12:13:17 Failed 0 inserts
```

In InfluxDB CLI, verify the new measurement tickers that are created:

```
> show measurements;
name: measurements
name
----
tickers
```

The SELECT statement is used to retrieve data points from one or more measurements. The InfluxDB query syntax is as follows:

```
SELECT <field_key>[,<field_key>,<tag_key>] FROM
<measurement_name>[,<measurement_name>] WHERE <conditional_expression>
[(AND|OR) <conditional_expression> [...]]
```

The following are the arguments for SELECT:

| Name | Description |
| --- | --- |
| `SELECT` | This statement is used to fetch data points from one or more measurements |
| `*` | This indicates all tag keys and field keys and the time |
| `field_key` | This returns a specific field |
| `tag_key` | This returns a specific tag |
| `SELECT "<field_key>"::field,"<tag_key>"::tag` | This returns a specific field and tag; the `::[field \| tag]` syntax specifies the identifier's type |
| `FROM <measurement_name>,<measurement_name>` | This returns data from one or more measurements |
| `FROM <database_name>.<retention_policy_name>.<measurement_name>` | This returns a fully qualified measurement |

| | This returns specific database measurement with default RP |
|---|---|
| `FROM <database_name>..<measurement_name>` | |

Let's look at some examples for a better understanding.

The query selects all of the fields, tags, and time from `tickers` measurements:

```
> select * from tickers;
name: tickers
time close company high low open ticker volume
---- ----- ------- ---- --- ---- ------ ------
2017-11-27T05:00:00Z 174.05 APPLE INC 174.105 174.05 174.06 AAPL 34908
2017-11-27T05:00:00Z 98.42 JPMorgan Chase & Co 98.44 98.4 98.4 JPM 7904
2017-11-27T05:00:00Z 1065.06 Alphabet Inc 1065.06 1065.06 1065.06 GOOGL 100
[....]
```

The query selects the `field` key and `tag` key from the `tickers` measurements:

```
> select ticker, company, close, volume from tickers;
name: tickers
time ticker company close volume
---- ------ ------- ----- ------
2017-11-27T05:00:00Z AAPL APPLE INC 174.05 34908
2017-11-27T05:00:00Z JPM JPMorgan Chase & Co 98.42 7904
2017-11-27T05:00:00Z GOOGL Alphabet Inc 1065.06 100
2017-11-27T05:01:00Z JPM JPMorgan Chase & Co 98.365 20155
[...]
```

The query selects the `field` key and `tag` key based on the identifier type from `tickers` measurements:

```
> SELECT ticker::tag,company::field,volume::field,close::field FROM tickers
limit 3;
name: tickers
time ticker company volume close
---- ------ ------- ------ -----
2017-11-27T05:00:00Z AAPL APPLE INC 34908 174.05
2017-11-27T05:00:00Z JPM JPMorgan Chase & Co 7904 98.42
2017-11-27T05:00:00Z GOOGL Alphabet Inc 100 1065.06
```

The query selects all of the fields based on the identifier type from `tickers` measurements:

```
> SELECT *::field FROM tickers limit 3;
name: tickers
time close company high low open volume
---- ----- ------- ---- --- ---- ------
2017-11-27T05:00:00Z 174.05 APPLE INC 174.105 174.05 174.06 34908
2017-11-27T05:00:00Z 98.42 JPMorgan Chase & Co 98.44 98.4 98.4 7904
2017-11-27T05:00:00Z 1065.06 Alphabet Inc 1065.06 1065.06 1065.06 100
```

The query selects fully qualified ticker measurements:

```
> SELECT ticker, company, volume, close FROM market.autogen.tickers limit
3;
name: tickers
time ticker company volume close
---- ------ ------- ------ -----
2017-11-27T05:00:00Z AAPL APPLE INC 34908 174.05
2017-11-27T05:00:00Z JPM JPMorgan Chase & Co 7904 98.42
2017-11-27T05:00:00Z GOOGL Alphabet Inc 100 1065.06
```

The following is a list of arguments for WHERE:

| WHERE supported operators | Operation |
|---|---|
| = | equal to |
| <> | not equal to |
| != | not equal to |
| > | greater than |
| >= | greater than or equal to |
| < | less than |
| <= | less than or equal to |
| Tags:<br>`tag_key <operator> ['tag_value']` | Single quote for tag value, since tag value is of string type |
| timestamps | The default time range is between `1677-09-21 00:12:43.145224194` and `2262-04-11T23:47:16.854775806Z` UTC |

Using any of =, !=, <, >, <=, >=, <> in the SELECT clause yields empty results for all types.

Let's look at some examples of this argument for a better understanding.

The query returns all `tickers` when high is larger than `174.6` and `ticker` is `AAPL`:

```
> SELECT * FROM tickers WHERE ticker='AAPL' AND high> 174.6 limit 3;
name: tickers
time close company high low open ticker volume
---- ----- ------- ---- --- ---- ------ ------
2017-11-27T14:30:00Z 175.05 APPLE INC 175.06 174.95 175.05 AAPL 261381
2017-11-27T14:31:00Z 174.6 APPLE INC 175.05 174.6 175 AAPL 136420
2017-11-27T14:32:00Z 174.76 APPLE INC 174.77 174.56 174.6003 AAPL 117050
```

The query performs basic arithmetic to find out the date when the ticker is JPM and high price is more than the low price by 0.2%:

```
> SELECT * FROM tickers WHERE ticker='JPM' AND high> low* 1.002 limit 5;
name: tickers
time close company high low open ticker volume
---- ----- ------- ---- --- ---- ------ ------
2017-11-27T14:31:00Z 98.14 JPMorgan Chase & Co 98.31 98.09 98.31 JPM 136485
2017-11-27T14:32:00Z 98.38 JPMorgan Chase & Co 98.38 98.11 98.12 JPM 27837
2017-11-27T14:33:00Z 98.59 JPMorgan Chase & Co 98.59 98.34 98.38 JPM 47042
2017-11-27T14:41:00Z 98.89 JPMorgan Chase & Co 98.9 98.68 98.7 JPM 51245
2017-11-29T05:05:00Z 103.24 JPMorgan Chase & Co 103.44 103.22 103.44 JPM
73835
```

InfulxDB supports group by. The GROUP BY statement is often used with aggregate functions (COUNT, MEAN, MAX, MIN, SUM, AVG) to group the result set by one or more tag keys.

The following is the syntax:

```
SELECT_clause FROM_clause [WHERE_clause] GROUP BY [* |
<tag_key>[,<tag_key]]
```

The following are the arguments for the `GROUP BY TAG_KY`:

| | |
|---|---|
| `GROUP BY *` | Groups by all tags |
| `GROUP BY <tag_key>` | Groups by a specific tag |
| `GROUP BY <tag_key>,<tag_key>` | Groups by multiple specific tags |
| Supported Aggregation functions:<br>`COUNT(),DISTINCT(),INTEGRAL(),MEAN(),`<br>`MEDIAN(),MODE(),SPREAD(),STDDEV(),SUM()` | |
| Supported Selector functions:<br>`BOTTOM(),FIRST(),LAST(),MAX(),`<br>`MIN(),PERCENTILE(),SAMPLE(),TOP()` | |

Consider the following example:

The query finds all tickers' maximum volumes, minimum volumes, and median volumes during 10-19, November 27, 2017:

```
> select MAX(volume), MIN(volume), MEDIAN(volume) from tickers where time
<= '2017-11-27T19:00:00.000000000Z' AND time >=
'2017-11-27T10:00:00.000000000Z' group by ticker;
name: tickers
tags: ticker=AAPL
time max min median
---- --- --- ------
2017-11-27T10:00:00Z 462796 5334 32948
name: tickers
tags: ticker=GOOGL
time max min median
---- --- --- ------
2017-11-27T10:00:00Z 22062 200 1950
name: tickers
tags: ticker=JPM
time max min median
---- --- --- ------
2017-11-27T10:00:00Z 136485 2400 14533
```

By change `group by *`, it will group the query result for all tags:

```
> select MAX(volume), MIN(volume), MEDIAN(volume) from tickers where time
<= '2017-11-27T19:00:00.000000000Z' AND time >=
'2017-11-27T10:00:00.000000000Z' group by *;
name: tickers
```

```
tags: ticker=AAPL
time max min median
---- --- --- ------
2017-11-27T10:00:00Z 462796 5334 32948
name: tickers
tags: ticker=GOOGL
time max min median
---- --- --- ------
2017-11-27T10:00:00Z 22062 200 1950
name: tickers
tags: ticker=JPM
time max min median
---- --- --- ------
2017-11-27T10:00:00Z 136485 2400 14533
```

InfluxDB supports the arguments for GROUP BY - time interval, the following is the syntax:

```
SELECT <function>(<field_key>) FROM_clause WHERE <time_range> GROUP BY
time(<time_interval>),[tag_key] [fill(<fill_option>)]
```

| Syntax | Descrption |
|--------|------------|
| time_range | Range of timestamp field, time > past time and < future time |
| time_interval | Duration literal, group query result into the duration time group |
| fill(<fill_option>) | Optional. When time intervals have no data, it can change to fill the value |

Let's look at some examples for a better understanding.

Find stock trade volumes' mean value during 10-19, November 27, 2017, and group the results into 60-minute intervals and `ticker` tag key:

```
> select mean(volume) from tickers where time <=
'2017-11-27T19:00:00.000000000Z' AND time >=
'2017-11-27T10:00:00.000000000Z' group by time(60m), ticker;
name: tickers
tags: ticker=AAPL
time mean
---- ----
2017-11-27T10:00:00Z
2017-11-27T11:00:00Z
2017-11-27T12:00:00Z
2017-11-27T13:00:00Z
2017-11-27T14:00:00Z 139443.46666666667
2017-11-27T15:00:00Z 38968.916666666664
```

```
2017-11-27T16:00:00Z 44737.816666666666
2017-11-27T17:00:00Z
2017-11-27T18:00:00Z 16202.15
2017-11-27T19:00:00Z 12651
name: tickers
tags: ticker=GOOGL
time mean
---- ----
2017-11-27T10:00:00Z
2017-11-27T11:00:00Z
2017-11-27T12:00:00Z
2017-11-27T13:00:00Z
2017-11-27T14:00:00Z 6159.033333333334
2017-11-27T15:00:00Z 2486.75
2017-11-27T16:00:00Z 2855.5
2017-11-27T17:00:00Z
2017-11-27T18:00:00Z 1954.1166666666666
2017-11-27T19:00:00Z 300
name: tickers
tags: ticker=JPM
time mean
---- ----
2017-11-27T10:00:00Z
2017-11-27T11:00:00Z
2017-11-27T12:00:00Z
2017-11-27T13:00:00Z
2017-11-27T14:00:00Z 35901.8275862069
2017-11-27T15:00:00Z 17653.45
2017-11-27T16:00:00Z 14139.25
2017-11-27T17:00:00Z
2017-11-27T18:00:00Z 14419.416666666666
2017-11-27T19:00:00Z 4658
```

InfluxDB supports the `INTO` clause. You can copy from one measurement to another or create a new database for measurement.

The following is the syntax:

```
SELECT_clause INTO <measurement_name> FROM_clause [WHERE_clause]
[GROUP_BY_clause]
```

| Syntax | Description |
| --- | --- |
| `INTO <measurement_name>` | This helps you to copy data into a specific measurement. |
| `INTO <database_name>.<retention_policy_name>.<measurement_name>` | This helps you to copy data into a fully qualified measurement. |
| `INTO <database_name>..<measurement_name>` | This helps you to copy data into a specified measurement with a default RP. |
| `INTO <database_name>.<retention_policy_name>.:MEASUREMENT FROM /<regular_expression>/` | This helps you to copy data into a specified database with RP and using regular expression match from the clause. |

Let's take a look at some examples for a better understanding.

Copy the aggregate mean of all of the field values into a different database and create a new measurement:

```
> use market
Using database market
> SELECT MEAN(*) INTO market_watch.autogen.avgvol FROM /.*/ WHERE time >=
'2017-11-27T00:00:00.000000000Z' AND time <=
'2017-11-27T23:59:59.000000000Z' GROUP BY time(60m);
name: result
time written
---- -------
1970-01-01T00:00:00Z 8
> use market_watch
Using database market_watch
> show measurements;
name: measurements
name
----
avgvol
tickers
> select * from avgvol
name: avgvol
time mean_close mean_high mean_low mean_open mean_volume
---- ---------- --------- -------- --------- -----------
2017-11-27T05:00:00Z 435.3618644067796 435.43688926553676
435.27535762711864 435.33908870056507 16300.42372881356
2017-11-27T14:00:00Z 448.45324269662916 448.67904269662927
448.16110786516856 448.42909325842686 60777.84269662921
2017-11-27T15:00:00Z 446.46472277777775 446.5794283333334 446.3297522222223
446.4371933333333 19703.03888888889
2017-11-27T16:00:00Z 445.9267622222222 446.0731233333333 445.7768644444446
445.9326772222222 20577.522222222222
2017-11-27T18:00:00Z 447.22421222222226 447.29334333333327
447.1268016666667 447.1964166666667 10858.56111111111
2017-11-27T19:00:00Z 440.0175634831461 440.1042516853933 439.9326162921348
440.02026348314615 11902.247191011236
2017-11-27T20:00:00Z 447.3597166666667 447.43757277777786 447.2645472222222
447.3431649999999 19842.32222222222
2017-11-27T21:00:00Z 448.01033333333334 448.43833333333333
448.00333333333333 448.29333333333335 764348.3333333334
```

# Query pagination

InfluxDB supports powerful query pagination using offset and limit. Pagination is a common use case in web applications when dealing with large data. Google shows you 10 search results at a time, Amazon may show 20 results per page, and software logs tracking UI may show 20-100 items on the UI. By getting a total count, we can easily get a total page number using the following formula:

*Total page = (total result count / page size)*

If the *page size* is *n*, then the initial page displays records starting from *0-n-1*. When you click on **Next** or scroll to next (using the infinity scroll bar), the next page will display records from *n-2n-1*, and so on. In InfluxDB, we can use the limit to define how many data points we want to fetch per query, offset moves data point records from *0*, to *n*, to *2n* until the end of records.

The following is the syntax:

```
SELECT_clause [INTO_clause] FROM_clause [WHERE_clause] [GROUP_BY_clause]
[ORDER_BY_clause] LIMIT_clause OFFSET <N> [SLIMIT_clause]
```

Consider the upcoming examples.

Assume we will query the `ticker` information. The UI page will display 10 records at a time. The following queries show how to achieve this goal:

```
> select count(*) from tickers;
name: tickers
time count_close count_company count_high count_low count_open count_volume
---- ----------- ------------- ---------- --------- ---------- ------------
1970-01-01T00:00:00Z 3507 3507 3507 3507 3507 3507
> SELECT ticker,company, volume, close FROM tickers LIMIT 10 OFFSET 0
name: tickers
time ticker company volume close
---- ------ ------- ------ -----
2017-11-27T05:00:00Z AAPL APPLE INC 34908 174.05
2017-11-27T05:00:00Z JPM JPMorgan Chase & Co 7904 98.42
2017-11-27T05:00:00Z GOOGL Alphabet Inc 100 1065.06
2017-11-27T05:01:00Z JPM JPMorgan Chase & Co 20155 98.365
2017-11-27T05:01:00Z GOOGL Alphabet Inc 1500 1064.93
2017-11-27T05:01:00Z AAPL APPLE INC 27891 174.0652
2017-11-27T05:02:00Z GOOGL Alphabet Inc 1700 1065.12
2017-11-27T05:02:00Z AAPL APPLE INC 20390 174.0957
2017-11-27T05:02:00Z JPM JPMorgan Chase & Co 42901 98.37
2017-11-27T05:03:00Z AAPL APPLE INC 21059 174.05
> SELECT ticker,company, volume, close FROM tickers LIMIT 10 OFFSET 10
```

```
name: tickers
time ticker company volume close
____ _____ _____ _____ _____
2017-11-27T05:03:00Z JPM JPMorgan Chase & Co 11095 98.31
2017-11-27T05:03:00Z GOOGL Alphabet Inc 2000 1065.24
2017-11-27T05:04:00Z JPM JPMorgan Chase & Co 14955 98.3
2017-11-27T05:04:00Z GOOGL Alphabet Inc 1600 1063.67
2017-11-27T05:04:00Z AAPL APPLE INC 23365 174.0215
2017-11-27T05:05:00Z GOOGL Alphabet Inc 1302 1063.93
2017-11-27T05:05:00Z AAPL APPLE INC 34056 174.03
2017-11-27T05:05:00Z JPM JPMorgan Chase & Co 14515 98.32
2017-11-27T05:06:00Z AAPL APPLE INC 28192 174.01
2017-11-27T05:06:00Z JPM JPMorgan Chase & Co 24609 98.2501
> SELECT ticker,company, volume, close FROM tickers LIMIT 10 OFFSET 20
name: tickers
time ticker company volume close
____ _____ _____ _____ _____
2017-11-27T05:06:00Z GOOGL Alphabet Inc 2900 1064.06
2017-11-27T05:07:00Z JPM JPMorgan Chase & Co 16332 98.28
2017-11-27T05:07:00Z GOOGL Alphabet Inc 662 1064.93
2017-11-27T05:07:00Z AAPL APPLE INC 11298 174.04
2017-11-27T05:08:00Z GOOGL Alphabet Inc 720 1064.91
2017-11-27T05:08:00Z AAPL APPLE INC 12963 174.0236
2017-11-27T05:08:00Z JPM JPMorgan Chase & Co 12674 98.255
2017-11-27T05:09:00Z AAPL APPLE INC 25547 173.9851
2017-11-27T05:09:00Z JPM JPMorgan Chase & Co 7442 98.2301
2017-11-27T05:10:00Z AAPL APPLE INC 17162 173.99
```

# Query performance optimizations

In the data model section, we have listed some best practices. Tags in InfluxDB are indexed. When the query has certain search fields frequently used, consider storing it as a tag. Many GROUP BY aggregations are expensive, for those GROUP BY fields, consider storing as a tag. For very dynamic values, you should store as fields. Since tags could be a large string, too many series that cause high memory usage, can impact performance.

Each measurement is indexed by time and sorted. Any time-bound related query will be quite efficient. Some of the plugins might automatically create a measurement by adding very long strings, for example, server.cluster.someid.time. This will impact query performance. In such a case, consider renaming them to a shorter concise measurement name.

When writing data records into measurement, we need to check whether the time precision matches the actual dataset. For example, when dealing with market high frequency trading data, mostly it needs at least millisecond precision. But if time in measurement is second precision, some data will conflict, which may cause a loss of data and the time may be set to default `1970-01-01T00:00:00Z`. On the other hand, if the data only needs second-level precision, but time in measurement is defined in nanoseconds, it will increase the size of the data on the disk, slowdown the write throughput, and timestamps may be stored as a wrong value.

In the case of a slow query, try to run `show queries` to list which query is slower. `show queries` display query ID, query text, and duration of current running queries in the current instance. Consider the following example:

```
> show queries;
qid query database duration
--- ----- -------- --------
10 SELECT SUM(somefield) FROM ameasurement where.. group by.. sampled 6 s
```

In certain cases, for very long run queries, you may want to kill it, you can run `KILL QUERY`. It will terminate the running query.

# Interaction via Rest API

InfluxDB supports a powerful HTTP API that runs by default on port `8086` with reading and writing capabilities. Since InfluxDB does not require a schema-defined upfront, this allows applications client store data and pulls data through HTTP API. It is very useful in many use cases, such as DevOps. It can automatically pull data from Jenkins to InfluxDB.

InfluxDB has four end points for interaction with, `/ping`, `/debug/requests`, `/query`, and `/write`.

The `/ping` command provides a simple way to verify that a source computer can communicate over the network with a remote InfluxDB instance. It can check the status and version information. It also supports both `GET` and `HEAD HTTP` requests.

Consider the upcoming example:

If you are in the same instance of InfluxDB, try this `curl -sl -I`
`http://localhost:8086/ping`:

```
curl -sl -I http://localhost:8086/ping
HTTP/1.1 204 No Content
Content-Type: application/json
Request-Id: 91306baa-d710-11e7-800b-000000000000
X-InfluxDB-Version: 1.5
```

`204` mean success status. If you are in the window client, you can use Postman (HTTP RESTful tool) to send HTTP rest APIs to InfluxDB. You will get the same `204` response from the InfluxDB instance.

Postman can be downloaded from here `https://www.getpostman.com/apps`.

When you send the request from the client, you need to get the IP address or hostname to replace the localhost: `http://yourInstanceDBHostnameOrIPaddress:8086/ping`.

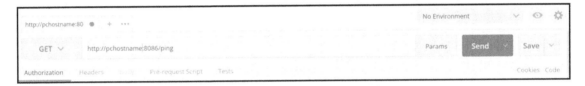

In the following example, we will use the command-line tool to test:

`/debug/requests`

This request checks the user request information.

Consider the upcoming example.

Open two Unix Terminals. In one Terminal, enter `debugs/request`.

```
http://localhost:8086/debug/requests?seconds=60
```

It will show all the user requests in the past 60 seconds. The other Terminal runs the following query command a few times:

```
curl -G 'http://localhost:8086/query?db=market' --data-urlencode 'q=SELECT
* FROM tickers limit 5'
```

The following is the result for `debug/request` after 60 seconds:

```
curl http://localhost:8086/debug/requests?seconds=60
{
"127.0.0.1": {"writes":0,"queries":3}
}
```

It shows that there are three query requests sent from a user and zero write requests. The sender IP address is `127.0.0.1`.

If the query seconds is equal to 60, the parameter is not added to the URL and the default 10 seconds will be used.

In the previous example, we have a demo of a simple `/query` request, which is used to get data from `tickers` measurement in the market database. `/query` is very powerful. You can use this to retrieve data points, handle retention points, users, and even manage the database. `/query` supports the GET and POST HTTP methods. SELECT and show keywords can run under the `/query` GET method.

The POST method handles cluster admin functions, ALTER, CREATE, DELETE, DROP, GRANT, KILL, and REVOKE.

Therefore, we need to be very careful when we use POST to handle database DDL operations. This kind of request must be as a cluster admin.

Let's look at an example of creating a database for a better understanding:

```
$ curl -i -XPOST http://localhost:8086/query --data-urlencode "q=CREATE
DATABASE testdb"
HTTP/1.1 200 OK
. . .
```

Verify that the `testdb` database is created by running the SHOW command:

```
~$ curl -G 'http://localhost:8086/query' --data-urlencode 'q=SHOW DATABASES
'
{"results":[{"statement_id":0,"series":[{"name":"databases","columns":["nam
e"],"values ":[["_internal"],["market"],["market_watch"],["testdb"]]}]}]}
```

Let's look at an example of deleting a database for a better understanding:

```
~$ curl -i -XPOST http://localhost:8086/query --data-urlencode "q=DROP
DATABASE testdb"
..
~$ curl -G 'http://localhost:8086/query' --data-urlencode 'q=SHOW
DATABASES'
{"results":[{"statement_id":0,"series":[{"name":"databases","columns":["nam
e"],"values":[["_internal"],["market"],["market_watch"]]}]}]}
```

To run multiple queries, just use a semicolon to separate out these queries:

```
~$ curl -G 'http://localhost:8086/query?pretty=true' --data-urlencode
"db=market" --data-urlencode "q=SELECT c ount(*) FROM tickers WHERE
ticker='JPM';SELECT MEAN(close) FROM tickers WHERE ticker='GOOGL'"
{
"results": [
{
"statement_id": 0,
"series": [
{
"name": "tickers",
"columns": [
"time",
"count_close",
"count_company",
...
],
"values": [
[
"1970-01-01T00:00:00Z",
1172,
1172,
..
]
]
}
]
},
{
"statement_id": 1,
"series": [
{
"name": "tickers",
"columns": [
"time",
"mean"
],
```

```
"values": [
[
"1970-01-01T00:00:00Z",
1056.9267642857149
]
]
}
]
}
]
}
```

`/write` : The write end point is used to write data to the database measurement through the `POST` method.

Consider the upcoming example.

Let's create a sample database `testdb` used in the previous example and then run the `write` command to insert two data points for weather data under `testdb` and separate each point data with a new line:

```
$ curl -i -XPOST 'http://localhost:8086/write?db=testdb' --data-binary
'weather_report,city=NYC
temp=44.1,windchill=42.5,humidity="58%",pressure="30.59
in",winddir="variable",windspeed="3.5 mph" 1511361000000000000
weather_report,city=NYC
temp=41.3,windchill=39.2,humidity="62%",pressure="30.65
in",winddir="NE",windspeed="Calm" 1511361060000000000'
HTTP/1.1 204 No Content
. .
```

Two data points are loaded to the `weather_report` measurements:

```
> select * from weather_report
name: weather_report
time city humidity pressure temp windchill winddir windspeed
---- ---- -------- -------- ---- --------- ------- ---------
2017-11-22T14:30:00Z NYC 58% 30.59 in 44.1 42.5 variable 3.5 mph
2017-11-22T14:31:00Z NYC 62% 30.65 in 41.3 39.2 NE Calm
```

# InfluxDB API client

InfluxDB supports many popular programming languages as an application client to interact with the database. In any case, you may need to write the application client code to load and get the data from InfluxDB. Here are basic examples for Java, Python, and Go application clients that interact with InfluxDB.

In this example, we will write Apache logs to measure and query results from InfluxDB.

The following are the steps in the code:

1. Connect InfluxDB.
2. Create or use the database.
3. Create the points.
4. Write the points to measurement.
5. Query the saved results.

# InfluxDB with Java client

Assume that you have installed JDK on your local system. If not, you can go to the Oracle site to download it and follow the instructions for installation. Once the installation is successful, type `java -version`. You should see the current version of JDK as shown in the following URL:

`http://www.oracle.com/technetwork/java/javase/downloads/index.html.`

1. First, we need to create a maven project and define Maven `pom.xml` with the following dependency library and add InfluxDB-related dependencies:

```
<dependencies>
<dependency>
<groupId>org.InfluxDB</groupId>
<artifactId>InfluxDB-java</artifactId>
<version>2.7</version>
</dependency>
<dependency>
<groupId>com.squareup.okhttp3</groupId>
<artifactId>okhttp</artifactId>
<version>3.9.1</version>
</dependency>
<dependency>
<groupId>com.squareup.retrofit2</groupId>
<artifactId>retrofit</artifactId>
```

```
<version>2.3.0</version>
</dependency>
<dependency>
<groupId>com.squareup.retrofit2</groupId>
<artifactId>converter-moshi</artifactId>
<version>2.3.0</version>
</dependency>
</dependencies>
```

2. Write a Java program:

```java
publicclass InfluxDBApiTest {
publicstaticvoid main(String[] args) throws Exception {
InfluxDB InfluxDB =
InfluxDBFactory.connect("http://yourInfluxDBInstanceIPAddress:8086"
, "root", "root");
String dbName = "testdb";
InfluxDB.createDatabase(dbName);
InfluxDB.setDatabase(dbName);
Point point1 =
Point.measurement("apachelog_java").time(1511361120000000000L,
TimeUnit.NANOSECONDS)
.addField("http", "GET /cgi-bin/try/ HTTP/1.0").addField("status",
200).addField("duration", 3395)
.addField("ip", "192.168.2.20").build();
Point point2 =
Point.measurement("apachelog_java").time(1511361180000000000L,
TimeUnit.NANOSECONDS)
.addField("http", "GET / HTTP/1.0").addField("status",
200).addField("duration", 2216)
.addField("ip", "127.0.0.1").build();
InfluxDB.write(point1);
InfluxDB.write(point2);
Query query = new Query("SELECT * FROM apachelog_java", dbName);
InfluxDB.query(query, 20, queryResult ->
System.out.println(queryResult));
}
}
```

3. After running this program, it will print out two records, which are written to the new `appachelog_java` measurement:

```
QueryResult [results=[Result [series=[Series [name=apachelog_java,
tags=null, columns=[time, duration, http, ip, status],
values=[[2017-11-22T14:32:00Z, 3395.0, GET /cgi-bin/try/ HTTP/1.0,
192.168.2.20, 200.0], [2017-11-22T14:33:00Z, 2216.0, GET /
HTTP/1.0, 127.0.0.1, 200.0]]]], error=null]], error=null]
```

# InfluxDB with a Python client

In this example, we will set up a python environment and run InfluxDB with a python client.

1. Install Python.

   Assume that you have Python installed. Python 3 is installed by default on modern versions of Ubuntu, type `python3 -V` to verify. If not, run the following command to install Python 3:

   ```
   sudo apt-get install python3
   ```

2. Install InfluxDB-Python.

   Install InfluxDB-python by entering the following command:

   ```
   $ pip install InfluxDB
   ```

   On Debian/Ubuntu, you can install it with the following command:

   ```
   sudo apt-get install python-InfluxDB
   ```

3. Write a Python program.

   Type `python` on the Terminal. It will load the Python shell. Enter the following Python codes line by line. It will print out two records, which are written to the `appachelog_py` measurement:

   ```
   >>> from InfluxDB import InfluxDBClient
   >>> json_body = [{
   ... "measurement": "apachelog_py",
   ... "time": 1511361120000000000,
   ... "fields": {
   ... "http": "GET /cgi-bin/try/ HTTP/1.0",
   ... "status": 200,
   ```

```
... "duration": 3395,
... "ip": "192.168.2.20" }
... }, {
... "measurement": "apachelog_py",
... "time": 1511361180000000000,"fields": {
... "http": "GET / HTTP/1.0",
... "status": 200,
... "duration": 2216,
... "ip": "127.0.0.1"
... }}]
>>> client = InfluxDBClient('localhost', 8086, 'root', 'root',
'testdb')
>>> client.write_points(json_body)
True
>>> result = client.query('select * from apachelog_py;')
>>> print("Result: {0}".format(result))
Result: ResultSet({'(u'apachelog_py', None)': [{u'duration': 3395,
u'ip': u'192.168.2.20', u'status': 200, u'http': u'GET /cgi-
bin/try/ HTTP/1.0', u'time': u'2017-11-22T14:32:00Z'},
{u'duration': 2216, u'ip': u'127.0.0.1', u'status': 200, u'h ttp':
u'GET / HTTP/1.0', u'time': u'2017-11-22T14:33:00Z'}]})
```

# InfluxDB with Go client

In the example shown next, we are going to set up a Go environment to run InfluxDB with Go client.

1. Install Go.

   Install Go by following the golang installation guide available at:

   https://golang.org/doc/install

   Set up GOROOT and GOBIN:

   ```
   sudo apt install golang-go
   export GOROOT=/usr/lib/go
   export GOBIN=/usr/bin/go
   ```

   Set up $GOPATH:

   ```
   mkdir ~/go
   export GOPATH=~/go
   export PATH=$PATH:$GOPATH/bin
   export PATH=$PATH:$GOROOT/bin
   ```

Check the Go version:

```
$ go version
go version go1.6.2 linux/amd64
```

2.  Install the InfluxDB Go client library:

```
go get github.com/InfluxDB/InfluxDB
```

You should see a message similar to the following:

```
package github.com/InfluxDB/InfluxDB: code in directory
/home/user/go/src/github.com/InfluxDB/InfluxDB expects import
"github.com/influxdata/InfluxDB"
```

3.  Write the Go program:

```go
package main
import (
"log"
    "time"
    "github.com/influxdata/InfluxDB/client/v2"
)
const (
database  = "testdb"
username = "root"
password = "root"
)
func main() {
    c, err := client.NewHTTPClient(client.HTTPConfig{
        Addr:     "http://localhost:8086",
        Username: username,
        Password: password,
    })
// Create a new point batch
bp, err := client.NewBatchPoints(client.BatchPointsConfig{
        Database: database,
        Precision: "s",
    })
// Create a point and add to batch
tags := map[string]string{}
    fields1 := map[string]interface{}{
"http": "GET /cgi-bin/try/ HTTP/1.0",
"status": 200,
"duration": 3395,
"ip": "192.168.2.20",
    }
    pt1, err := client.NewPoint("apachelog_go", tags, fields1,
```

```
time.Unix(0, 1511361120000000000))
    bp.AddPoint(pt1)
    fields2 := map[string]interface{}{
"http": "GET / HTTP/1.0",
"status": 200,
"duration": 2216,
"ip": "127.0.0.1",
    }
    pt2, err := client.NewPoint("apachelog_go", tags, fields2,
time.Unix(0, 1511361180000000000))
    bp.AddPoint(pt2)
// Write the batch
if err := c.Write(bp); err != nil {
    log.Fatal(err)
}
 }
 }
```

4. Run the Go program as follows:

```
go run goclientInfluxDBtest.go
```

Once the program has successfully run, you should see a new measurement—apachelog_go is created in the database and two data points are inserted.

```
> show measurements
name: measurements
name
----
apachelog_go
apachelog_java
apachelog_py
weather_report
> select * from apachelog_go
name: apachelog_go
time duration http ip status
---- -------- ---- -- ------
2017-11-22T14:32:00Z 3395 GET /cgi-bin/try/ HTTP/1.0 192.168.2.20
200
2017-11-22T14:33:00Z 2216 GET / HTTP/1.0 127.0.0.1 200
```

# InfluxDB ecosystem

InfluxDB is a NoSQL database. In many real-world projects, it typically needs to develop data collect applications to collect and send data to the process engine, and then the process engine will process the collected matrix to save in the database. Fortunately, InfluxDB provides this kind of ecosystem to make development much easier. In typical InfluxDB ecosystem components, Telegraf is the agent to collect and send data. Kapacitor is a real-time streaming data process engine. Chronograf is a dashboard tool and is used for visualizing time-series data. In this section, we will discuss Telegraf and Kapacitor:

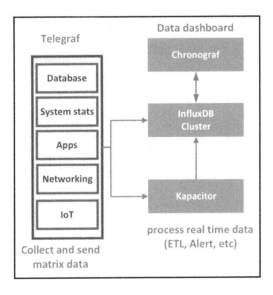

# Telegraf

Telegraf is a plugin-driven agent for collecting, processing, aggregating, reporting, and writing matrix. It has more than 100 plugins. It is written in Go and compiled as a standalone library; it doesn't have external dependency. The plugin development is easy. You can write your own plugins. This plugin-driven architecture can easily fit into your application workflow to push or pull metrics. This architecture design makes Telegraf easy to use and flexible.

Telegraf can be used to collect and send metrics time-series data from various resources:

- Databases such as MySQL and MongoDB connect to these data sources and pull data
- System level matrixes such as disk usage, logs, CPU, and system events
- IoT allows you to collect and send the sense devices matrix

## Telegraf data management

Telegraf gets input from input plugins, and then processes data via filter and transformation. After the process step is complete, it will start the aggregation step and run the aggregation functions to get results, and finally use the output plugin to write data into InfluxDB:

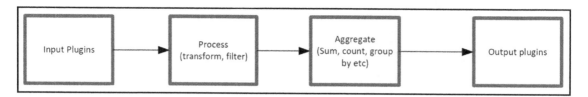

Consider the upcoming example. Let's use Telegraf to collect a matrix from a UNIX system CPU, memory, and swap usage and load it onto InfluxDB. Here are the detailed steps:

1. Create a new database in InfluxDB:

   ```
   create database telegraf
   ```

2. Install Telegraf:

   ```
   $ wget http://get.InfluxDB.org/telegraf/telegraf_0.10.2-1_amd64.deb
   $ sudo dpkg -i telegraf_0.10.2-1_amd64.deb
   ```

3. Generate `telegraf.conf` using the `sample-config` option. Define the input filter for cpu, mem, and swap. Define the output filter as InfluxDB:

   ```
   $ telegraf -sample-config -input-filter cpu:mem:swap -output-filter
   InfluxDB > telegraf.conf
   ```

Quick review generates the configuration file (`telegraf.conf`). It contains the related input and output configuration:

```
[[inputs.cpu]], [[inputs.mem]],[[inputs.swap]] and output
configuration: [[outputs.InfluxDB]].
```

4.  Run Telegraf with the generated configuration file:

```
$ telegraf -config telegraf.conf
```

5.  Check the data in InfluxDB to verify that the data is loaded:

```
> use telegraf;
Using database telegraf
> show measurements;
name: measurements
name
----
cpu
mem
net
swap
> select cpu, host, usage_softirq, usage_steal, usage_system,
usage_user from cpu limit 3;
name: cpu
time cpu host usage_softirq usage_steal usage_system usage_user
---- --- ---- ------------- ----------- ------------ ----------
2017-12-03T00:08:00Z cpu-total bwu-pc 0 0 0.20046775810221984
3.1406615436011274
2017-12-03T00:08:00Z cpu2 bwu-pc 0 0 0 3.3066132264534605
2017-12-03T00:08:00Z cpu1 bwu-pc 0 0 0.20060180541627498
3.2096288866598295
```

Now, Telegraf is integrated with InfluxDB.

# Kapacitor

Kapacitor is a real-time data processing engine. It can process stream and batch data from InfluxDB. Similar to Telegraf, it has a plugin-driven design. This makes Kapacitor very flexible. It can easily integrate with many open source libraries and engines. The user can define their own plugins. It is used to publish the subscribed event-driven design pattern, which helps Kapacitor to easily handle streaming real-time data.

Consider the upcoming example.

Use Kapacitor triggering alerts and set up an alert on high CPU usage.

We use the previous telegraf example and send the CPU data to InfluxDB. Then Kapacitor pulls the data from InfluxDB using `ticker` script, which defines the rules and tells Kapacitor to generate the alert log:

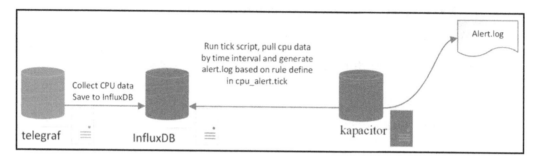

Install Kapacitor using the following command:

```
wget https://dl.influxdata.com/kapacitor/releases/kapacitor_1.3.3_amd64.deb
sudo dpkg -i kapacitor_1.3.3_amd64.deb
```

For other environments, refer to the following installation link:

```
https://portal.influxdata.com/downloads
```

Once the install is successful, start Telegraf using the following command:

```
sudo systemctl start telegraf
```

Start Kapacitor and check the status using the following command:

```
sudo systemctl start kapacitor
sudo systemctl status kapacitor
```

View the Kapacitor logs using the following command:

```
sudo tail -f -n 128 /var/log/kapacitor/kapacitor.log
```

Define a TICKscript. A TICKscript is a **domain-specific language** (DSL) that defines the tasks. It tells Kapacitor how to process the pipeline. Create a file by the name `cpu_alert.tick`:

```
stream
// Select just the cpu measurement from our example database.
|from()
.measurement('cpu')
|alert()
.crit(lambda: int("usage_idle") < 100)
// Whenever we get an alert write it to a file.
.log('/tmp/alerts.log')
```

Use Kapacitor's CLI tool to define the `cpu_alert` task and provide the stream type, tick file, database, and RP:

```
$ kapacitor define cpu_alert
> -type stream
> -tick cpu_alert.tick
> -dbrp telegraf.autogen
```

Enable the `cpu_alert` task using the following command:

```
$ kapacitor enable cpu_alert
```

Verify that the `cpu_alert` task is created and enabled in the tasks list:

```
$ kapacitor list tasks
ID Type Status Executing Databases and Retention Policies
cpu_alert stream enabled true ["telegraf"."autogen"]
```

Now, we have set up the task; it is time to record the stream data using the `cpu_alert` task. We set up the duration as 60 s; it will return the task ID:

```
$ kapacitor record stream -task cpu_alert -duration 60s
f5943f37-bb49-4431-8ab1-fd27a772a7de
```

Check the task recording status by returning the task ID using the following command:

```
f5943f37-bb49-4431-8ab1-fd27a772a7de:
$ kapacitor list recordings f5943f37-bb49-4431-8ab1-fd27a772a7de
ID Type Status Size Date
f5943f37-bb49-4431-8ab1-fd27a772a7de stream finished 1.1 kB 02 Dec 17 21:00
EST
```

Check the end point InfluxDB send data to Kapacitor:

```
$ curl -G 'http://localhost:8086/query?db=telegraf' --data-urlencode
'q=SHOW SUBSCRIPTIONS'
{"results":[{"statement_id":0,"series":[{"name":"_internal","columns":["ret
ention_policy","name","mode","destinations"],"values":[["monitor","kapacito
r-736ab512-4d00-408a-b852-
c3a17dc5ffd1","ANY",["http://localhost:9092"]]]},{"name":"market","columns"
:["retention_policy","name","mode","destinations"],"values":[["autogen","ka
pacitor-736ab512-4d00-408a-b852-
c3a17dc5ffd1","ANY",["http://localhost:9092"]]]},{"name":"market_watch","co
lumns":["retention_policy","name","mode","destinations"],"values":[["autoge
n","kapacitor-736ab512-4d00-408a-b852-
c3a17dc5ffd1","ANY",["http://localhost:9092"]]]},{"name":"testdb","columns"
:["retention_policy","name","mode","destinations"],"values":[["autogen","ka
pacitor-736ab512-4d00-408a-b852-
c3a17dc5ffd1","ANY",["http://localhost:9092"]]]},{"name":"telegraf","column
s":["retention_policy","name","mode","destinations"],"values":[["autogen","
kapacitor-736ab512-4d00-408a-b852-
c3a17dc5ffd1","ANY",["http://localhost:9092"]]]}]}]}
```

From InfluxDB log, we can see Kapacitor start recording the data:

```
[InfluxDB] 2017/12/03 01:37:56 D! linking subscriptions for cluster
localhost
[httpd] 127.0.0.1 - - [03/Dec/2017:01:38:00 -0500] "POST
/write?consistency=&db=telegraf&precision=ns&rp=autogen HTTP/1.1" 204 0 "-"
"InfluxDBClient" 81766872-d7f4-11e7-8a93-000000000000 294[cpu_alert:alert2]
2017/12/03 01:38:00 D! CRITICAL alert triggered id:cpu:nil msg:cpu:nil is
CRITICAL data:&{cpu map[cpu:cpu0 host:bwu-pc] [time usage_guest
usage_guest_nice usage_idle usage_iowait usage_irq usage_nice usage_softirq
usage_steal usage_system usage_user] [[2017-12-03 06:38:00 +0000 UTC 0 0
95.97989949747311 0.10050251256280458 0 0 0 0 0.3015075376884316
3.618090452262322]]}
```

Finally, check `/tmp/alert.logs`. The ones defined as critical events are flushed into `alert.log` as follows:

```
$ tail -f -n 100 /tmp/alert.logs
```

We just completed the end-to-end integration between Telegraf, InfluxDB, and Kapacitor!

# InfluxDB operations

In this section, we will discuss some InfluxDB operations, such as how to back up and restore data, what is the RP, how to monitor InfluxDB, clustering, and HA.

# Backup and restore

It is critical to backup your data and recover them in case problem occurs, such as system crashes and hardware failures. InfluxDB provides a variety of backup and restore strategies.

# Backups

Backup is a must in every production database. There are two types of backups in InfluxDB: metastore and database.

Metastore contains system information. You can back up a metastore instance by running the following command:

```
influxd backup <path-to-backup>
```

When backing up databases, each database needs to be backed up separately by running the following command:

```
influxd backup -database <mydatabase> <path-to-backup>
```

You can specify some arguments for retention, shard, and since as follows:

```
-retention <retention policy name> -shard <shard ID> -since <date>
```

If we change the `<path-to-back>` value with the remote IP address, InfluxDB will run the remote backup:

```
influxd backup -database mydatabase -host <remote-node-IP>:8088
/tmp/mysnapshot
```

# Restore

If you need to restore data, the `restore` command is as follows:

```
influxd restore [ -metadir | -datadir ] <path-to-meta-or-data-directory>
<path-to-backup>
```

Here, `metadir` points to the backup metastore location and `datadir` points to the backup database location.

# Clustering and HA

InfluxData (company developed InfluxDB) has InfluxEnterprise products, which provide highly scalable clusters on your infrastructure and management UI.

In InfluxEnterprise, we need to set up meta nodes and data nodes for cluster installation. Each meta node runs on its own server. At least three meta nodes need to be set up in a cluster; then join meta nodes to the cluster. There is no requirement for each data node to run on its own server; however, the best practices are to deploy each data node on a dedicated server. A minimum of two data nodes must be in a cluster for high availability and redundancy and to join data nodes to the cluster.

# Retention policy

**Retention Policy (RP)** specifies how much data should be available at any given time.

It is defined as follows:

- **Duration**: This is the time for how long InfluxDB keeps data
- **Replication factor**: This is the number of copies of the data that are stored in the cluster
- **Shard group duration**: This is the time range that is covered by shard groups
- **Shard groups**: This is the logical container for shards and shards contains actual data

If RP is not defined when we create the database, the default autogen RP will be applied.

Autogen has an infinity duration, where the replication factor is 1 and the shard group duration is 7. When RP duration is more than 6 months, InfluxDB will set the shard Group duration to 7 days by default.

# Monitoring

InfluxDB is a time-series database, which naturally supports real-time event-based data, but there are many tools that can easily integrate with InfluxDB. As we've discussed earlier, Kapacitor is a very useful tool used to process real-time data and generate warning base on tick scripts. It supports both batch and stream by querying the InfluxDB database and defining alert rules and output alert. Chronograf is another of InfluxData's open source tools for web visualization. It has tick components to monitor data for the InfluxDB database and easily generates visualization alerts in the dashboard. Chronograf offers a UI for Kapacitor, which is useful for monitoring infrastructure, databases, and so on.

# Summary

In this chapter, we introduced the concept of InfluxDB, how to install InfluxDB, and set up the configuration.

We also learned InfluxDB query language, HTTP API, and client API. You saw how to use Kapacitor and Telegraf to monitor system logs with InfluxDB. Finally, we discussed InfluxDB operations.

InfluxDB is an excellent choice for time-series based data. It provides efficient collection of data with query flexibility. Multiple language supports provide easy integration with many enterprise applications. With the TSM data storage engine, InfluxDB provides high throughput batch read and write performance. More and more plugins continually add in the ecosystem component and make it easy to use in many real-world projects and become popular.

# Other Books You May Enjoy

If you enjoyed this book, you may be interested in these other books by Packt:

**MongoDB Administrator's Guide**

Cyrus Dasadia

ISBN: 978-1-78712-648-0

- Install and deploy MongoDB in production
- Manage and implement optimal indexes
- Optimize monitoring in MongoDB
- Fine-tune the performance of your queries
- Debug and diagnose your database's performance
- Optimize database backups and recovery and ensure high availability
- Make your MongoDB instance scalable
- Implement security and user authentication features in MongoDB
- Master optimal cloud deployment strategies

## Learning Neo4j 3.x - Second Edition
Jérôme Baton, Rik Van Bruggen

ISBN: 978-1-78646-614-3

- Understand the science of graph theory, databases and its advantages over traditional databases
- Install Neo4j, model data and learn the most common practices of traversing data
- Learn the Cypher query language and tailor-made procedures to analyze and derive meaningful representations of data
- Improve graph techniques with the help of precise procedures in the APOC library
- Use Neo4j advanced extensions and plugins for performance optimization
- Understand how Neo4j's new security features and clustering architecture are used for large scale deployments

# Leave a review - let other readers know what you think

Please share your thoughts on this book with others by leaving a review on the site that you bought it from. If you purchased the book from Amazon, please leave us an honest review on this book's Amazon page. This is vital so that other potential readers can see and use your unbiased opinion to make purchasing decisions, we can understand what our customers think about our products, and our authors can see your feedback on the title that they have worked with Packt to create. It will only take a few minutes of your time, but is valuable to other potential customers, our authors, and Packt. Thank you!

# Index

Made in the USA
Monee, IL
01 March 2020